Collaborative Parish Leadership

Collaborative Parish Leadership

Contexts, Models, Theology

Edited by
William A. Clark and Daniel Gast

LEXINGTON BOOKS
Lanham • Boulder • New York • London

Published by Lexington Books
An imprint of The Rowman & Littlefield Publishing Group, Inc.
4501 Forbes Boulevard, Suite 200, Lanham, Maryland 20706
www.rowman.com

Unit A, Whitacre Mews, 26-34 Stannary Street, London SE11 4AB

Unless otherwise noted, references to the Bible are from the New Revised Standard
Version Bible, copyright 1989, Division of Christian Education of the National Council of
the Churches of Christ in the United States of America.

British Library Cataloguing in Publication Information Available

Library of Congress Cataloging-in-Publication Data

Names: Clark, William A. (William Anthony), 1958- editor.
Title: Collaborative parish leadership : contexts, models, theology / edited by William A. Clark and
    Daniel Gast.
Description: Lanham : Lexington Books, 2016. | Includes bibliographical references and index.
Identifiers: LCCN 2016044795 (print) | LCCN 2016045209 (ebook)
Subjects: LCSH: Christian leadership--Catholic Church. | Parishes. | Pastoral theology--Catholic
    Church.
Classification: LCC BX1913 .C61355 2016 (print) | LCC BX1913 (ebook) | DDC 253--dc23
LC record available at https://lccn.loc.gov/2016044795

ISBN 9781498533683 (cloth : alk. paper)
ISBN 9781498533706 (pbk. : alk. paper)
ISBN 9781498533690 (electronic)

♾™ The paper used in this publication meets the minimum requirements of American
National Standard for Information Sciences Permanence of Paper for Printed Library
Materials, ANSI/NISO Z39.48-1992.

Printed in the United States of America

This book is dedicated to those who support and enrich collaborative pastoral leadership in local parish communities during an era of challenge and change, including parishioners, pastors, priests and deacons, lay and religious ministers, diocesan ministers, and their bishops.

Contents

Acknowledgments

We owe great debts to persons and organizations that made possible both the publication of this book and the pastoral and scholarly work it presents.

We begin with the sponsors of the evaluative research grant program upon which many of the chapters are grounded. In the United States, the Lilly Endowment Inc. *Sustaining Pastoral Excellence* (SPE) program provided the initial funding to Loyola University Chicago and the Archdiocese of Chicago as an institutional partnership for the first five years of the collaborative pastoral leadership project, INSPIRE. We particularly express deep appreciation for the counsel and support of the Endowment's Dr. Craig Dykstra and Dr. John Wimmer.

SPE then supported another four years through a matching grant, joined by Loyola University Chicago and the Archdiocese of Chicago. In those institutions we particularly express gratitude to Dr. Peter Gilmour, Dr. Mary Elsbernd, Dr. Robert Ludwig, and Dr. Brian Schmisek and Mark Bersano at Loyola's Institute of Pastoral Studies. Dr. Gilmour and Dr. Elsbernd conceived and designed the project. They joined with Sr. Judith Vallimont and Dr. Joseph Bator at the Archdiocese of Chicago to propose and coadminister the grant program start-up. At the Archdiocese, Dr. Carol Fowler, director of Personnel Services, served as an invaluable mentor and codirector of the project's Lead Team. Dr. Carol Walters, Director of the archdiocesan Office for Lay Ecclesial Ministry, consistently enhanced the integrity of the project's services, reporting, and relationships.

In Germany, Dr. Karl Albrecht personally provided ongoing funding for the CrossingOver program led by Dr. Wilhelm Damberg at the Ruhr University Bochum, also institutionally partnered with the Diocese of Essen. Dr. Albrecht's funding included support of travel and pastoral visitation programs between Chicago and six German dioceses, conferences, and scholarly research that began in 2003 and continue to the present day. We believe that his zeal, passion, humility, and vision epitomize the spirit and pastoral imagination of our transatlantic conversations and learning. Here we also acknowledge the continuing relationships sustained by Graciela Sonntag at Crossing-Over, and by Dr. Matthias Sellmann and Dr. Andreas Henkelmann at the Center of Applied Research in Pastoral Theology at Bochum.

We also give thanks to persons who contributed significant support and learning to both projects, including Dr. Katarina Schuth, OSF, at the University of St. Thomas, Dr. Mary Gautier at CARA, the Center for Applied Research in the Apostolate at Georgetown, Dr. John Haughey, SJ, at Georgetown's Woodstock Theological Center, Dr. Robert Schreiter, CPPS, at Chicago's Catholic Theological Union, Dr. Eileen Daily, and Dr. David DeLambo.

In the preparation of the volume for publication, we are especially thankful for our editor at Lexington, Sarah Craig, for several acts of skilled advisement, encouragement, and service. At a point when we worried that circumstances beyond our control would end the project, Sarah remained supportive and kept the work moving forward. Special debts of gratitude are also owed to Dr. Peter Gilmour and to Cecily Abel, who at critical moments generously offered adept advisory and editorial interventions and mentoring. We are also grateful for the generous financial support for the editorial work that came from the Committee on Faculty Scholarship at the College of the Holy Cross, Worcester, Massachusetts, from the Engaged Scholars Studying Congregations Fellowship of the Congregational Studies Team (supported by the Lilly Endowment), and from benefactors of Sr. Viola Lausier, SCIM, of the Good Shepherd Sisters of Biddeford, Maine.

Finally, some deeply personal acknowledgments. We thank our families for several acts of support and long sufferance, especially Kathy Gast (Dan's wife), Paula Clark (Bill's sister), and Fr. John Savard, SJ, of the College of the Holy Cross. To all the members of the Jesuit communities at Loyola University Chicago and the College of the Holy Cross, Worcester, Massachusetts, for their continuing care, support, and indefatigable encouragement through some difficult times. Very special thanks is due to the many medical professionals and caregivers at Tufts Medical Center, Boston, Massachusetts, who made it possible for Bill to continue working through some very challenging circumstances. Bill also wants to express his lasting gratitude to Dan for joining in this project when a coeditor made all the difference between suspending or completing the project.

Foreword

Dr. Brian Schmisek,
Director of the Institute of Pastoral
Studies at Loyola University Chicago

The institutional partnership and exchanges begun in 2004 between Cross-ingOver at the Ruhr University in Bochum, Germany, and Project INSPIRE at the Institute of Pastoral Studies, Loyola University Chicago, are well known both in academic and pastoral circles. The generosity of Karl Albrecht in Germany and the Lilly Endowment in the United States was a potent combination spawning a number of positive outcomes. Not least of these was a collaboration that facilitated shared wisdom and best practices between two educational institutions seeking to learn from each other.

Both of our institutions are situated in vibrant and dynamic faith settings: the Diocese of Essen in Germany and the Archdiocese of Chicago in the United States. The intercultural exchanges enjoyed over the years have been rich and informative for all concerned, and they continue in that vein. The nearly decade-long fruitful dialogue culminated in the 2013 "Milestone Conference," held at Loyola University Chicago and the 2015 conference, "Taufbewusstsein und Leadership," held at the Ruhr University Bochum, Germany.

Through these exchanges we learned that parish life in North America and Europe continues to grow, adapt, and impact the global church. Parish life certainly includes pastoral care, team leadership, membership, and the vital relationship of leaders with their local church and parish communities. These are issues that we continue to address in significant ways.

We were pleased to learn that CrossingOver has become part of a new Center of Applied Research in Pastoral Theology. Our own INSPIRE project has developed into an office of Parish Leadership and Management Programs that builds on past successes while introducing additional resources in parish health and wellness, and courses in Spanish to meet yet other parish needs.

We look forward to continued exchanges with our German partners and other international voices for years to come. Something powerful and dynamic has been unleashed for the benefit of pastoral theology and the church.

Many thanks to the authors of this text and especially the editors, William A. Clark, SJ, and Dan Gast, who brought the manuscript to completion. It is our hope that these pages share some of the wisdom we have gained through our academic and pastoral enterprise and exchange. There is so much more—friendships, relationships, razed silos, and expanded horizons—that punctuates these years not written on these pages but written in our hearts.

We have engaged a shared enterprise. We have been changed. And we are grateful.

Foreword

Prof. Dr. Wilhelm Damberg, Professor of Medieval and Modern Church History, Faculty of Catholic Theology, Ruhr University Bochum

Since 2004, the Faculty of Catholic Theology at the Ruhr University of Bochum in the industrial heartland of Germany has hosted a unique project called CrossingOver. This project aims to find new insights and ideas for innovation in Catholic parish life by stimulating an intercultural learning process between Germany and the United States. It was initiated and financed by Karl Albrecht, a German businessman who had spent several years in the United States. CrossingOver started with the objective of organizing internships for German priests and lay ecclesial ministers in US parishes to provide new and enriching experiences, and thus help them to improve local parish life in Germany.

CrossingOver searched for an institution in the United States able to accompany and support these objectives. INSPIRE, a joint program of the Institute of Pastoral Studies at Loyola University Chicago and the Archdiocese of Chicago aimed at developing parish staffs into effective leadership teams, emerged as the appropriate partner. INSPIRE and CrossingOver both focus on parish life, both enjoy a university context, and both cooperate with an urban diocese, INSPIRE with the American Archdiocese of Chicago and CrossingOver with the German Diocese of Essen. A formal partnership between Loyola University Chicago and Ruhr University became the crucial factor for the success of CrossingOver.

After the initial CrossingOver program, participants returned to Germany with enthusiastic reports, and the exchange program was extended. Americans, many who had hosted the German priests and pastoral workers, were invited to German dioceses and parishes. A personal network of relationships grew from more than seven years of these CrossingOver exchange programs. From these experiences, scholarly research on the many aspects of this joint project emerged and became the main focus of CrossingOver. Currently four major comparative research CrossingOver projects are run by Linda Duerrich, Andreas Henkelmann, Rosel Oehmen-Vieregge, and Graciela Sonntag. Two of these researchers are contributors to this book.

As in the first phase of the CrossingOver project, the continuing institutional partnership with the Institute of Pastoral Studies at Loyola University Chicago is central to the success of this research work. The INSPIRE Milestone Conference of 2013 in Chicago imparted important insights. In 2015 CrossingOver was happy to host many researchers from INSPIRE and across the United States at the Ruhr University in Bochum, Germany, for another conference.

New developments are ongoing. CrossingOver will become part of a new "Zentrum für Angewandte Pastoralforschung" (Center of Applied Research in Pastoral Theology), directed by Matthias Sellmann. It should be noted that the creation of this center was also heavily influenced by INSPIRE.

The publication of this mission-driven book gives me on behalf of the team and all participants of CrossingOver the opportunity to thank the Institute of Pastoral Studies at Loyola University Chicago, the Archdiocese of Chicago, and INSPIRE for their welcoming, trusting, and fruitful cooperation. In addition, I thank the contributors, and especially the editors, William A. Clark, SJ, and Dan Gast, for all their tireless efforts to bring this book to publication.

Introduction

Collaborative Leadership for Local Church Communities

William A. Clark, SJ, and Daniel Gast

Traditional parishes, area clusters, chapel groups, small Christian communities—whatever form local church communities may take, they are an essential aspect of the life of the Church. These institutions and structures, however, are under great stress in many parts of the world, and are in need of careful, thoughtful reform in order to continue to serve the Church well. Amid these challenges, many of the customary styles of leadership in local communities are proving insufficient. The health of our church communities calls for collaborative approaches that engage and sustain contributions from across the rich spectrum of the Church's membership. Such approaches can only be developed through experimentation, continual practice, research, and reflection, which themselves include careful listening and cooperation. These, in broad outline, are the convictions that ground the essays presented in this volume.

The local faith community is the Christian church's most ancient form of organization. Beginning with the gathering around the apostles in Jerusalem (which itself emerged from the itinerant community of disciples around Jesus), and following on with the small groups of believers who began to spread out from there in all directions, Christians organized themselves in intimate, face-to-face communities for worship and mutual support, both pastoral and practical. In the New Testament, the Acts of the Apostles and, especially, the letters of Paul testify directly to the centrality and dynamism of personal relationships within these local "churches" (as Paul unhesitatingly calls them), as well as to the strong sense of spiritual unity each community shared with all the others. However it may have happened that the Greek word used for groups of resident aliens (*paroikia:* "a nearby dwelling") came to be applied to these local communities, they had been the embodiment of Christian life from the beginning.

The many centuries and varied circumstances of later developments have included every imaginable variation in size, location, function, official status, social importance, and theological standing of these local communities. These variations have often enough been rivals of one another in times of cultural and political transition (for example, house churches in tension with the development of the office of local bishop), and in later centuries across denominational lines (e.g., episcopal, presbyteral, and congregational forms of local organization). Through it all, however, the conviction has remained virtually unanimous that full and authentic Christian practice requires a visible faith community in order to flourish.

In Roman Catholicism, particularly as practiced in Europe and North America, parish organization (usually by territory, sometimes by "personal" criteria such as language or ethnicity) has long been normative. Current canon law reserves the word "community" for this level of organization, even while tending to refer to the larger diocese as "the local church." In the United States, parishes were the heart of the enormously successful system for creating and sustaining local church communities among huge numbers of new Catholic immigrants in the nineteenth and twentieth centuries. In Europe, the presence of parish churches often anchored and defined both rural villages and urban neighborhoods, even in times and places where the parish as such was understood more as an administrative unit than as a living community.

The relationship of the parish community to the other social entities to which parishioners belong (circles of family and friends and neighbors, spiritual or service confraternities or movements, guilds and trade organizations, civic groups, etc.) has often been complex and a matter of debate. By the end of the twentieth century, the very idea of "community" had become a cultural challenge, as mobility, communication, globalized economy, and mass culture reshaped age-old social patterns. Secularization throughout the culture, though its causes and meaning are certainly contested, is another undeniable feature of this era of change. So overall it is no surprise that "church community" is a particularly difficult challenge. While Catholic Christians continue to revere the Church as a divine gift, and long for dynamic and engaging personal and social experiences of Church at the local level, parish communities in many places find themselves struggling for survival. The pressures they face are cultural, financial, demographic, and administrative. Their rivals range from nondenominational megachurches to hospital chapels to informal faith-sharing groups to Sunday sports leagues, as people search among myriad alternatives for the personal balance and spiritual fellowship they need. Amid a prevailing culture of consumption and individual choice, the Church seeks ways of maintaining and strengthening its original impulse to be *community* as it seeks to live through, with, and in its Lord.

This challenging task has engaged the contributors to this volume for many years. We have been occupied with both pastoral practice and the theory which seeks to understand and guide it. Our work has been shaped by a number of common experiences, methods, and initiatives. Together, this common ground has helped us to keep our work focused on something that we take to be much more important than merely the promotion of some particular new ways to do parish leadership. What we see emerging, rather, is a new way of approaching *collaboratively* the whole field of study, experimentation, reflection, and practice in the leadership and development of local church communities. This approach gives central importance to receiving the steady input of the local communities themselves who are meant to benefit from the work, and soliciting insights from many different fields of expertise.

Contributors to this volume represent to some degree this diversity of interests and experience. Among the perspectives we bring are those of Pastoral Theology and Church History, which have been of great importance to the Church in Europe since the Second Vatican Council and are well represented by our academic colleagues from Germany. Closely related, but more focused on concrete practice than on integrating theory, is the field of Practical Theology which, especially in the United States, has begun to emerge as an important aspect of Catholic reflection on the Church's life and mission. Both Pastoral and Practical Theology seek to bring into dialogue the insights of the theological tradition and careful observation of the current situation of the Church as it pursues its mission in the actual cultural, social, and political circumstances of today. Such reflection sets up important arenas of interaction between theology and a variety of social sciences. Several of us, accordingly, bring extensive experience in qualitative social research, which seeks to build a fuller understanding of personal motivations and social contexts than is typically provided by statistical data alone, using such methods as case studies, interviews, and detailed observation techniques. Others have contributed important background study and experience in Organizational Development, which looks at the ways in which persons, processes, and structures deal with change. Finally, direct personal involvement in the life and leadership of local church communities has been of great importance to all of us.

The role of collaborative interaction among all these fields and methods can be seen also in some of the projects that for several of us have nurtured our interest in questions of parish mission and leadership. From the 1980s and earlier, increased attention to the changing circumstances of Christian communities spurred the development of a specialized area of Practical Theology that has become well-known as "Congregational Studies." This approach makes use of a wide variety of social research tools and theological

perspectives to recognize and understand in detail a community's local culture and circumstances, and it relies on the direct involvement of a congregation's members in the study. Originally developed among Protestant communities, Congregational Studies has more recently attracted Catholic pastoral
leaders and theologians as well, in response to the many new questions that
changing cultural circumstances have raised. Early in the twenty-first century, a group of scholars from several Christian traditions, known as the Congregational Studies Team, received funding from the Lilly Endowment Inc.
of Indianapolis for an initiative called the Engaged Scholars Project. This
initiative supported, with funding and mentoring, the work of younger scholars of religion, both sociologists and theologians, who set out to use the
methods of Congregational Studies to make a direct impact on the lives of
local church communities. Two contributors to the present volume, Rev.
William A. Clark, SJ, and Dr. Brett Hoover, were fortunate to participate as
research fellows in this program.

In recent years the Lilly Endowment *Sustaining Pastoral Excellence* program funded two other major projects making fundamental contributions to
the support of Catholic parishes. One of these, "Project INSPIRE," as an
institutional partnership of the Archdiocese of Chicago and Loyola University Chicago, set out to shape the formation of collaborative parish leadership
teams in the archdiocese. INSPIRE's hallmark was its focus on the local
pastoral teams' own work to build local cultures of collaboration among
ordained, lay professional, and volunteer staff members. For this task, it
deployed trained consultants, generated learning plans, and collected follow-
up progress reports from parish teams and from individual team members,
and organized frequent gatherings and other networking opportunities for the
pastoral leadership teams involved in the project. It was the thought-provok-
ing conversation at INSPIRE's closing Milestone Conference that first encouraged us to bring together this volume of essays.

During the same time, the Lilly Endowment also supported Emerging
Models of Pastoral Leadership, an extensive program of research, conferences, and publication on the many new approaches to parish leadership
emerging in US parishes. A notable feature of the work done by Emerging
Models was its extensive consultation with actual pastoral leaders at all levels, so that the models it described were deeply informed by long and detailed conversation among practitioners from multiple points of view. The
original directors of both these projects, Dan Gast of INSPIRE and Dr. Marti
R. Jewell of Emerging Models, contribute essays to this volume.

Our opening chapter, focused on trends in US parishes that call for careful
conversations among a wide variety of co-workers, makes use of the experience of Project INSPIRE, as well as important research on the current state of
Catholic ministry presented at the INSPIRE Milestone Conference by Dr.
Katarina Schuth, OSF, of St. Thomas University in St. Paul, Minnesota.

INSPIRE also provided a very promising experiment in development of collaborative parish leadership through the creation of a unique approach to parish consulting. Dan Gast, executive director of INSPIRE from 2003 to 2012, created a team of professional consultants who shared with him backgrounds in Organizational Development, experiences in pastoral life, and leadership on diocesan as well as parish levels. The consulting method they developed emphasized group process, open communication, naming and developing both individual and team strengths and values, and matching those team values to the local culture of the parish. Our second chapter is Gast's overview of this approach to consulting, written with Dr. Peter Gilmour, one of the originators of Project INSPIRE. They find the fundamental concepts of the method reaffirmed again and again by current developments in other areas of pastoral ministry and research.

The process of looking carefully at the results and effects of collaborative practice must also, we believe, involve collaborative methods. The Froehles' contribution provides us an engaging example of how qualitative research can be applied to understanding the actual effects of methods such as parish consultancy in the lives of parish communities. A prominent voice in the development of Practical Theology in the Catholic context, Dr. Bryan Froehle is director of the doctoral program in Practical Theology at the School of Theology and Ministry at St. Thomas University in Miami, Florida. His wife, Dr. Mary Froehle, is a professional counselor with extensive experience in pastoral education, including as an adjunct faculty member in the Institute of Pastoral Studies at Loyola University Chicago. She is assistant professor of Practical Theology at St. Paul Regional Seminary, Boynton Beach, Florida. Together, they conducted research on three Chicago parishes that participated in Project INSPIRE. Their chapter provides a case study in the ways collaborative approaches shaped the ministries of typical INSPIRE communities, and shaped the communities themselves.

The next several chapters use a variety of methods that take very seriously the "shape of communities" in assessing what pastoral experience reveals about collaborative leadership. Fr. Clark's essay on parish reorganization draws on research conducted while he held the INSPIRE Visiting Research Professorship at Loyola University Chicago. In recent decades, clustering, merging, and closing of parishes in the face of changing communities and declining numbers of priests have become unavoidable aspects of parish life in much of the United States and Europe. In large regions once strongly Catholic, where flourishing parishes could be found in nearly every town and city neighborhood, it has become common to see former Catholic schools, convents, rectories, halls, and church buildings either sold for other purposes, boarded up and left unused, or demolished. While specific circumstances of the decline, and types of resources available to address it, vary significantly from one locale to another, the tendency has often been to reorganize local communities on a diocese-wide basis. This wholesale approach has indeed led to revitalization for some particular parishes, but it has also needlessly disrupted many quite vital local communities. Failure to carefully construct collaborative processes for stewardship in times of significant change can lead to a great deal of anger and alienation when community members perceive themselves excluded from meaningful decision making. Looking at two parish clusters, seemingly quite similar but merged under very different circumstances and with very different results, Fr. Clark discusses the role that collaborative leadership can play when communities must be radically reorganized.

In the United States and elsewhere, another pastoral challenge presented by increased mobility and changing demographics has been the emergence of complex multicultural parish communities. Such communities can result from the arrival in one area of significant numbers of Catholic immigrants, or from diocesan attempts to provide ministry to more widely scattered Catholics of a particular language group, or from successful local outreach efforts to refugees, migrant workers, and others from outside a parish's established community. However they come about, such communities are faced with serious decisions about how to structure the relationships among two, three, or even more language groups using parish facilities and how to foster cooperation among these groups. It is a situation that cries out for collaborative approaches to leadership, but useful models are not always available for such complex social systems. Dr. Brett Hoover, assistant professor of Theological Studies at Loyola Marymount University in Los Angeles, and INSPIRE's first visiting research professor, conducted extensive research in a wide variety of multicultural parishes. His essay discusses the promises and challenges of collaborative leadership in such situations.

In many US dioceses, opportunities for cross-cultural collaboration of the type Dr. Hoover describes involve immigrants from Mexico. In recent decades, Mexican immigration to the Chicago area, for example, has increased to the point that nearly three-quarters of the large Latino population (which itself comprises nearly 30 percent of the city's residents) report Mexico as their country of origin. In the Catholic Church in Chicago, the percentage of native Spanish speakers now equals that of native English speakers, with Mexicans as the dominant national group. As visiting research professors for Project INSPIRE in Chicago, both Hoover and Clark spent significant amounts of time observing parishes with large Mexican populations. It has been important for us, therefore, to include among these chapters the contribution of Dr. Elfriede Wedam of the Department of Sociology and the McNamara Center for the Social Study of Religion at Loyola University Chicago. Dr. Wedam has long been involved with questions concerning the social functioning of congregations and other religious organizations in urban settings. In recent years she established a strong working relationship with Catholic leaders in Mexico City who are investigating the effects of rapid urbanization on the religious practices of Mexican Catholics and on the pastoral strategies of parish leaders. Her comparison of such apparently different social milieux as Chicago and Mexico City—and the similarity of both the challenges and the conclusions—yields strong indications that our overall theme of collaborative approaches to pastoral leadership remains relevant even across cultural and linguistic lines.

The international potential of this work started to become evident to INSPIRE team members when, quite early in the life of the project, Dan Gast was asked to participate in hosting a group of German pastors and lay associates. They were visiting Chicago to gain fresh perspectives on some of the common challenges facing parish communities. The program, sponsored by a prominent German layman with business experience in the Chicago area, was called CrossingOver, and it eventually brought dozens of German Catholic pastoral leaders and academics into contact with the church in Chicago. From the beginning, CrossingOver involved an important academic component as well, centered in the members of the Catholic faculty at the Ruhr University Bochum. Their efforts, now including a Center of Applied Pastoral Theology, have led to numerous publications on aspects of pastoral practice both in America and Germany, and have had a notable impact on the Catholic Church in Germany. Graciela Sonntag, a research associate for CrossingOver and a pastoral associate for the Diocese of Münster, and Dr. Andreas Henkelmann, a pastoral theologian associated with both CrossingOver and the Centre of Applied Pastoral Theology (ZAP), contribute analysis of recent German approaches to parish leadership.

The history of parishes as social institutions in Western Europe is of course much longer and more complex than in the United States. Nonetheless, descriptions of recent social changes that have resulted in the diminishment of ordained leadership, financial resources, and parish population in large areas of Europe have a clear ring of familiarity on both sides of the Atlantic. Despite the legacies of strong twentieth-century movements in liturgical and pastoral theology, and post–Vatican II efforts in some countries to build up a corps of highly trained nonordained pastoral workers, new conditions have prompted clustering and closing of many European parishes, and raised serious questions about appropriate leadership models. In the French Archdiocese of Poitiers, a startlingly new collaborative approach has emerged since the 1980s, by which small communities have been maintained in many villages and neighborhoods that would otherwise have seen their churches shuttered. The approach involves commissioning, by episcopal authority, of lay pastoral teams for each of these local communities, which are also grouped into "pastoral sectors" under the supervision of a priest pastor. The Poitiers arrangement has inspired and influenced similar adaptations in a number of regions worldwide. Prof. Dr. Reinhard Feiter explores the Poitiers

Model, and its influence in Europe and the world. Prof. Dr. Feiter is professor of Pastoral Theology and Religious Education and director of the Institute of Pastoral Theology at the Faculty of Catholic Theology of the Westfälische Wilhelms-University Münster, Germany.

The collaborative spirit of Practical Theology, which makes it such a useful tool in the overall development of local pastoral practice, is further demonstrated in Dr. Marti R. Jewell's exploration of the work of collaborative leadership and its interplay with the Tradition. Using the expertise that she honed in her service as the director of the Emerging Models of Pastoral Leadership project throughout its most active period, Dr. Jewell grounds her theological reflection in the lived experience of many diverse local communities throughout the United States. She considers this experience in light of scripture, Church history, and the doctrine of the Trinity. In this way, she seeks an approach to local pastoral leadership that is both theological and practical, able to meet contemporary challenges while growing respectful cooperation between clergy and laity. The practical note sounded here is picked up again in the last chapter, in which the book's editors return to the question of "talking about parish" posed in the first chapter. Here, with particular reference to Gast's expertise in the area of Organizational Development, we look at context, motivation, and strategies for carrying forward the conversations suggested throughout this volume. We sincerely hope that the strategies presented here will stimulate the actual praxis of collaborative pastoral leadership.

In an "Afterword," Fr. Clark presents a brief sketch of an overall "Theology of Collaborative Leadership," reflecting on the deeper connections between the Christian tradition and the various themes suggested by the chapters. Without losing focus on the local church community, he attempts to open a wider lens, looking at the concepts of communion and revelation, sacrament and incarnation, collaboration and mission. His hope is to link the whole work of collaborative pastoral leadership to some of the most central truths of the Christian faith.

Chapter One

Talk about Parish

Toward Conversations of Consequence

Daniel Gast and William A. Clark, SJ

EDITORS' NOTE

Pope Francis has called Catholic parishes throughout the Church to a process of "self-renewal and constant adaptivity." In the United States, trends observed over the past few decades make clear that parishes are in significant transition with respect to membership, structures, ministers and ministries, and staffing patterns. Priests are fewer in number and many become pastors soon after ordination. Their ability to grow collaborative expressions of pastoral leadership depends on more than personal attitudes about priestly function. Pastors and their pastoral staffs must be skilled as managers, a requisite that prepares them to lead. They lead parishes that are often increasing in size and complexity, often due to diocesan restructuring (clustering, merging, etc.), but also due to important demographic changes. Their communities are aging, changing or blending culturally and socioeconomically, yet populated with discernible age-cohorts who expect different forms of participation, pastoral care, and pastoral leadership. This chapter offers recent data on the self-identification, values, and best practices of ordained and lay ecclesial ministers. It also briefly reviews recent data regarding parish transitions and membership. We propose that the more persons we engage in exploration and learning, the better chance that critical realities will not go unaddressed.

Mr. Daniel Gast directed Project INSPIRE from its launch in 2004 until his retirement in 2013. A project to build collaborative forms of pastoral leadership in parishes, INSPIRE was a partnership initiative of Loyola University Chicago and the Archdiocese of Chicago made possible by a generous grant from the Lilly Endowment Inc. *Sustaining Pastoral Excellence* (SPE) program. Dan has served in several church settings locally and nationally including parish ministry, catechetical ministry, Catholic schools, higher education, diocesan ministry, and Catholic publishing.

Dr. William A. Clark, SJ, is associate professor of religious studies at the College of the Holy Cross, Worcester, Massachusetts. He was INSPIRE's visiting research professor at Loyola University Chicago from 2011 to 2013. Fr. Clark served as a pastor and in other pastoral ministry roles in New England and in Jamaica (West Indies). He is author of *A Voice of Their Own: The Authority of the Local Parish*, published in 2005 by Liturgical Press. He holds a doctoral degree from Weston Jesuit School of Theology (now Boston College School of Theology and Ministry).

"A COMMUNITY OF COMMUNITIES"

In 2013 the Church was blessed with a pope who writes and exhorts in plain language. Still firm in papal fidelity to tradition, mission, and teaching, Pope Francis has modeled an invitational and conversational posture. That is particularly evident in his approach to the life and work of parishes. In his Apostolic Exhortation *Evangelii Gaudium*, Francis writes:

> The parish is not an outdated institution; precisely because it possesses great flexibility, it can assume quite different contours depending on the openness and missionary creativity of the pastor and the community. While certainly not the only institution which evangelizes, if the parish proves capable of self-renewal and constant adaptivity, it continues to be "the Church living in the midst of the homes of her sons and daughters." This presumes that it really is in contact with the homes and the lives of its people, and does not become a useless structure out of touch with people or a self-absorbed group made up of a chosen few. The parish is the presence of the Church in a given territory, an environment for hearing God's word, for growth in the Christian life, for dialogue, proclamation, charitable outreach, worship and celebration. In all its activities the parish encourages and trains its members to be evangelizers. It is a community of communities, a sanctuary where the thirsty come to drink in the midst of their journey, and a centre of constant missionary outreach. We must admit, though, that the call to review and renew our parishes has not yet sufficed to bring them nearer to people, to make them environments of living communion and participation, and to make them completely mission-oriented.[1]

Pope Francis here introduces several ideas and images of parish communities that, in the course of the document (and certainly elsewhere in his writing and speaking), he develops into persistent themes.

In chapter 2 of *Evangelii Gaudium* he reminds his readers, "The Gospel tells us constantly to run the risk of a face-to-face encounter with others."[2] Here, the Pope assumes that the character of the parish is such that it is indeed a primary place in the Church for such encounters. (He warns, of course, that this can only be true if the parish "really is in contact with the homes and the lives of its people.") A second theme flows from this first, that parishes present the Church as a people of *many* faces, the communities displaying "quite different contours" amid the "flexibility," "openness," and "creativity" which they display at their best. Third, convinced that "the joy of evangelizing always arises from grateful remembrance,"[3] he draws the parish as a place where that evangelical remembrance is forged, "an environment for hearing God's word, for growth in the Christian life . . . a sanctuary where the thirsty come to drink." Fourth, the ideal parish is a model for Francis's "Church that goes forth," for it is "a centre of constant missionary outreach" which, as he has already reminded his readers, "embraces human life, touching the suffering flesh of Christ in others."[4] Finally, as he will explain, in order to be renewed as an "environment of living communion and participation," the parish must be "a mystical fraternity, a contemplative fraternity . . . capable of seeing the sacred grandeur of our neighbour, of finding God in every human being, of tolerating the nuisances of life in common by clinging to the love of God."[5]

NURTURING PARISH COMMUNITIES

The hopefulness and vision that have been such a clear element of Pope Francis's style, as well as both his invitation to renewal and his critique of insularity, make this an important time for conversation about parish communities in the universal Church. If they are indeed to be renewed, to be nurtured and grown as attractive gatherings of effective, mission-focused people of resilient faith, they must face up to new challenges. Researchers have uncovered a number of critical issues that impact Catholic parish life in the United States. Some trends represent positive opportunities, others pose threats; some are well known, others remain less identified or less considered among parishioners and even among those in active ministry. It is our conviction that none of the threats posed are ultimately destructive, *unless* they remain untreated or taken for granted, and the accompanying opportunities unexploited.

In this chapter, and those to follow, we invite readers to an attitude of critical reflection, self-assessment, and sharing, and to keep three questions in play: What shall become of our local parish communities? Who are the various constituencies able to play a role in that future? How might each of them contribute to understanding the opportunities and challenges, and then to shaping and stewarding the transitions the future holds?

A JOB OR A MINISTRY?

In the United States, if given the choice of describing what they do as "their job" or "their ministry," parish staff members will overwhelmingly favor "ministry." Most could offer personal stories about being "called to ministry" as ordained or as laypersons.[6] Delegation by the bishop or pastor begets roles and titles that identify parish ministers as people dedicated to lives and life-styles of service that seldom know a 40-hour workweek. They perform acts of service, witness, and presence that acknowledge the sustaining nurture of Word and sacrament in their daily lives.

When one follows most any of them throughout their days, however, it becomes hard to deny that ministry is also hard work. Days and evenings are riddled with tasks, carved up with schedules that declare good intentions if not ultimate results, interrupted by phone calls, texts, and doorbells. It is quite an achievement if a pastor, for instance, is able to work at one task for an unbroken fifteen minutes, unless it is late in the evening. Lay ministers have it much the same. It is significant that, when the US Conference of Catholic Bishops issued a formal declaration about lay ecclesial ministers, they chose to lead with imagery of Jesus' classic parable about work and time, naming their text, *Co-Workers in the Vineyard of the Lord: A Resource for Guiding the Development of Lay Ecclesial Ministry.*[7] Ministerial work is God's work.

The document's subtitle implies that shaping and ordering ministerial work is itself more work. Such effort must develop coherent, effective rela-tionships that yield supportive, measured, mission-focused ministry. "Col-laborative pastoral leadership" relies on such relationships and on a shared mission and vision held by persons who bring to the "co-working" different threads of knowledge, different virtues and skills, different values. Moreover, collaboration in pastoral leadership generates working relationships through-out a community. The mission of Church is thereby engaged, as its amazing breadth across space and time receives unique expression within local parish communities. Forming, nurturing, and sustaining such communities, how-ever, requires pastoral ministers to focus attention, somewhat ironically, away from "the work" and toward one another. For these people whose gifts include aptitudes for nurturing human spirits and community, "teamwork" often appears to be neither instinctive nor intuitive. There is just too much "real work" to do. The challenges, though, are even more complex than that.

TODAY'S PASTORAL LEADERS

A recent large research project on Christian pastors and the quality of their leadership describes a tension well known within—but rarely outside of—rectories, parsonages, and parish offices. Pastors across all denominations—including Catholic pastors—report very high levels of satisfaction with, and enduring commitment to their life vocations. This is true even of pastors serving in difficult or conflicted communities.[8] Nevertheless, pastors addi-tionally report two groups of stressors that put health and perceptions of achievement at risk. These include experiences of community demands, criticism, conflict, and incompatible perceptions of the pastor's role. Ahead of all that, however, and topping out the list of stressors, pastors report experiences of isolation and loneliness.[9] Pastoral work can be permeated with people and yet lonely.

In Catholic parishes that joined in the INSPIRE project,[10] the work that pastoral associates and lay ministers do appeared to pose similar stressors and experiences. Generally, urban Catholic parishes are not tiny communities; most have distinct populations and cohorts within them, each with particular needs and expectations. Weeks and calendars are full, days can go very long, and one's pastoral work is focused on the immediate task and the particular persons served. Any wider focus may only extend to the next approaching task and deadline. For most members of a pastoral staff, unremitting successions of tasks blur any sense of the larger and longer view.

The parish school principal walks into the office somewhere around sunrise. The associate pastor and pastoral associate make morning rounds and evening appointments. The director of religious education meets with parents and catechists, puts lunch on hold for parent check-ins, and develops adult formation activities, usually held on evenings and weekends. The youth minister strives for later morning arrival, leads weekend events and summertime trips for young people and youth leaders, and turns out the parish center lights late into the evening. Deacons might be full or part time in any of these roles; some hold down "day jobs" and are at their pastoral work in off hours. The liturgical director and/or music minister plans, rehearses, and leads in a wide range of worship settings that in a single week ritualize occasions of joy and hopefulness, daily faith, finality and grief. The pastor knows he is "welcome" to be everywhere, to affirm all the good works with acts of presence and gratitude, but it's a scramble from altar to office to appointments to council and commission meetings. It is easy to see how the work itself, good work all of it, can divide and isolate persons, and quell collaborative intentions.

From parish to parish there can be myriad other positions with pastoral delegation: bereavement ministers, business managers, Rite of Christian Initiation of Adults (RCIA) ministers, family ministers, senior assistance ministers, associates serving specific ethnicities in the parish, and so on. A fuller staff portrait would also include those who support the work of pastoral leaders: receptionists, secretaries, and custodial or building managers. Pastors in some INSPIRE parishes requested these persons' participation in the project, thus widening ownership of mission and collaborative participation. Truth be told, there is no "typical" parish pastoral ministry scenario. US parishes vary greatly in terms of staffing, ministries, priorities, and profiles, even when compared to their closest neighboring parishes.

Varied roles bring life and foster vibrant communities. Any ministry can simultaneously drain and enrich the minister, requiring long hours but immersing one in purposeful work and significant relationships. INSPIRE interviewers found pastoral workers who love the work they do. They also found many of the same workers spiritually tapped out at the end of long days, some who also balance family lives, homework (their children's and sometimes their own), meals, laundry, and soccer. Neither were rectory living quarters safe havens from all of this. Interviewers and observers also noted that forms of isolation such as ministerial "silos" (disconnection from the work of other team members) and episodes of loneliness seemed to be taken for granted as coming with the territory.

Pastoral work is resplendent with contrasting perceptions of joy and of burden. When pastoral leaders aren't too busy to look for it, they get to see the difference they make in peoples' lives. They also cope with limited resources, cultural and social forces that diminish parish vitality. They often experience conflicting expectations from their own people or even from church authorities. To hold both the work and each other under such conditions requires much more of team members than intention and resolve. Collaboration in pastoral leadership grows through ministers' commitments to align their works and measure achievements against the mission they proclaim. It is a skilled performance. Collaborative leadership requires a continuous repertoire of practice, substantive conversation, and evaluation. This shared learning cycle generates awareness of being valued as a colleague, openness to new commitments, and more fully shared practice.

SIGNS OF THE TIMES IN THE US CHURCH

Pastoral learning must be accountable to the signs of the times, and the present day poses particular challenges. For this reason, sociological studies of Church institutions and church life are critically important today. Evolving, varied parish profiles and rapidly changing circumstances challenge researchers, theologians, bishops, and others who seek the broad view. Parishes in the United States express great variation, even when compared to their geographical neighbors, and their diversity and organizational complexity can befuddle laypersons and skilled organizational analysts alike.

Annual diocesan reports reveal certain numbers and trends—for instance, that through consolidations and mergers parishes are getting larger, or that more of them are shared by two or more cultural-linguistic groups, or that increasing numbers of laypersons occupy ministerial and administrative roles.

What, however, underlies those numbers and trends? How do parishes achieve and sustain vitality? What causes them to stagnate or wither? Who among the critical actors in parish communities is able to make a real difference? What are their best practices and, perhaps most critically, what goes on in their hearts and minds? Contextual insight from Dr. Katarina Schuth, OSF, allowed participants in Project INSPIRE's Milestone Conference (Chicago, October 2013) to place INSPIRE's qualitative data (gathered via observation, interviews, and narrative reports) against a more comprehensive backdrop of data from national research.[11] To her own analysis of the state of pastoral formation in US seminaries and religious orders, Dr. Schuth added several quantitative studies from CARA (Georgetown University's Center for Applied Research in the Apostolate) and several independent researchers.[12]

In a succinct paragraph, Dr. Schuth's report summarizes the evolving complexity, pastoral challenges, and emerging realities of parish life in the United States.

> Broadly speaking, parish life in the United States has changed drastically since 2002, characterized especially by merging and clustering parishes. As a consequence larger parish units are being formed, often calling for more members on pastoral teams, including full and part-time members. At the same time, a smaller pool of experienced priests is available; younger priests who need mentoring are becoming pastors shortly after ordination, and the crisis brought on by clergy who sexually abused youth is having a long-term impact. As the Church continues to experience growth in immigrant numbers, language and cultural barriers are exacerbated not only among parishioners, but also among priests coming to serve from other countries. All of these changes require staff development and mentoring.[13]

OVERVIEW OF US PARISH MINISTRY

Then Dr. Schuth—to borrow from the child's play-rhyme—opens the doors to see *all* the people, the ones serving and those worshiping, but also to note the ones missing. The ones serving include a decreasing number of priest pastors and associate pastors, smaller numbers of religious men and women, an increasing count of ordained deacons, and a dramatically increasing number of laypersons.

Profiles for key leadership roles are themselves changing. The largest generational cohort of pastors now approaches and passes retirement age. International priests, recruited from other countries and sometimes not formed in US seminaries, constitute almost a fifth of those serving. Younger priests with less experience become pastors, and associate pastors are an increasingly endangered population. As a group, younger priests tend to describe themselves as traditional, put great stock in the indelible spiritual character of their ordination, and express less enthusiasm for collaborative working arrangements with laypersons. A recent CARA study depicted in

Table 1.1 offers sobering attitudinal profiles of generational cohorts that comprise US priesthood. [14]

Table 1.1. Attitudes of Priests from Four Different Generations

	Pre–Vatican II Priests	Vatican II Priests	Post–Vatican II Priests	Millennial Priests
Open to discussion about collaborating with lay ministers	83%	78%	76%	65%
Open to discussion about working with lay administrators in parishes	76%	65%	63%	56%
The Church should allow women greater participation in all lay ministries.	84%	85%	82%	65%
Ordination makes a priest essentially different from the laity	75%	61%	77%	88%

From *Same Call Different Men: The Evolution of the Priesthood since Vatican II,* by Mary L. Gauthier, Paul M. Perl, and Stephen J. Fichter, 2012.

Accumulated data show one ministerial cohort that is growing and projected to grow further, while most others decline or grow marginally: laypersons in church ministry, most of them women. Table 1.2 reports the percentages of parish ministers drawn from various groups over fifteen years. [15]

Table 1.2. Parish Ministers 1990 to 2005

Ecclesial Status	1990	1997	2005	% Change 1990 to 2005
Religious Brothers	<1%	<1%	<1%	_____
Religious Sisters	41%	28%	16%	-25%
Laywomen	44%	54%	64%	+20%
Laymen	14%	17%	20%	+6%

From *Lay Parish Ministers,* David DeLambo. New York: National Pastoral Life Center, 2005, p. 45.

A subsequent report identifies patterns of decline for the number of diocesan priests and growth for deacons and for laypersons in ministry and leadership settings:

> Although the number of diocesan priests and Catholic parishes in the United States has declined in the last two decades, the number of other parish leaders has continued to grow along with the overall Catholic population. The number of US diocesan priests declined by 19 percent from 1992 to 2010 and the number of parishes dropped by 9 percent (a net difference of -1,751 parishes). As parishes have consolidated and now contain larger communities, on average, parish staffs have been growing in the United States as well. The number of professionally trained lay ecclesial ministers (LEM) increased by 76 percent between 1992 and 2010 and the number of permanent deacons serving the Church expanded by 62 percent.[16]

In Figure 1.1, Dr. Schuth provides a striking visual portrait of laypersons in ministry, culled from several recent sources.[17]

Meanwhile, enrollment figures for programs offering formal and advanced preparation of laypersons offer a stark contrast. Dr. Schuth's Figure 1.2 illustrates the sharp drop that occurs during the years when the sexual abuse crisis went public and US dioceses were forced to make financial settlements. In Figure 1.3, a "drill-down" look at those years makes clear the precipitous drop and subsequent stagnation of lay ministry enrollments.[18]

Moreover, unsurprisingly in proportion to trends of loss in the general Catholic population, fewer young adults prepare for lay ministries and pastoral work.

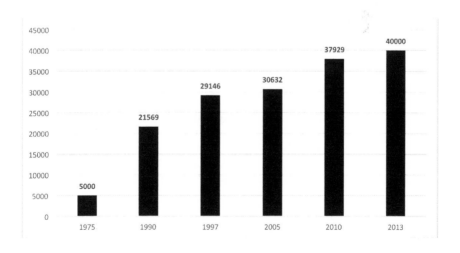

Figure 1.1.   Lay Ecclesial Ministry in the United States

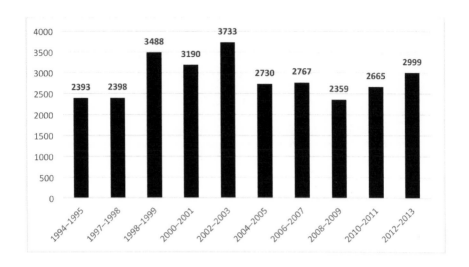

Figure 1.2. All Lay Ecclesial Ministry Students 1994–2013

Unlike any of the three older cohorts, the *Millennial Generation* is characterized by a significant loss of Catholic identity. Born between 1979 and 1987,
only seven percent [see themselves] as highly committed to the Catholic
Church. Many of them raise questions about the importance of being Catholic,
the substance of the faith, and the porous boundaries they see between Catholics and others. The sex abuse scandal was a traumatic shock for these young
people, some of whom responded with disgust and removed themselves from
the Church. Ideological differences within this group have created a split, with
a small percentage highly committed and ideologically conservative and most
others estranged and more progressive. How the Church responds to this
youngest generation will make all the difference in their future association
with the Church.[19]

Resources for advanced preparation have become threatened by economic
and institutional realities. As a matter of Church policy, enrollments preparing persons for lay ministry in diocesan seminaries have ceased or studies
and formation have been segregated.[20] More recently, pastoral studies programs at colleges and universities face uncertainty, compromise, or institutional thinning. High matriculation costs and expectations about lay minister
compensation proffer dim prospects for returning one's investment or secur-
ing employment that can be counted on to support a stable standard of living,
let alone family life.

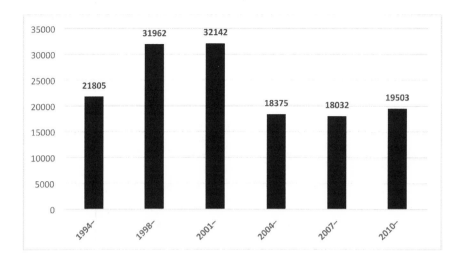

Figure 1.3.   Drill-Down of Lay Ecclesial Ministry Enrollments 1994–2010

PARISHIONERS

Parishioner profiles are equally dramatic. While the US Catholic population has increased by almost 24 million since 1965, that growth is supported by an increasingly Hispanic influx that masks a comparative decline in Anglos and Anglo Europeans. A 2010 report from the CARA observed, "Taking into account differences in parish size and the racial and ethnic changes reported by pastors, 40 percent of all growth in registered parishioners in US parishes from 2005 to 2010 was among Hispanic/Latino(a)s."[21]

US Catholics live in interesting times. From macro to on-the-ground perspectives, Catholic parishes are complex and dynamic as communities and as organizations. Profiles of parish staffs are likewise intricate and diverse. Catholic pastoral ministers are not cut from the same cloth. Even US-born priests of successive generational cohorts vary in their approach to pastoral office and commitments. In the United States, priests are supported and sometimes relieved in certain assignments by deacons, lay ecclesial ministers, business managers, or international priests, each of whom bring comparatively different administrative and ministerial skill sets and cultural profiles.

These ministers serve communities that are ever more diverse in socioeconomic, cultural, and generational profiles. So, too, are the varied communities to whom ministers and parishioners would extend invitations and expressions of hospitality. Indeed, effectively communicating such messages requires graceful competence in performances ranging from personal encounter and witness to navigating the whitewater worlds of social media. In any form, being present is not what it used to be. Catholics are challenged to grow the Faith in an era of unprecedented social, technological, and cultural transition.

CRITICAL CONVERSATIONS

We believe, therefore, that a wide array of conversations is in order, involving hierarchy, academia, and all other relevant institutions and communities, but most especially the local parish communities themselves. Parishioners may inquire and learn from researchers, theologians, ministers, bishops, and other Church leaders, but they themselves also have crucial insights to contribute. While each of these groups itself constitutes a community with its own disciplines and perspectives, and must pursue lively internal conversations, church members also need to discover how to talk "across borders." We contend that each of these perspectives—lay, ministerial, and professional, however we name them—is important and consequential. Should one or more miss out on the learning and discernment, the Church will suffer the consequences when the time comes for co-ownership of hard decisions and implementations. Together, we can provide shaping, substance, and commitments to fill futures with hope and possibility that replace regret and resignation.

BIBLIOGRAPHY

Carroll, Jackson W., with Becky R. McMillan. *God's Potters: Pastoral Leadership and the Shaping of Congregations*. Grand Rapids, MI: William B. Eerdmans, 2006.

DeLambo, David. *Lay Parish Ministers*. New York: National Pastoral Life Center, 2005.

Elsbernd, Mary. "Listening for a Life's Work: Contemporary Callings to Ministry," in *Revisiting the Idea of Vocation: Theological Explorations*. Edited by John C. Haughey, SJ. Washington, DC: Catholic University of America Press, 2004.

Francis, Pope. Apostolic Exhortation, *Evangelii Gaudium*, Joy of the Gospel. Libreria Editrice Vaticana, November 24, 2013. Accessed May 2016, at http://w2.vatican.va/content/francesco/en/apost_exhortations/documents/papa-francesco_esortazione-ap_20131124_evangelii-gaudium.html.

Gray, Mark. "Perspectives from Parish Leaders: U.S. Parish Life and Ministry." Washington, DC: Center for Applied Research in the Apostolate at Georgetown University, 2012. Also published by the Emerging Models Project at the National Association for Lay Ministry, Washington, DC, 2012.

Gray, Mark, Mary Gautier, and Melissa A. Cidade. "The Changing Face of Catholic Parishes." Washington, DC: Center for Applied Research in the Apostolate at Georgetown University, 2009. Also published by the Emerging Models Project at the National Association for Lay Ministry, Washington, DC, 2011.

Schuth, Katarina, OSF. "INSPIRE: Implications for Ministry in the U.S. Church." From proceedings of the INSPIRE Milestone Conference, Loyola University Chicago, 2013.

————. "Pastoral and Seminary Education Panel Report." INSPIRE Milestone Conference, 2013.

US Conference of Catholic Bishops. *Co-Workers in the Vineyard of the Lord: A Resource for Guiding the Development of Lay Ecclesial Ministry*. Washington, DC: USCCB, 2005.

NOTES

1. Pope Francis, Apostolic Exhortation, *Evangelii Gaudium*, Joy of the Gospel (November 24, 2013), §28. (Hereafter cited as "EG.")
2. EG, §88
3. EG, §13.
4. EG, §24.
5. EG, §92.
6. See Mary Elsbernd, "Listening for a Life's Work: Contemporary Callings to Ministry," in *Revisiting the Idea of Vocation: Theological Explorations*, John C. Haughey, SJ, ed. (Washington, DC: Catholic University of America Press, 2004).
7. US Conference of Catholic Bishops, *Co-Workers in the Vineyard of the Lord: A Resource for Guiding the Development of Lay Ecclesial Ministry* (Washington, DC: USCCB, 2005).
8. Jackson W. Carroll with Becky R. McMillan, *God's Potters: Pastoral Leadership and the Shaping of Congregations* (Grand Rapids, MI: Wm. B. Eerdmans, 2006), 159–178.
9. Ibid., 179–180.
10. The project leveraged funding from the Lilly Endowment Inc. *Sustaining Pastoral Excellence* (SPE) program to identify pastors and staffs who wished to build upon their successes by forming themselves as pastoral leadership teams. The next two chapters describe INSPIRE's collaboration-focused methodologies, learning, and outcomes.
11. Dr. Katarina Schuth, OSF, holds the endowed chair for the Social Scientific Study of Religion at St. Paul Seminary School of Divinity and the University of St. Thomas in St. Paul, Minnesota.
12. Dr. Schuth authored or collaborated on several seminal studies of Catholic pastoral formation and practice including *Priestly Ministry in Multiple Parishes* (2006); *Educating Leaders for Ministry: Issues and Responses* with V. Klimoski and K. O'Neil (2005); *Reason for the Hope: The Futures of Roman Catholic Theologates* (1989); *Seminaries, Theologates, and the Future of Church Ministry: An Analysis of Trends and Transitions* (1999); and *Seminary Formation: Recent History-Current Circumstances-New Directions* (2016).
13. Schuth, "INSPIRE: Implications for Ministry in the U.S. Church," paper prepared for the INSPIRE Milestone Conference, Loyola University Chicago, October 2013.
14. Ibid., 19.
15. David DeLambo, *Lay Parish Ministers* (New York: National Pastoral Life Center, 2005), 45. See also Mark Gray, Mary Gautier, and Melissa A. Cidade, "The Changing Face of U.S. Catholic Parishes" (Washington, DC: Center for Applied Research in the Apostolate [CARA] for the Emerging Models of Pastoral Leadership project with funding from the Lilly Endowment Inc., 2009).
16. Mark Gray, "Perspectives from Parish Leaders: U.S. Parish Life and Ministry" (Washington, DC: CARA for the Emerging Models of Pastoral Leadership project with funding from the Lilly Endowment Inc., 2012).
17. DeLambo as reported by Schuth, "Implications for Ministry."
18. Schuth, "Pastoral and Seminary Education," Panel Report at INSPIRE Milestone Conference, October 2013.
19. Schuth, "Implications for Ministry," 24.
20. "The Congregation is firm on this point: seminaries exist for the formation of candidates for the priesthood (cf. *Pastores Dabo Vobis*, n. 61). Thus, the laity should not routinely be admitted to share the seminarians' classes or their living spaces (their dining area, the chapel, the library, and especially not the living quarters). If circumstances require the seminary to educate the laity (which really ought to take place elsewhere), it must arrange to do so in such a way that the integrity of the seminary is not compromised." Congregation for Catholic Education, Letter on Apostolic Visitation (2005–2006), 2009. Accessed June 2016, http://www.vatican.va/phome_en.htm.
21. Gray, Gautier, Cidade, "Changing Face of U.S. Catholic Parishes," 54.

Chapter Two

INSPIRE Learning about Parish Consulting

Daniel Gast and Peter Gilmour

EDITORS' NOTE

Project INSPIRE ("Identify, Nurture, and Sustain Pastoral Imagination through Resources for Excellence"), a pastoral leadership development effort shared in partnership by the Archdiocese of Chicago and Loyola University Chicago, provides the lens for this chapter. The authors served on the project's Lead Team during its active phase between 2004 and 2013. Their aim in this report is to build a case and groundwork for a new form of consulting to parishes, pastoral teams, and leadership persons in parish communities. They also profile the unique capacities and particular kind of intelligence one must bring to such consulting. They contend that forming and growing persons who can provide parishes with mission-oriented consultation should become an institutional priority for church leaders.

Daniel Gast was executive director of Project INSPIRE from 2003 to 2013. (See previous chapter editors' note for further details.)

Dr. Peter Gilmour collaborated with colleagues at Loyola University Chicago and the Archdiocese of Chicago to design and propose Project INSPIRE to the Lilly Endowment Inc. and thereafter served as the principal investigator on the project's Lead Team. He is professor emeritus at Loyola University Chicago's Institute for Pastoral Studies. Prior to his retirement Dr. Gilmour served as graduate program director of the master of arts degree in religious education. His publications include *The Emerging Pastor* (Sheed and Ward, 1986), *The Wisdom of Memoir* (St. Mary's Press, 1997), and *Growing in Courage* (St. Mary's Press, 1998).

OVERVIEW

INSPIRE used experienced organizational consultants, deployed to work on-site with parish-based pastoral staffs. The consultants assisted pastors and their many different configurations of staff persons in the work of growing collaborative pastoral leadership.[1] In the terminology of the INSPIRE project, pastoral staffs worked to form themselves as "Pastoral Leadership Teams." The project's promise to the sponsoring Lilly Endowment Inc. *Sustaining Pastoral Excellence* (SPE) program was to build expressions of collaborative pastoral leadership in no fewer than thirty-six parishes of the Archdiocese of Chicago.

When the original SPE grant program ended after five years, the project had actually developed iterations of Pastoral Leadership Teams in forty-six parishes and also among a team of directors from the archdiocesan chancery. The larger number of parishes is due to four clustered interparish enrollments, but also subtracts one staff that withdrew from the project. In a four-year Sustaining Grant program the project would re-enroll two pastoral teams in parishes that had merged during their original enrollment. It would also enroll six new parishes and one episcopal vicar, his deans and staff.

This chapter is based on the director's conference report with appendices distributed electronically to enrolled participants prior to the October 2013 Milestone Conference at Loyola University Chicago. In what follows, we draw upon documentation about organizational consultation accrued over nine years of work with pastors, priests, deacons, lay ecclesial ministers, and other laypersons on parish staffs, in archdiocesan offices, and episcopal leadership in the Archdiocese of Chicago. Source materials include written reports from some of these persons and from the project's parish consultants, as well as interview data. We offer a project leadership perspective, including our own recollections and interpretations of issues and events. Most of the written reports and digitally recorded and transcribed interviews are organized in a digital database now held at the Center for the Study of Religion at the Loyola University Chicago Department of Sociology.

We frame our inquiries about parish consulting with four questions and one assertion. What organizational literature informed the process INSPIRE developed as "Parish Consultation"? What did INSPIRE stakeholders learn about organizational consultation with pastors and their staffs? What expressions of collaborative pastoral leadership mark the transition from pastoral staff to Pastoral Leadership Team? How can consultative relationships assist that development? Compared to the consulting praxis in corporate, community, and nongovernmental organization (NGO) settings in the United States and Europe, is organizational consulting in Catholic parishes strikingly different, or at least somehow nuanced? (Yes, we will assert, it is "strikingly nuanced" with respect to content, flow, application. The case will be supported by narrative drawn from INSPIRE data.)

We begin with a brief orientation to the organizational literature that informs such consultation. Then we will tour INSPIRE's application of the team learning concepts and related disciplines so critical in today's business and nonprofit service sectors.[2] Readers will see how the Church's organization, together with critical religious thinking and free discourse and discovery, creates fruitful interactions leading to transformation, conversion, and action.[3]

Team learning among parish staff persons both invites and relies upon praxis, the process of action-oriented reflection and dialogue about Church and parish mission. Skilled praxis embraces critical tensions between theory and practice for the purpose of refining and improving pastoral care and pursuing mission. Over years of commitment to such personal and shared learning, INSPIRE's gifted pastoral leadership teams generated particular disciplines and best practices for collaborative pastoral leadership. We will round out our analysis with consideration of how these disciplines and practices can grow both pastoral teams and the parish communities they serve.

CONSULTATION FOR PASTORAL TEAMS

Two distinct but complementary pastoral formation agendas converged to "inspire" the consultation that emerged in our project. The Lilly Endowment Inc. *Sustaining Pastoral Excellence* (SPE) program called attention away from problem-focused or corrective processes, and thus beyond concern for simple ministerial formation and performance. The challenge to those applying for an SPE grant: propose ways to support those who are *already* succeeding as pastors. The Endowment leadership boldly proclaimed the *E*-word, "Excellence," as the focus of a national project.[4] Assessing data from their recently sponsored studies, the Lilly Endowment leadership seemed keenly aware of one big looming constant in parish and congregational ministry: inevitably, pastoral work gets lonely, isolating, de-energizing even for those who show traits of pastoral excellence. What if, the Endowment implied, we were to front-load resources that at least mitigate the stressors that cause burnout, that at best strengthen and grow persons so they exude pastoral excellence? It is no surprise that a large majority of successful proposals to SPE promised to establish and cultivate pastoral peer groups or build networks among pastoral persons, and no surprise that most peer-gathering projects succeeded.

Two leaders in Chicago expanded the SPE agenda. Dr. Mary Elsbernd, OFM, and Sr. Judith Vallimont, SSpS, called to the Endowment's attention the pastoral excellence of laypeople serving in pastoral assignments in the

Chicago Catholic Church. While an important document from the US Conference of Catholic Bishops, *Co-Workers in the Vineyard of the Lord: A
Resource for Guiding the Development of Lay Ecclesial Ministry*,[5] was in
embryonic form—it would not be formally issued until late 2005—Dr. Elsbernd and Sr. Judith, along with Dr. Joseph Bator and Dr. Peter Gilmour
cowrote a proposal to identify "excellent" pastoral *staffs* in the archdiocese
and build their capacities for collaboration in excellent pastoral leadership.
The Chicago proposal team promised to develop Pastoral Leadership Teams
on-site and to supplement with occasional large group gatherings.

It is easy to miss the proposal's nuance. It expressed a university/archdio-
cese institutional partnership formed to do something more than assert the
posture of laypeople in Catholic pastoral ministry. The INSPIRE project
would call attention to the important contribution of ordained and laypersons
who "cowork" as colaborers in parish communities. That is, the principal
focus would not be on distinct performances of individual pastoral ministers,
but on their capacity to perform excellent pastoral leadership collaboratively.
INSPIRE, we would often advise pastors and staffs, is first about forming
collaborative relationships in ministry. Pastoral team members could pursue
certain performance competencies, but we would work to position those
skills to enhance the integrity and collaborative capacity of the pastoral team.

THE INSPIRE PROMISE

To honor its commitment to the *Sustaining Pastoral Excellence* program,
Loyola University Chicago and the Archdiocese of Chicago formed a Partnership Initiative that would bring organizational development expertise and
collaborative pastoral leadership to parish staffs in the Church of Chicago.
Before they approved the project, Endowment leaders asked the partnership
to reconfigure implementation strategy away from reliance on academic programming and training efforts. Project leaders proposed a delivery system
prioritizing on-site services. In brief detail, the process began with application by the pastor and staff, assignment of a consultant who would help them
understand the work ahead and discern their commitment, personal and team
interviews that would lead to learning plans, assignment of funding to support the work, implementation with checkpoints, and evaluation. The project
would also bring the pastoral teams together for in-service and encourage
networking among them.[6] The unique institutional partnership pledged to
serve people willing to strive for pastoral excellence as individual ministers
and as pastoral teams:

> INSPIRE serves as a resource connecting pastoral leaders who currently pastor
> with distinction, with those who can be mentored and coached to one day
> display excellence of their own. INSPIRE offers programming leading to a

transformation, over time, in the culture of the archdiocese, so that excellence is cultivated and nurtured in all of the archdiocese's pastoral leaders.

> —Michael Garanzini, SJ. *Letter of introduction to the Lilly Endowment*
> *Sustaining Pastoral Excellence program director, September 2003*

INSPIRE will unite the resources of a university-based Catholic school of ministry (Institute of Pastoral Studies—Loyola University Chicago) and one of the nation's largest concentrations of Roman Catholics (Archdiocese of Chicago). . . . INSPIRE aims to strengthen the essential unity of ministries in the Archdiocese, to promote a shared ecclesial vision, and to foster a team-based sense of responsibility for pastoral excellence among Pastoral Leadership Teams of the Catholic Church in Chicago.

> —*Proposal to Sustaining Pastoral Excellence (SPE) program*
> *of the Lilly Endowment Inc., 2003.*

OD MEETS CHURCH AND PARISH

INSPIRE's leadership determined to bring organizational development (OD), leadership development, and organizational psychology to the Catholic parish setting. They drew from a base of literature in these fields with the intention to adapt corporate practices to serve Church mission and complement the Chicago Catholic ecclesial culture. The three disciplines are relative newcomers to the enterprises of corporate and community organizations, if only because the concept of "organization" is itself a largely mid-twentieth century accommodation. Organizational management authority Peter Drucker found seeds of "the organization" in the early Industrial Age but asserted that ideas of organizing, managing, and leading "organizations" began gaining traction only after World War II and the early Information Age through the late twentieth century.[7] He described the movement from "command and control" models of "scientific management" to forms of management and articulations of leadership that invite the practical "knowledges" and the wisdom of "workers" into the processes that shape and advance the ordering of structures, production of goods and services, and even declarations of corporate mission.

INSPIRE's Lead Team, a group of five persons from Church and University, challenged themselves to respect the differences between corporate or community organizations and the particular organization that we identify as the Catholic parish. Parishes do not exist to produce a product or provide a particular social service; they are faith communities formed to express Eucharistic thanksgiving and praise, to ground people's lives in faithful living, and to further the mission of Christ to all the world. They certainly perform work, starting with the work of sacraments and sacramentality, and they render service in many forms in their communities and beyond. In the course of expressing their institutional commission from their local Church (the diocese) and the universal Church, they give authoritative witness and amplify a message to secular society that often runs counter to purely profit-centered or humanist or capitalist or socialist agendas. William Clark summarizes their unique authority to give this witness:

> In thus conforming to the authority of Christ the local community demonstrates to the church and the world how authority can be expressed not merely as universal pronouncements that enter from outside the boundaries of a community, but rather *intimately,* in innumerable details of human life together.[8]

That is, they express the Church's communal mission in service of the Gospel, witnessing to an ongoing narrative of personal and corporate encounters with the grace of God. In their efforts to reconcile failures, heal, serve, and work in the world as servants and witnesses, members of a parish community are "filled with the hope that arises in the concrete proclamation of the reign of God in word, sacrament and mission."[9]

INSPIRE longed for and attempted to move toward a comprehensive "ecclesiology of the local parish community," and the above remarks are intended only to hint at the broadest contours of that challenge. Here, we wish only to describe the context of our caution against wholesale adoption of assumptions and practices from corporate culture. Parish ministers adroitly practice the hermeneutic of suspicion. They rightly bristle at interventions with "business" or corporate and organizational agenda that discount or appear to patronize their faith-oriented, pastoral, and prophetic agendas.

The consultative work we did in INSPIRE, however, rose out of that corporate world. Selectively and briefly, we want now to identify the insights and practices we engaged, and some of the theorists and writers from that North American/European corporate milieu—most of them at one time or another consultants themselves. This, however, we present as more than acknowledgment. We propose that Catholic church leaders and especially pastoral educators attend to this body of work,[10] so that some of its principles and practices move from novelty to routine in pastoral praxis.[11]

We begin by recognizing the contribution of Dr. Homer Johnson, who founded and led the Loyola University Chicago Center for Organizational Studies at the Institute for Workplace Studies. The Center educated and trained several INSPIRE parish consultants. Dr. Johnson's book, *Basic Principles of Effective Consulting*, coauthored with Loyola's Dr. Linda K. Stroh, is a mainstay for consultation practitioners.[12]

We chose consultants with career histories that included church and parish-based ministries, but who were also credentialed and proficient in the organizational disciplines.

Stroh and Johnson (2006) assert a twofold division to the population of organizational consultants.[13] Some are "experts" bringing a specific knowledge or skill to an organization. Others are "facilitators" whose services apply awareness of relational and communicative dynamics to decision making, learning, planning, and problem solving. Most, the authors acknowledge, tend to bring both kinds of services—expertise and facilitation—to a consultation. This would hold true for INSPIRE's parish consultants, but their profiles, instincts, and intentions would skew toward facilitative agenda.

Parish consultation is systems-oriented.[14] Organizational writers like converted biochemist Margaret Wheatley (1992), similarly converted aero-space engineer Peter Senge (1990), and well before them management pioneer Peter Drucker read from the scientific literature and applied new insights to organized human enterprise. Drucker left Nazi Germany for London and then the United States. His published writings spanned from 1939 to 2008, three years after his death. He wrote keen observations of how businesses, corporations, and industries form, reform, deteriorate, and innovate.

All three writers admonish readers to step back and make the effort to understand a wider view, the relationships, dynamic forces, and balances within their own institutional systems and with other systems in their environment. All prescribe paying attention to relationships. Drucker, Senge, and Wheatley propose that taking extra time and making the effort to grow shared vision is, in the age of information and learning organizations, the pathway to achieving objectives and animating mission.

Others would raise up the organic nature of institutions as dynamic systems.[15] Notably, Arie de Geus furthered the case for approaching organizations as living entities, as "living working communities."[16] His schema inspired thinking about the health, vitality, and survivability of companies, in other words the organics of organizational stewardship. "Parish vitality" would become a popular topic of inquiry among INSPIRE's enrolled pastoral teams.

Still other writers would apply systems concepts to institutional leadership, managerial supervision, and planning. Tom Peters authored a series of books advocating organizations that could respond to "whitewater" change by deconstructing command and control rubrics and enlisting workers as partners in the pursuit of excellence.[17] Colleagues Chris Argyris and Donald Schön mapped the rhythms of organizational communication and learning, and established team learning protocols to grow adaptive communities and achieve actionable knowledge.[18]

At the Project INSPIRE 2004 start-up, new writing about ethnic and multiethnic cultures in organizations and communities had yet to inform the project's work, but arose during the project's later years. Juana Bordas' *Salsa, Soul, and Spirit*[19] on leadership in Latino/a, African-American, and Native American cultures brought an unprecedented representation of pastoral ministers from Chicago's multiethnic parishes to INSPIRE's 2011 leadership programming.

TOOLS AND LEARNING PRACTICES

INSPIRE programming would leverage this broad scope of organizational thinking by enlisting learning and assessment tools that arose out of it. (A reference listing of the following writers, resources, and other influential contributions appears at the end of this chapter.) During World War II, the daughter-mother team of Isabel Briggs Myers and Catherine Cook Briggs initiated the development of the Myers-Briggs Type Indicator (1956) based on the psychological personality traits identified by Swiss psychologist Carl Jung. Similar patterns of implementation appeared with the use of other personality or communication profiles, such as DISC (Dominance, Inducement, Submission, Compliance) based on the work of Marston (1928).

Several other writers became direct contributors to consulting and team learning activities in the project. Stephen Covey's books on the *Seven Habits of Highly Effective People* (1989), the "Eighth Habit" (cultivating voice), time management, and principle-centered leadership became consultant-staff conversation items and team reading staples for some pastoral teams. Scenario planning at rectory tables, in parish halls, and at INSPIRE convocations drew from the insights of Peter Schwartz (1991), Kees van der Heijden (1996), and Gill Ringland (1998). Writings of William Isaacs (1999) and Daniel Yankelovich (1999) guided efforts to form pastoral teams adept at conversation and dialogue. Futures exploration at a major INSPIRE convocation implemented the conversation-driven "World Café" (2005) developed by Juanita Brown and David Isaacs. Daniel Goleman's (1995 ff.) "emotional intelligence" markers became a basis from which INSPIRE consultants built behavioral descriptions of parish teams able to demonstrate collaborative pastoral leadership.

Finally, the work of Peter Block informed design and approach to facilitative consulting conceived by the project's director and Lead Team. Block's description of the consulting stages from intake to implementation, engagement, and termination gave us the framework with which we would introduce the project, build contracts and learning plans, and grow continuing relationships with INSPIRE's first thirty-six pastoral leadership teams. Updates to his seminal work, *Flawless Consulting*, continued to inform our later work. His reflection with John McKnight on asset-based consulting and community development in *Community, the Structure of Belonging* opened new horizons for our reflections on parish communities during the Sustaining Grant years after 2009.[20]

APPLYING OD TO CHURCH

Experiences of reticence from the client community affirmed our own hesitation to adopt "OD" practices wholesale. One enrolling pastor expressed a typical concern: the title identifying the project's parish visitors, "consultants," sounded too "businessy" to his ear. Review of our practices in the first two years shows us doing mostly what had been done by other pastoral leaders with similar challenges for several decades: we added prayer. Into significant events like enrollments, decision-making moments, and conversations about difficult topics we added rituals and reflection based on scripture.

However, we have little doubt that when consultants and pastoral teams were sincere and transparent in taking the time to abide in prayer, there was already the beginning of a climate, an openness or readiness to build uncommon common ground. Facilitative consultants initially work to create reflective, conversational climates; they aim to get their clients to slow down their thinking, rather than increase speed and efficiency. They strive to produce safe, comfortable silences. The insertion of prayer and ritual into facilitation was therefore a natural for the client population, but by itself it risked becoming a somewhat artificial, add-on device.

INSPIRE TEAM LEARNING AGENDA

Two persons from Loyola's Institute of Pastoral Studies (IPS) and two directors of the archdiocesan continuing formation ministries composed INSPIRE's original Lead Team. Well before initiation of the project and hiring a director they crafted, we believe, a brilliant response to bridge the gap between corporate world and ecclesial world. They built a simple but sophisticated personal learning and team-learning schema.

The designers declared a project agenda of growing "Pastoral Leadership Teams" possessing "a sustained, mindful peculiar integration of knowledge, spirituality, skill and experience." These objectives formed "the curricular matrix of INSPIRE."[21] The project would support the aim of the Lilly Endowment's SPE grant program, the development of "pastoral imagination." The term appeared as a guiding theme in SPE literature, conceived by Dr. Craig Dykstra as "a peculiar intelligence that involves . . . capacities of mind, spirit and action that are specific to pastoral ministry itself."[22] By the end of the project's first year, the INSPIRE team had developed and refined the concept.

Recognizing and sustaining pastoral excellence became a matter of creating ways to promote Pastoral Imagination. Pastoral Imagination is identified as "a peculiar intelligence born of a unique integration of knowledge, skill, experience, and spirituality both in individuals and in Pastoral Leadership Teams."[23]

Personal learning would complement team learning, both forms supported by grant funding. Learning plans would aim to cultivate persons and teams of pastoral imagination by weaving into the plans four "broad, interrelated areas essential to Pastoral Leadership Teams:

1. human/personal formation
2. spiritual life and formation
3. intellectual/theological rootedness
4. skills for ministry.[24]

Each of these four learning areas would be addressed as both personal and team activities. INSPIRE's learning schema thus applied a twofold adaptation of Pope John Paul II's four-part priestly formational agenda in the apostolic exhortation, *Pastores Dabo Vobis.* [25] It thereby evinced not only its own pastoral imagination but the pastoral wisdom of a deeply respected voice within the Catholic milieu.

The designers understood the kinds of personal and collective challenges to which the project would call lay and ordained ministers. Collaborative pastoral leadership aims to make persons, families, and communities whole. Pastoral persons must understand themselves and each other as grounded persons of emotional and spiritual depth. As teams, they must become adept at much more than communication. To co-labor, to work together, they must share inquiry, conversation, truth exploration, and dialogue. They must acquire the technical skills of shared strategic, mission-focused planning. At times they must become appreciative custodians of their own limitations and failures.

The particular genius of the INSPIRE learning agenda, we propose, is that it makes explicit each of the first two learning areas: personal and team integration; personal and shared spirituality. In the following and subsequent pages, we share from written reports submitted as "nonconfidential" by parish team participants.

> So for me, what I felt I really could use, going into priesthood and what not, is a retreat experience. So I did that. . . . There's a famous phrase that you can't give what you don't have. As ministers, as pastoral people, our lives are about giving. But if we don't have a tank, it's going to be hard to do it.
> —Interview, newly ordained associate pastor, suburban parish

> I have used some of the personal funds to work with a personal trainer to learn more about flexibility and strengthening. For me the experience to date has been one of coming to know more about the mind/body connection. Just

setting the time aside each week for these past six weeks has become important. It is a real respite in a busy schedule.

—Interview, senior pastor, city parish

When first asked to be part of the pastoral team, I wasn't quite sure that as the facilities manager I should be. But after our first overnight I had really started to understand that what I do is actually a ministry. . . . The whole experience has helped bring me closer to not just the staff but also with the parishioners.

—Interview, facilities manager, suburban parish

The first learning area suggests the importance of "personal wholeness." When engaged by teams, it addresses their capacities to give and take, speak and listen, and to appreciate gifts, languages, perceptions, and contributions that are not one's own. On the individual level, it includes matters of personal health and physical stamina in addition to psychological wellness and integration. It includes the permission—rather, the necessity—to explore one's own creative and intellectual passions that round out one's personhood. Human formation as a team means cultivation of healthy relationships and a respect for the talents, limits, and intentions that each member brings to the shared mission. Members of such teams undergo tempering and experience personal growth.[26] They take that maturity into the team setting.

It was something that really struck me. . . . We realized we were truly a team. . . . Fr. Rich came with his ideas and we got down to what goals we really wanted. . . . And in our conversation of a couple of those things, he found and we found we were going in a different direction, and he literally took his paper and turned it over and started over. . . . And that was a really big moment for us.

—Interview, school principal, suburban parish

As INSPIRE consultants and teams engaged the spiritual learning activities, we began to understand the unique advantage that pastoral teams have over their corporate and community peers. The identification of spirituality as a critical learning area offers a pastor and staff an asset for both personal and collaborative grounding that could be hard won in secular settings.[27] Catholic pastoral teams gather persons who draw inspiration from liturgical worship and a common text, a shared faith tradition and narrative that affirms their unusual life dedications. They can draw from a common scriptural well. They can process matters of the heart and faith encounters that brought them to parish work. Each can readily name the *why* of personal mission, and so build the collective appreciation of the *what* and *how* of the work they share.

> We spend a good deal of time in prayer at our meetings. We begin with the
> upcoming readings or the gospel to engage in conversation. They're meaning-
> ful and they are prayerful conversations.
>   —Continuation of interview with school principal, suburban parish

Ironically, spiritual depth is what parishioners assume their pastoral people naturally have, and actually most do demonstrate exceptional spirituality.
Their spiritual lives, however, tend to erode in the daily grind of church
work. Many spend days bereft of serene moments, filled to the brim with
tasks, deadlines, and interruptions. Their roles and workdays breed experiences of isolation.[28] Chicago clergy, we discovered, could usually point to
important resources to help them nurture spirituality: peer groups, annual
retreats, and routine practices like the breviary and liturgical calendar. We
noticed, however, that lay ministers named less of these kinds of supports,
and more of the stresses between ministry in the parish and ministering to
their own families. For them most days ended with feelings of being spiritually tapped out. We found that lay ministers would be most likely to select
the learning area of spiritual formation as their first area of desired growth.
Staff retreat days also emerged as popular early team learning activities.

By the time we began to enroll the second cohort of six pastoral staffs in
2005, some INSPIRE parish consultants noted a significant difference between consultation in corporate settings and parish settings. In the former,
developing a sense of spirit and cultivation of spirituality usually came, if at
all, after "more urgent" matters of strategy and execution were addressed. In
parish settings, spirituality is the gateway.[29]

The third learning area, identified by the designers as "theological/intel-
lectual rootedness" went through several name changes, as consultants attempted to describe and attract learning commitments. For some persons, the
original term appeared off-putting and academic. Some others did, however,
catch the sense of the terms and sought enrollment in formal studies at
Loyola University Chicago Institute of Pastoral Studies (IPS) or Chicago's
Catholic Theological Union (CTU). Still others sought to build their understanding of Catholic teaching and tradition. For personal learning some
would identify programs offered by the archdiocesan catechetical and school
offices. By the end of the project's second year, the study area was simply
referenced as "Tradition" or "Immersion in Catholic Tradition." At the end
of the project's third year, a reflection developed for the National Association for Lay Ministry (NALM) profiled the span of "theological/intellectual
rootedness" activities:

> Tradition: Personal immersion into the Church's rich theological, liturgical,
> doctrinal, and moral teaching is concomitant with one's dedication to pastoral
> service. Personal learning activities chosen by INSPIRE participants range
> from conferences and study days to enrollment in continuing education and

degree programs. Teams read and share perceptions of books with theological or pastoral titles. Some engage seminary or university professors to conduct one-day programs designed for on-site delivery. Despite wide differences in most teams' levels of formal education, when teams learn to share theological reflection, there are remarkable outcomes. One team still follows a three-year-old commitment to engage common learning that connects Eucharist with Catholic Social Teaching. The encounter continues to critique and reshape both the parish mission and personal commitments to that mission.

The fourth learning area, "skills for ministry," seemed clear and wide open enough that consultants believed they had little to do but ask the question, "So, what are the skills you want to grow to enhance your ministry?" Many responses were unsurprising: the Director of Religious Education (DRE) who felt the need to build personal capacity in adult education; the pastoral associate who wanted to learn conversational Spanish; and the pastoral team that wanted to build a parishioner leadership development process. This is the area that brought us some wonderful anecdotes. One pastor confided behind a closed door that he wanted personal training "off hours" that would help him learn how to work the computer at his desk. A year later he shared an annual report with staff and parishioners featuring his first computer-generated slideshow presentation.

Implementation of this "technical learning" area, however, revealed two important dynamics about pastoral development in Catholic parishes. There were more people than the one pastor checking to see if the door was closed. Several lay ministers expressed concern about their certification requirements, coursework or training they needed to document. They needed to certify knowledge acquisition or performance competencies for their particular ministry. This sort of learning had been anticipated and supported by the INSPIRE guidelines for personal learning. It only stood out in relief when we observed another kind of learning objective sought by other participants.

INSPIRE's learning program was deliberately open-ended, rather than restricted to learning objectives aimed at developing required competencies for any particular ministry. Since our consultants were helping people establish learning programs that could enhance personal integration, they asked questions that probed personal desires and passionate pursuits. One of the earliest enrolled associate pastors, whom many considered one of the best homilists in the archdiocese, listened to his consultant, and then chose to pursue advanced work in homiletics.

Over the project's nine years, we watched people take delight in enrolling themselves in some ministerial pursuit that was either beyond the minimum certification standard or significantly outside of their ministry assignment. Three pastors expressed desire to return to doctoral dissertations long left behind when they responded to pastoral service calls. School principals returned to programs that strengthened their leadership or administrative skills or built stronger theological capacities. Reflection on this phenomenon prompted consultant awareness that institutional cultures can promote entry-level standards that unintentionally may also be ceilings.

More important, these experiences set us up to understand and cultivate a form of consultation that seeks purposes other than addressing deficiencies or responding to problems and crises. It is certainly not that remediation-focused consultation is unnecessary; competency-based forms of development assure communities of a certain quality and benchmarked standards for ministry. Nevertheless, pastors and staff persons thanked us for asking questions and affirming ministerial possibilities they had seldom or never been asked to consider. We further appreciated the Lilly Endowment's designation of a program that quite explicitly called over sixty projects nationally to aim for "pastoral excellence." The experience would prepare us in later years to pay attention to asset-based organizational development.[30]

TAKING STOCK

How would we evaluate, how would we offer to stakeholders what the Endowment's SPE program called "signs of success" in the pursuit of collaborative pastoral leadership? We would have to allow our early enrolling teams to show us what collaboration looks like in pastoral praxis.

We followed our first twelve pastoral teams as they positioned themselves for, attempted, backed away from, or grew collaborative behaviors among themselves. What does it look like when parish teams demonstrate collaborative pastoral leadership? Our first efforts at getting feedback from the teams themselves were hampered by the bulky reporting and accountability instruments we gave them. As we eventually got wise and went digital, however, we recorded and transcribed interviews with pastors and team members and later collected "three sentence" reports (described below) from teams, many who often wrote at greater length and in richer detail than strictly required. Finally, we employed *NVivo*, a narrative reporting and data organizing software that gave us an increased storage, retrieval, and assessment facility.[31]

ESTABLISHING SAFE SPACE

Early on, therefore, the best feedback about collaborative behavior came through consultant observations and the conversations they generated. An early supposition about the INSPIRE consultation effort projected limited consultant engagements. Pastors and staffs, we assumed, would work with a consultant until learning and reporting plans were complete; then the consultant might refer the clients to appropriate providers for personal and team learning activities. We did not anticipate a critically important human dynamic: the accelerated trust building that goes on when clients see the consultant as a "safe outsider" who will not be reporting to official superiors in the local administrative hierarchy. Most teams bonded with their original consultant, and others tended to change consultants until one became the familiar and trusted advisor.

We began to understand outsider identity as a considerable aspect of the "safe space" dynamic in facilitative pastoral consultation. The project director's initial apprehension about consultants continuing with their assigned teams gave way to this significant relational driver.[32] Collaboration is a pleasant sounding state of affairs that nevertheless, we discovered, involves laying aside fears, accepting vulnerability, building trust, building protocols for dealing with failure, and indeed sometimes facing up to personal or collective demons. During our early enrollments, especially in personal interviews, discernments, and planning sessions, we witnessed pastoral ministers and staff persons sharing highly personal confidences, sometimes as early on as the second or third session.[33] Learning plans would sometimes be submitted as confidential documents, especially when the learning—as would happen occasionally—involved therapeutic work, personal or marriage counseling, or interventions.

The importance, however, of the safety dynamics is that they also allowed INSPIRE consultants and leaders to learn what it takes to grow collaborative pastoral leadership and understand what it looks like in practice. That is, consultants were the frontline observers when persons and teams dealt with threat, eschewed face-saving routines, or tempered passions for the supreme importance of their own particular ministries. They were there to advise and encourage when pastoral ministers learned the collaborative arts of give and take, budget paring, coaccountability, and making space in programs and public events for another's contribution and recognition.

EARLY "SIGNS OF SUCCESS"

A consultant reporting on work in a particular parish during the project's second and third years provides a typical scenario of staffs on their way to becoming pastoral leadership teams. It shows how consultants engaged with staffs after the learning plans were built, the exceptionally wide range of learning commitments, spirituality dynamics, "healthy parish" imagery, and the moments of struggle that persons and teams confronted rather than avoided.

> Personal learning plans included activities such as spiritual direction, mentoring and coaching in leadership, gym membership, chiropractic care, spiritual

retreats, young adult conference, jazz guitar lessons, attendance at the PAAC Conference, and the purchase of a bicycle.

The principal consultant engagement consists of meeting with the team on a regular basis for the first three months after the discernment process to create their group and personal learning plans. Once the learning plans were in place, I facilitated their overnight retreat. Then we met every two months for a time for them to share their personal learning/growth with each other; to review the learning plan to make sure we were still on the right track; and for them to step back from their daily tasks to re-focus their attention on their INSPIRE goal.

Major achievements for [Parish Name] includes creating stability and good will in a team that underwent (1) frequent change in staffing and (2) working through strife that existed between two team members.

Significant obstacles for [Parish Name] include the team addressing a feud between a long time team member and a new team member. These two team members had different ideas on how the parish should operate. Their personalities clashed but nobody wanted to talk about it, including the two parties involved. After completing some of the activities the new team member commented that it was much easier to work with the other team members when you get to know them on a personal level, not just professional.

The team teaches us about collaborative pastoral leadership by reminding us that to work collaboratively, parish teams needs to spend their work time both serving parishioners and working on building the inner team structure and dynamics. Doing both helps ensure a healthy parish, creating a healthy Church.

As a Parish Consultant, I've learned that each person on a team wants a variety of things from their work—fulfillment, appreciation, fair pay, to feel like they are an important part of the group—that they make a difference in the group—that the group would be "less than" if they weren't there and mostly each person is focused on serving the Lord. [34]

In the early years, the project gathered consultants to share observations about the process and perceived outcomes. By the beginning of 2007, an overnight consultant "pullaway" allowed consultants to distill learning from the first two and one-half years, after the first eighteen pastoral staffs had enrolled. Following is a sampling from director and consultant perceptions of what collaborative expressions of pastoral leadership look like in everyday practice. [35]

"They pray together, plan together, and talk mission. There are several instances of joined work going on at one time. Individual persons say they feel supported, challenged, sustained by their colleagues. People can 'come to work' and know they can bring their own spirits along."

"I see first of all a sense of safety and trust in the group. Therefore they are not fearful of feedback."

". . . high—or good—energy in the group."

"A collaborative leadership relationship exists when both leader and followers base their interactions, efforts and planning on a true sense of '*communio*.'"

"[Team members] who understand the overall picture and see how their ministries are related . . . , members who do not see 'competitors' but 'collaborators.'"

"A team that . . . , isn't afraid to bring up risky topics or make honest comments . . . , they know how to disagree and make something useful happen."

The project's feedback procedures advanced significantly as a web-based reporting system came online and teams developed their Internet skills. Some teams designated a reporter who would get written reports to log or who would interview team members at the computer desk. Individuals and teams were asked to log in to the private area of the project website to enter their "Three Sentence Reports." We made the process secure and user friendly and, of course, the entry window for the three sentence deliveries would simply scroll infinitely past that level. Fairly often people would get on a roll; some reports lengthened to over five hundred words, giving us rich detail. The project's narrative storage system counts almost four hundred personal and one hundred fifty team reports, and one hundred learning plans entered electronically. Following are two sample reports[36] that illustrate the two kinds of learning:

REPORT ON TEAM LEARNING received March 2, 2010
Personal Experience: Yesterday (March 1) we had a[n] Inspire-team meeting and we discussed [a] serious issue that was holding the staff back in making important decisions for our community of faith. As a Hispanic, I was not sure how to use or understand the idiom "the elephant in the room." As a result of our meeting and open discussion led by Carol (parish consultant), the team could openly discussed [sic] a big issue that was always present in our staff meetings but overlook[ed] as a problem by us as a team. As a result I feel more equipped to deal with the situation. I feel liberated somehow. Thank you so much for this opportunity. I think [it] is great!

REPORT ON PERSONAL LEARNING received March 2, 2010
Personal Experience: One result of our group process, evaluating and clarifying staff roles and responsibilities, was an expansion of my position in the parish. Our consultant, Tony, suggested that I would benefit from some coaching as I began to assume this new role. Tony assigned me some reading, asked me to take notes, and use my notes to help me prepare, in particular, for meetings. We also did some exploration of emotional intelligence models to help me identify ways that I would be more effective (and happier!) in my new role.
The work has proven very helpful. I am learning techniques that help me actively listen, keep my emotional responses in check and influence my colleagues. My confidence has grown, which helps in situations that I would previously have found threatening.
Tony has helped me think about "keeping it down here"—his shorthand for leveling out my emotional responses, especially to adversity. This has proven to work very well in conjunction with another aspect of my INSPIRE

> personal growth work: Pilates classes. Pilates has helped me regain my center
> physically—and that helps me hold on to my center emotionally.

Individual team members would enact most of the personal learning work
and then report to the project or the consultant. Over longer periods, however, consultants would mentor, coach, or counsel one or more persons on their
teams. It would not be uncommon to see personal learning plans reevaluated
and rewritten. Common team learning activities included consultants observing team meetings and debriefing the dynamics with their teams. Typically,
team development would take well over a year to achieve collaborative behaviors that a team could claim as routine.

Moreover, there would commonly be cycles of engagement and disengagement, and teams would often be tempted to return to their "real work"
patterns of isolation and task-oriented performances. ("The difference between consulting with Fortune 500 organizations and parishes . . . ," reported
one consultant privately, "parishes are slow.") Being busy, or being too busy
to "do their INSPIRE work" was a commonly reported blockage, often informally noted as a greeting when a consultant walked into a team meeting
room for a check-in consultation. The phenomenon of pastoral ministers'
task-orientation was the project's number one finding, reported our first
INSPIRE Research Professor, Dr. Brett Hoover.[37]

Thus, there would be occasions of deconstructing blockages and moving
toward reorientation. Moments of tacit avoidance or outright impasse would
occur. Teams would "get stuck" (as one consultant called it) or lose energy
and withdraw. Consultants could be tempted to see this as a failure in their
own performances and, like the teams, gloss over the stalemate episodes in
their reports. Over time most consultants became familiar with the backing-
off behaviors, and we realized that many times a consultant could see the
forestalling behaviors begin to form. They would work toward the right
moment to point out curious behaviors, silences, comments, and ask their
teams, "What just happened?"

Pastoral team members recognized that such moments might require potentially painful and time-consuming engagement, often about episodes of
conflict or failure. However, we began to understand that impasse itself was
many times an opportunity or gateway to a team's learning the art and conversation involved in managing conflict, negotiating, holding persons and
relationships in safe space, and achieving dialogue and best practice commitments. An early-enrolled team actually asked their consultant to help them
build and then lead an overnight retreat that would allow them to acknowledge and reconcile their scapegoating of a senior team member. Such are the
predictably unpredictable passages that lurk below the neatly arranged pathway scenarios constructed over the project's nine years.

PARISH CONSULTATION

The broad answer to "What do parish consultants do?" references typical OD consulting in any corporate or NGO setting. Facilitative consultation fosters interdependence, alignment, and coordinated execution. It points clients to the corporate mission and assists them, as they order themselves and the work they do, toward some resolution or some change that serves common goals. Consultants seek shared perceptions, agreements, declarations of intention, and commitments. They may assist persons and even hold them accountable as they build structural arrangements and personal capacities that contribute to common mission.

The role of parish consultant as it evolved during INSPIRE, however, exhibits some critical differences. One is the starting point. Organizational development literature tends to conceive consultation as a skilled response to a client's presentation of a problem.[38] As any pastor or minister can attest, awareness of big problems can surely be the case in any church setting. The Lilly Endowment SPE program, however, challenged project stakeholders to attract pastors and ministers who are perceptibly successful and then "sustain" their excellence. INSPIRE consultants thus began with a process that acknowledged their clients as persons and teams of "pastoral excellence."

The "learning plan" agenda introduced reflections on personal and team integrity. Participants more immediately understood themselves as part of a success story than as part of a problem. This may be another factor in the unusually rapid trust built between project consultants and their pastoral team clients. In most cases that bonding became a critical resource, as consultants and then clients later detected and acknowledged "elephants in the room" and other face-saving or avoidance dynamics that forestall truly collaborative team development. Teams and consultants could then leverage the trust and safety dynamics they had established early in the process. This relational positioning, and a bank of several years' worth of aggregate knowledge about the potential for struggle, informed how we would develop a consultant performances inventory and organize the categories summarized below.

- *Collaborative Pastoral Excellence:* Consultants provide the grounding and energy for pastoral team development by structuring experiences, discussions, and reflections that grow pastoral team leadership. Consultants seek commitments of confidentiality and arrange interviews and meetings built for conversation, reflection, and discovery. They coach or teach approaches to healthy group process and meeting skills that serve communication and conflict management. They promote self and team identity as pastoral leaders. Over time consultants transfer responsibility for monitoring and accountability from themselves to the team.

- *Interpersonal Competence:* Consultants apply strong relational skills to individual counseling and facilitation of group activities. They establish positive working relationships that inspire trust, mutual respect, transparency, and honesty. They use active listening and observation of nonverbal communication to feed perceptions back to a team and then invite interpretive discussion. Consultants model and assist development of emotional maturity. They also make personal use of professional coaching or mentoring relationships to assess their own actions and intentions.

- *Change Agency:* Consultants act as catalysts and guides. They help team members understand their pastoral leadership as a unique skilled stewardship of change in the lives of persons and in the community. Consultants demonstrate personal *savior faire* for the process, motivate by modeling, and affirm and debrief both small and significant achievements on the pathway toward collaborative pastoral leadership. They seek out and recommend to their teams persons who can act as resources to team members, such as senior mentors, executive coaches, and pastoral leadership teams from other parishes.

- *Personal and Team Learning:* Consultants assist persons and teams as they form specific intentions to grow personal and team integrity, spirituality, Catholic sensibility, and skills that serve parish work. Consultants promote transformative learning experiences: reflection that suspends assumptions; immersion into the vast resources of Christian spirituality and tradition; and practice in the art of slowing down one's thinking to engage reflection, inquiry, discussion, conversation, and dialogue.[39] Pastoral team members broaden their understanding of learning: learning means building new or deepened skills, but it also means learning to understand and appreciate each other; learning may involve solitary study or therapeutic work, but it also includes times for play and social interaction. Learning focuses on "the work we do together," parish and Church mission. Learning breeds pastoral imagination.

- *Leadership Development:* Consultants help persons understand themselves as leaders and stewards of leadership within the community. They encourage team members to see leadership as a widely shared transformative resource in healthy parish communities. Through teaching and coaching, using community development exercises like scenario planning, town hall nights, and small group process, consultants help pastoral ministers expand their performance of pastoral leadership. As team members develop ways to share spotlight, podium, and joint programming responsibilities, they learn to take delight in collaborative expressions of pastoral leadership.

- *Sharing Faith and Spirituality:* Consultants model attractive, accessible approaches to spiritual practice. They seek to learn and appreciate the spiritual traditions of other cultures. They help pastoral team members build spiritual sharing practices that bridge gaps between levels of theological learning, sophistication, and culture. They challenge overly busy ministers to make room in their days and weeks for spiritual exercises. They connect persons to centers and resources that provide spiritual direction, retreats, reading, and networking.

* *Parish Mission:* Consultants facilitate the appropriation of the parish mission, vision, and values for the concrete tasks of parish programming, worship, education, and social outreach. They inspire conversations about call and baptismal identity that ripple throughout the parish community. They ask questions about preferred futures, plausible commitments, community assets, and the human needs present both inside and outside the parish boundaries. Teams learn to grow and declare institutional identity that orders and provokes expressions of pastoral imagination.

PASTORAL LEARNING COMMUNITIES

SPE sought project proposals to support successful pastors. As we described earlier, designers of INSPIRE audaciously attempted and achieved an expanded focus. They presented INSPIRE as a project to sustain not only pastors, but their staffs of ordained and lay associates, other delegated lay ministers, support staff, and in some cases select lay parishioner leaders. The project designers intended to sustain and nurture the relational bonds that join ministries. Even so, the project was able to address but one sector of the parish systems in one specific effort: to transform parish staffs into "pastoral leadership teams." The project's purview excluded the parish council and the myriad "lay ministry" and social organizations that drive US parish life and mission. Applying many of the project's consultative practices in more inclusive settings is, we contend, the next critical step in growing vital, resilient parishes.

In practice, moreover, organizational consulting typically has a more limited scope and short-term engagement, for example, to assist resolution of conflicts, to help organize a program or build planning, to organize a strategic transition, or just to improve the ways that staff or team meetings are prepared and conducted. In church settings, any of these less intense consultative engagements can benefit from applying what we learned about parish-focused organizational consulting. We propose that there are already persons who work in ministry settings who could be trained or certified for specific consultative services.

BIBLIOGRAPHY

Argyris, Chris, and Donald A. Schön. *Organizational Learning II: Theory, Method and Practice*. Reading, MA: Addison-Wesley, 1996.

Block, Peter. *Flawless Consulting: A Guide to Getting Your Expertise Used*. San Francisco: Pfeiffer, 2011.

———. *Community: The Structure of Belonging*. 3rd Edition. San Francisco: Berrett-Koehler, 2008.

Bordas, Juana. *Salsa, Soul, and Spirit: Leadership for a Multicultural Age*. San Francisco: Berrett-Koehler, 2007.

Carroll, Jackson W., with Becky R. McMillan. *God's Potters: Pastoral Leadership and the Shaping of Congregations*. Grand Rapids, MI: Wm. B. Eerdmans, 2006.

Clark, William. *A Voice of Their Own: The Authority of the Local Parish*. Collegeville, MN: Liturgical Press, 2005.

de Geus, Arie. *The Living Company*. Boston, MA: Harvard Business School Press, 1997.

Drucker, Peter. *Post-Capitalist Society*. New York: Harper Business, 1993.

Fleischer, Barbara. "Mezirow's Theory of Transformative Learning and Lonergan's Method in Theology: Resources for Adult Theological Education." *Journal of Adult Theological Education* 3, no. 2 (2006): 147–162.

John Paul II, Post-Synodal Apostolic Exhortation, *Pastores Dabo Vobis*. Libreria Editrice Vaticana, 1992.

Jones, L. Gregory and Kevin R. Armstrong. *Resurrecting Excellence: Shaping Faithful Christian Ministry*. Grand Rapids, MI: Wm. B. Eerdmans, 2006.

McKnight, John, and John Kretzman. *Discovering Community Power: A Guide to Mobilizing Local Assets and Your Organization's Capacity*. Chicago: ACTA, 2005.

Peters, Thomas J., and Nancy Austin. *A Passion for Excellence*. New York: Warner Books, 1986.

Peters, Thomas J., and Robert H. Waterman. *In Search of Excellence: Lessons from America's Best-Run Companies*. New York: Harper & Row, 1982.

Senge, Peter M. *The Fifth Discipline: The Art and Practice of the Learning Organization*. New York: Doubleday/Currency, 1990.

Stroh, Linda K., and Homer H. Johnson. *The Basic Principles of Effective Consulting*. Mahwah, NJ: Erlbaum, 2006.

United States Conference of Catholic Bishops (USCCB). *Co-Workers in the Vineyards of the Lord: A Resource for Guiding the Development of Lay Ecclesial Ministry*. Washington, DC: USCCB, 2006.

Wheatley, Margaret J. *Leadership and the New Science: Learning about Organization from an Orderly Universe*. San Francisco: Berrett-Koehler, 1992.

REFERENCES

Principal works referenced in chapter currently in print; later editions available for many.

Adams, John D. *Transforming Leadership: From Vision to Results*. Alexandria, VA: Miles River Press, 1986.

———, ed. *Transforming Work: A Collection of Organizational Transformation Readings*. Alexandria, VA: Miles River Press, 1984.

Argyris, Chris. *Knowledge for Action: A Guide to Overcoming Barriers to Organizational Change*. San Francisco: Jossey-Bass, 1993.

Bridges, William. *Managing Transitions: Making the Most of Change*. Reading, MA: Addison-Wesley, 1991.

Brown, Juanita, and David Isaacs. *The World Café: Shaping Our Futures through Conversations That Matter*. San Francisco: Berrett-Koehler, 2005.

Covey, Stephen R. *The 8th Habit: From Effectiveness to Greatness*. New York: Free Press, 2005.

———. *The 7 Habits of Highly Effective People: Restoring the Character Ethic*. New York: Simon and Schuster, 1989.

Covey, Stephen R., A. Roger Merrill, and Rebecca R. Merrill. *First Things First: To Live, to Love, to Learn, to Leave a Legacy*. New York: Simon & Schuster, 1994.

Deal, Terrence E., and Allan A. Kennedy. *Corporate Cultures: The Rites and Rituals of Corporate Life*. Reading, MA: Addison-Wesley, 1982.

Deming, W. Edwards. *The New Economics for Industry, Government, Education*. Cambridge, MA: Massachusetts Institute of Technology, Center for Advanced Engineering Study, 1993.

———. *Out of the Crisis*. Cambridge, MA: Massachusetts Institute of Technology, Center for Advanced Engineering Study, 1986.

De Pree, Max. *Leadership Is an Art*. New York: Doubleday, 1989.

Drucker, Peter F. *Managing in a Time of Great Change*. New York: Truman Talley Books/Dutton, 1995.

Egan, Gerard. *The Skilled Helper: A Problem-Management and Opportunity-Development Approach to Helping*. Pacific Grove, CA: Brooks/Cole, 2002. Several workbooks and resources complement this text.

Goleman, Daniel. "An EI-Based Theory of Performance." In *The Emotionally Intelligent Workplace*. Edited by C. Cherniss and Daniel Goleman. San Francisco: Jossey-Bass, 2001.

———. *Emotional Intelligence*. New York: Bantam Books, 1995.

Handy, Charles B. *The Age of Unreason*. Boston, MA: Harvard Business School Press, 1989.

Helgesen, Sally. *The Web of Inclusion: A New Architecture for Building Great Organizations*. New York: Currency/Doubleday, 1995.

Hesselbein, Frances, and Rob Johnston. *On Mission and Leadership: A Leader to Leader Guide*. San Francisco: Jossey-Bass, 2002.

———. *Hesselbein on Leadership*. San Francisco: Jossey-Bass, 2002.

Isaacs, William. *Dialogue and the Art of Thinking Together: A Pioneering Approach to Communicating in Business and in Life*. New York: Currency, 1999.

Johnson, Homer H., Peter F. Sorensen, and Therese F. Yaeger. *Critical Issues in Organization Development: Case Studies for Analysis and Discussion*. Charlotte, NC: Information Age, 2013.

Juran, J. M., and Frank M. Gryna. *Juran's Quality Control Handbook*. New York: McGraw-Hill, 1988.

Kuhn, Thomas S. *The Essential Tension: Selected Studies in Scientific Tradition and Change*. Chicago: University of Chicago Press, 1977.

———. *The Structure of Scientific Revolutions*. Chicago: University of Chicago Press, 1996. The 50th Anniversary edition (2012) is available from University of Chicago Press.

Likert, Rensis, and Jane Gibson Likert. *New Ways of Managing Conflict*. New York: McGraw-Hill, 1976.

———. *The Human Organization: Its Management and Value*. New York: McGraw-Hill, 1967.

Marston, William Moulton. *Emotions of Normal People*. London: Kegan Paul, Trench, Trübner, 1928.

Mintzberg, Henry, Bruce W. Ahlstrand, and Joseph Lampel. *Strategy Safari: A Guided Tour through the Wilds of Strategic Management*. New York: Free Press, 1998.

———. *The Rise and Fall of Strategic Planning: Reconceiving Roles for Planning, Plans, Planners*. New York: Free Press, 1994.

Myers, Isabel Briggs, and Peter B. Myers. *Gifts Differing: Understanding Personality Type*. Mountain View, CA: Consulting Psychologists Press, 1980.

Parks, Sharon Daloz. *Leadership Can Be Taught: A Bold Approach for a Complex World*. Boston, MA: Harvard Business School Press, 2005.

Ringland, Gill. *Scenario Planning: Managing for the Future*. Chichester, England: Wiley, 1998.

Rost, Joseph C. *Leadership for the Twenty-First Century*. New York: Praeger, 1991.

Schein, Edgar H. *Organizational Culture and Leadership*. San Francisco: Jossey-Bass, 1985.

Schwartz, Peter. *The Art of the Long View*. New York: Doubleday/Currency, 1991.
Sofield, Loughlan, and Carroll Juliano. *Collaborative Ministry: Skills and Guidelines*. Notre Dame, IN: Ave Maria Press, 1987.
Sweetser, Thomas P. *The Parish as Covenant: A Call to Pastoral Partnership*. Lanham, MD: Sheed and Ward, 2001.
van der Heijden, Kees. *Scenarios: The Art of Strategic Conversation*. Chichester, England: Wiley, 1996.
———. *Sixth Sense: Accelerating Organizational Learning with Scenarios*. Chichester, England: Wiley, 2002.
Whitehead, James D., and Evelyn Eaton. Whitehead. *The Promise of Partnership: Leadership and Ministry in an Adult Church*. San Francisco: HarperSanFrancisco, 1991. Available in reprint from iUniverse.com (2000).
Yankelovich, Daniel. *The Magic of Dialogue: Transforming Conflict into Cooperation*. New York: Simon and Schuster, 1999.

NOTES

1. In US parishes, the composition of pastoral staffs, their roles and relationships, is anything but standardized. Economics in the local community tend to join with the pastor's discretion in influencing the number of persons, full-time or part-time or volunteer, and the roles to be filled. During the application and selection periods, pastoral teams in each parish self-identified their ranks and participating membership.

2. Peter Senge, *The Fifth Discipline: The Art and Practice of the Learning Organization* (New York: Doubleday, 1990), 233–249. In Senge's introduction of team learning, persons engage trusting conversations and dialogue to share vision and mental models, test assumptions, and use systems thinking, in order to structure commitments and action toward mutually identified ends. Team learning is a discipline that involves sharing observations and forming questions among persons with differentiated skill sets and knowledge references.

3. Barbara Fleischer, "Mezirow's Theory of Transformative Learning and Lonergan's Method in Theology: Resources for Adult Theological Education," *Journal of Adult Theological Education* 3, no. 2 (2006): 147–162. Adult educator Jack Mezirow and theologian Bernard Lonergan develop processes of inquiry and reflection that veer learners toward conversion and reorientation of commitments. "Conversion, for Lonergan, thus necessarily involves what Mezirow calls a transformation of meaning perspectives. It is a radical shift of perspective that transforms all further experiencing, understanding, judging, and deciding" (157).

4. Soon after our enrollment in SPE, the Endowment provided the project director with recommended reading. Through the *Pulpit and Pew* project at Duke University, L. Gregory Jones and Kevin R. Jones coauthored *Resurrecting Excellence: Shaping Faithful Christian Ministry* (Grand Rapids, MI: Wm. B. Eerdmans, 2001).

5. US Conference of Catholic Bishops, *Co-Workers in the Vineyard of the Lord: A Resource for Guiding the Development of Lay Ecclesial Ministry* (Washington, DC: USCCB, 2006).

6. The revised strategic agenda also suggested that Pastoral Leadership Teams would mentor and form other teams, presumably those from neighboring parishes. Because of the nature of pastoral ministry commitments, and the number one finding about pastoral staff persons in Chicago (that they are deeply task-oriented and settled into work in the parish that is always pressing), the director and Lead Team abandoned this scenario by midway through the second year.

7. Peter Drucker, *Post-Capitalist Society* (New York: Harper Business, 1993), 49–53.

8. William Clark, *A Voice of Their Own: The Authority of the Local Parish* (Collegeville, MN: Liturgical Press, 2005), 200.

9. Ibid.

10. In the following overview of organizational literature, we supply dating of the earliest text, pertinent to the subject specified, in an author's bibliography. All these authors developed and refined their thought in later writing. Many are still active in writing, research, and publish-

ing. At the conclusion of this paper we offer a selective bibliography, mostly texts that are more readily accessible in book or e-book form.

11. We are indebted to Dr. Barbara Fleischer for conversations about theologian David Tracy's appeal to "mutually critical correlation" and for stirring our interest in practical theology as an INSPIRE resource.

12. Linda Stroh and Homer Johnson, *Basic Principles of Effective Consulting* (Mahwah, NJ: Erlbaum, 2006).

13. Ibid., 4–8. They also distinguish external consultants from those employed as internal consultants. As will be demonstrated below, INSPIRE consultants were effective precisely because of their external identification, as "safe outsiders."

14. Awareness of process and the interactions of different actors and systems was first raised among observers from multiple scientific disciplines: science biographer James Gleick (1987) on chaos, biologist Ludwig von Bertalanffy (1968) on systems theory, and physicist/science historian Thomas Kuhn (1968) on the social dynamics of introducing new scientific paradigms (1968) are examples of philosophers who wrote with scant or no intention to inform the management and leadership of organizations.

15. Joseph Juran (1951/1962) and W. Edwards Deming (1982) developed practical approaches to measuring, promoting, and sustaining quality in the workplace. Economist and social researcher Rensis Likert (1961, 1967) applied advanced metrics to studies of human relationships in managerial performance, advancing the establishment of organizational psychology as a discipline.

16. Arie de Geus, *The Living Company* (Boston, MA: Harvard Business School Press, 1997).

17. See especially Tom Peters and Robert H. Waterman, *In Search of Excellence: Lessons from America's Best-Run Companies* (New York: Harper & Row, 1982), and Tom Peters and Nancy Austin, *A Passion for Excellence* (New York: Warner Books, 1986).

18. Chris Argyris and Donald A. Schön, *Organizational Learning II: Theory, Method and Practice* (Reading, MA: Addison-Wesley, 1996).

19. Juana Bordas, *Salsa, Soul, and Spirit: Leadership for a Multicultural Age* (San Francisco: Berrett-Koehler, 2007).

20. Peter Block, *Flawless Consulting: A Guide to Getting Your Expertise Used* (San Francisco: Pfeiffer, 2011), and *Community: The Structure of Belonging* (San Francisco: Berrett-Koehler, 2008).

21. Proposal to the Lilly Endowment Inc. *Sustaining Pastoral Excellence* program (September 15, 2003), 12. The proposal was supported by an early 2002 survey of Loyola IPS alumni, mostly nonordained laywomen and men, by data from the national Center for Applied Research in the Apostolate (CARA); and by a 2001 archdiocesan Office for Formation in Ministry consultation with episcopal vicars and agency directors; and by a 2003 survey of active pastoral associates.

22. Spring 2001 Newsletter of the Lilly Endowment Inc. Dr. Dyksta's appeal to pastoral imagination took seriously the multiple intelligences proposed by Howard Gardner. Successful applications (sixty-six of well over four hundred submitted to SPE) would support the Endowment's challenge to identify and support ministers whose already successful service demonstrated personal capacity for pastoral imagination and excellence.

23. INSPIRE 2004 Annual Report, 13–14.

24. Proposal to the Lilly Endowment, 4–8.

25. John Paul III, Apostolic Exhortation *Pastores Dabo Vobis*, On the Formation of Priests (PDV) (Libreria Editrice Vaticana, 1992), §42–59. The Holy Father's four "Areas of Priestly Formation" are titled Human Formation, Spiritual Formation, Intellectual Formation, and Pastoral Formation.

26. The INSPIRE continuing formation agenda echoed the Holy Father's concerns for future priests' balance, relational capacity, and affective maturity in PDV:

> Future priests should therefore cultivate a series of human qualities, not only out of proper and due growth and realization of self, but also with a view to the ministry.

These qualities are needed for them to be balanced people, strong and free, capable of bearing the weight of pastoral responsibilities.

Of special importance is the capacity to relate to others. This is truly fundamental for a person who is called to be responsible for a community and to be a "man of communion." This demands that the priest not be arrogant, or quarrelsome, but affable, hospitable, sincere in his words and heart, prudent and discreet, generous and ready to serve, capable of opening himself to clear and brotherly relationships and of encouraging the same in others.

In this context affective maturity, which is the result of an education in true and responsible love, is a significant and decisive factor in the formation of candidates for the priesthood. (PDV, excerpted, §43)

27. Workplace spirituality, however, has long been an agenda for many in corporate settings. See Richard McKnight, "Spirituality in the Workplace" in *Transforming Work: A Collection of Organizational Transformation Readings*, ed. J. D. Adams (Alexandria, VA: Miles River Press, 1984), and James Ritscher, "Spiritual Leadership" in *Transforming Leadership: From Vision to Results*, ed. J. D. Adams (Miles River Press, 1986).

28. Isolation haunts ministry. See Jackson Carroll's important study of Catholic and Protestant clergy, *God's Potters: Pastoral Leadership and the Shaping of Congregations* (Grand Rapids, MI: Wm. B. Eerdmans, 2006), 177–180.

29. In parish staff settings with perceptible significant tensions or relational obstacles, however, consultants saw less attraction to *team* spiritual formation agenda. Instead, people expressed the need to learn how to "communicate better" or sought to pursue only *personal* learning activities including spiritual formation.

30. Cf. Peter Block, *Community: The Structure of Belonging* (San Francisco: Berrett-Koehler, 2008); and John McKnight and John Kretzman, *Discovering Community Power: A Guide to Mobilizing Local Assets and Your Organization's Capacity* (Chicago: ACTA, 2005). Also see Block, *Flawless Consulting*, 3rd ed., ch. 12.

31. NVivo software grows a researcher's capacity to build comparative narrative data. As reports are entered, the program engages a researcher to build "information nodes" of associated words and phrases that bring selected activities into focus, http://www.qsrinternational.com/what-is-nvivo (accessed May 2016).

32. The decision to allow consultants to continue with their teams was a trade-off. Often continuance meant that teams would hire a consultant to provide training, team formation activities, retreats, coaching, and so on. The danger would be creation of consultant accountability to the client as a provider, potentially clouding the consultant's facilitative perspective or mitigating the consultant's ability to give direct and honest feedback. Now the consultant could be in the position of needing to please the client rather than challenge at points of disengagement or impasse. Impasse, we shall see later, is a critical milestone marker for many teams when they get close to true collaboration behaviors.

33. Participants would be advised that consultants would normally review their notes with the project director, but were allowed to designate information that would not be shared in this way. Consultant-director coaching and review meetings were treated as confidential matter.

34. Profile of Consultant-Team Engagement by consultant Phyllis DiFuccia from INSPIRE Consultant In-Service workshop, March 2007.

35. Excerpt from the project's 2007 Annual Report, distributed to sponsors and key stakeholders.

36. When reporting, participants indicated the degree of confidentiality assigned to each report. These statements about team and personal learning were marked "Not Confidential," and sent with permissions to share with the parish consultants.

37. Cf. Brett Hoover, *2010–2011 Final Report, INSPIRE Research Project*, Appendix D of 2011 Annual Report to *Sustaining Pastoral Excellence* program.

38. Block, *Flawless Consulting*, approaches the goals of consulting in terms of the consultant acting as "expert" or "an extra pair of hands" or taking on a "collaborative role" in problem solving (19–29). Stroh and Johnson allow that an expert or a facilitative consultant may be asked either to assist a project or to solve a problem. At the point of beginning a consultative

implementation, they posit the work of "diagnosing the problem" and defining the problem as it may play out at different organizational levels (60–67). Setting the question in terms of a stated "problem" allows an initial separation between the client and an objectified "problem." When the consultative focus eventually delves into the systemic issues, that separation usually becomes untidy, and clients must learn how they themselves participate in the problem.

39. These last three are skilled performances for collaborative communication. Discussion allows the making of points and sharing of counterpoints. So, "it rhymes with percussion," and can be a spirited exchange. Conversation involves "turning over" of ideas for shared exploration and understanding. Dialogue requires mutual agreements to suspend assumptions, allow time for silences, and entertain attempts to connect once disparate or conflicting ideas, or to leap into new insights and propose new action.

Chapter Three

Build Collaboration, Build Church?

Bryan Froehle and Mary Froehle

EDITORS' NOTE

Drs. Bryan and Mary Froehle have longstanding interests in congregational life and research. Having been involved at various stages of Project INSPIRE, they were asked at the close of the project's active phase to conduct a study of several representative parishes from among the more than sixty communities that benefited from INSPIRE's work. This chapter is abridged from the report they presented to the INSPIRE Milestone Conference.

Dr. Bryan Froehle directs the PhD program in practical theology and is professor of practical theology at the School of Theology and Ministry, St. Thomas University (Miami, Florida). He previously served on the faculty of Dominican University, River Forest, Illinois, and at the Center for Applied Research in the Apostolate (CARA). He holds a doctorate in sociology (University of Michigan, 1993). Dr. Froehle conducts much of his research at the intersection between theology and the social sciences, focusing on Catholic pastoral life and public theology.

Dr. Mary Froehle is assistant professor of practical theology, St. Vincent de Paul Regional Seminary, Boynton Beach, Florida, where she is director of the Office of Institutional Research and Evaluation (OIRE) and Instructional Technology. She serves as adjunct faculty member of the Institute of Pastoral Studies at Loyola University Chicago. She is also a licensed clinical professional counselor and a pastoral counselor in private practice.

SUMMARY

The authors assessed INSPIRE's work in three selected parishes, using a mix of in-depth personal interviews and focus groups and data from INSPIRE archives. The data suggest that for pastoral leadership team development, the pastor's support and pastoral vision are the most critical background vari-

ables. The most critical interventions provided by INSPIRE were consultants, access to networks, and financial resources, in that order. These elements depended on the staff's conduct of regular meetings, cultivation of
mutual respect, and engagement in contextually appropriate collaborative
practices. Such collaborative efforts critically enhanced parish pastoral staffs,
in turn producing more vibrant parishes. The study suggests opportunities for
continuing what INSPIRE began, particularly for academic institutions interested in partnering with dioceses and parishes.

PROJECT BACKGROUND

INSPIRE Origin, Mission, and Vision

INSPIRE was designed to advance pastoral team effectiveness in parish ministry within selected parishes in the Archdiocese of Chicago. Its leaders
described the project as a "partnership initiative" between the Archdiocese of
Chicago and Loyola University Chicago, particularly between the Archdiocesan Office of Human Resources and the Institute of Pastoral Studies at
Loyola. INSPIRE's grounding in the archdiocese and University modeled the
project's vision of collaboration from its earliest stages. Contemporary ministerial skill sets, including those for which Loyola University Chicago's Institute of Pastoral Studies is particularly known, strongly emphasize collaborative skills and teamwork. The strategic plan of the Archdiocese of Chicago,
developed toward the final years of INSPIRE's work, also reflects such a
focus.[1]

INSPIRE pursued the mandate of the Lilly Endowment's *Sustaining Pastoral Excellence* program to identify successful pastors and their staffs in the
archdiocese and assist their development as effective pastoral ministry teams.
An agenda of pastoral team effectiveness would require collaborative, interdependent utilization of talents, insight, and initiative of all team members in
promoting parish mission (see explanatory note).[2] Such a goal is particularly
appropriate for contemporary church life, marked as it is by fewer but larger
parishes with relatively larger and more complex parish teams than in the
past. These teams are increasingly composed of fewer priests and more lay
ecclesial ministers, some part-time and most serving in specialized ministries. Staff turnover tends to be relatively frequent, particularly for priests
other than the pastor.

The INSPIRE vision flows from contemporary research on team building,
leadership, and management in general. It resonates with emerging spiritual-
ities and theologies of collaborative ministry and leadership. Individual parish team members were therefore expected to develop themselves and their
gifts for the good of the pastoral team even as the team worked to reflect best
practices. The project arrived at a time when church leaders looked out at

corporate and nongovernmental organizations (NGOs) that routinely turn toward a team approach. Simultaneously, new forms of parish life and ministry were emerging.

INSPIRE's vision from the start was to integrate critical skill sets, theologies of ministry, and leadership research so as to build a new collaborative model for invigorating Catholic parish life. Both the challenges that IN-SPIRE confronted and the types of relationships it built have been familiar, perhaps even typical, in some other congregationally based Christian denominations. However, most Catholic parishes remain unfamiliar with these realities. Skill sets included pastoral planning, conducting meetings, and advancing personal development so as to promote more effective team functioning. Parish consultants facilitated skill development and modeled effective practices like respectful conversations. They provided much of the training and coaching as parish staff members transitioned into more effective pastoral leadership teams.

Research Goals and Design

Presenters at the INSPIRE Milestone Conference (October 2013) spoke to the operation and vision of INSPIRE, practical theological aspects of pastoral staffs serving within merged parishes, and challenges for staff effectiveness in multicultural parishes. The primary challenge guiding this summative qualitative evaluation was to identify critical practices and narratives related to pastoral staff collaboration within INSPIRE parishes. The goal was to understand the nature of INSPIRE's contributions and sort out best practices that could be adopted by parishes in the future.

Research methods were qualitative and based on semistructured interviews, both one-on-one and group interviews. The design called for selection of three different parishes where INSPIRE had been successful, presumably in somewhat distinctive ways within these different parish contexts. The selected parishes differ considerably as to demographic factors and their specific goals for INSPIRE. (INSPIRE's approach to staff development relied on commitments to respect the distinctiveness of each parish and each pastoral team.) Researchers focused on one parish from a Chicago Near West Side Hispanic neighborhood, another from a suburban middle-class setting, the third from a culturally diverse, recently merged city parish. This sort of analysis depends on an assumption that the three parishes whose staffs were selected for interviews represent some comparable practices observed in many parishes that partnered with INSPIRE. Such a claim is theoretical, not statistical, and no claim of statistical representativeness is given.

The primary data in this evaluation project were interviews with individual parish staff members at the three selected parishes, supplemented with a focus-group–type interview of available staff members at each parish. Additional data included INSPIRE's files regarding each parish's participation in INSPIRE, as well as materials maintained locally by the various parish teams. Interviews were arranged by INSPIRE leadership to include those persons INSPIRE staff deemed integral to the study. A total of seventeen interviews were conducted, three of which were focus group interviews, resulting in a total of 363 transcribed pages.[3]

CRITICAL CONTEXTUAL FACTORS FOR INSPIRE'S SUCCESS

Three critical contextual factors were identified as foundational to the development of pastoral leadership teams. The first addresses the need for effective leadership in times of transition, whether change is desired or perceived as unwelcome. Transitions are relatively common in Catholic parish life in the United States today, certainly within the parishes of the Archdiocese of Chicago where INSPIRE was located. The second and third factors are uniquely expressed in particular parishes but absolutely essential for improving collaboration and effectiveness in parish ministry teams. They are the pastor's commitment developing staff for team leadership, and his vision or expectations aligned with those of the parish pastoral team, as together they identify outcomes and collaborations that everyone really wants.

Parish Life and the Church Today

When INSPIRE was first planned in 2002, challenges for parishes and pastoral leadership in the Catholic Church in the United States had grown particularly acute: parishes were merging and the remaining parishes were getting larger, even as parish teams were larger, less stable, and with a greater mix of people of different backgrounds, skill sets, and combinations of full-time and part-time employment. All of this was against a backdrop of the sexual abuse crisis and declining credibility for the church, coupled with dramatically diminishing numbers of priests in active ministry.

> The truth is that the talent pool of the priests and the numbers are diminishing; without INSPIRE, we're headed for trouble. I really mean this: that we're sending guys ordained one year to become pastors—one year! . . . [When you're named pastor, they don't ask you what your experience is and how do you like to handle the finances. You go in with all kinds of assumptions. I think these guys who are being named and if they don't have a process like this, if they don't have some type of mentoring, if they don't have [someone who] says, "You know what? You need to spend money on staff development," that is going to be a real problem. That's going to be a real problem because we're already sending guys in who have language barriers. We have guys who have lack of experience. It's going to be a problem. They have got to get some support somewhere.

The Pastor's Leadership

The role of the pastor emerged as a critically necessary, though not sufficient, factor in INSPIRE's success in the three parishes studied. Pastors had a sense of commitment and investment in INSPIRE in part because they chose to do it and to lead their staffs into it.

> I think the key thing [is that] . . . you have to have a leader who's open to this. If we didn't . . . I think the dynamic would have been very different and the outcome could have been very different.

In each of the three parishes where interviews were conducted, pastors initiated the relationship with INSPIRE and the staff followed the lead of the pastor. An examination of INSPIRE archives suggests that this was the case in general: the three pastors appear to represent the norm, not the exception. This finding suggests that the pastor's buy-in and commitment are crucial aspects of the process.

The Pastor's and Pastoral Team's Vision

A related, and we believe important, finding determines how far the work of improving pastoral staff effectiveness might go. The pastor's vision of enhanced staff effectiveness could mark the boundary at which work on its improvement ends. In every case, diminishment of engagement in INSPIRE seems to have occurred when the pastor felt that the needs for which he engaged the project had been largely addressed. This is not to suggest that ceasing participation relied on a single decision of one person. Rather, the pastor's vision seemed to inform that of the pastoral staff as a whole during the INSPIRE process.

Engagement requires a sense of commitment to the possibilities for enhanced pastoral team effectiveness. Offering something like INSPIRE gives pastors and parish staffs as a whole an opportunity to renew their commitment and vision.

> We were hungry for change, so INSPIRE had willing participants. We were ready to do something. We had the support and the direction of our leader, of our pastor. . . . [T]hose two things were instrumental.
> Kudos to our pastor because he set the tone. He set the tone for open, honest communication and a trusting environment. He also empowered us. . . . [W]e were his colleagues. . . . He truly set a team atmosphere. . . . I think it was that he was leading by example, so by setting that tone of team leadership, then we in turn, witnessed that . . . and then we would do the same thing in all our own ministry.
> INSPIRE only works . . . , if the people that are going to be a part of it are serious about it. . . . Our issue was oftentimes we'd get together and have these

> great events and growth, but then to implement it—I think that's where our
> downfall was. It's like, oh yeah, we need to do this and this is what's missing
> in the parish. Then we'd get back in the business of our lives and parish life.

In other words, the vision sets the pace for the team to move forward, which
is critical because the team is inevitably affected by a natural tendency toward fragmentation or isolation as individual, task-based approaches are tak-
en up by stakeholders of separate, specialized ministries. Pastoral vision thus
engenders a sense of an endpoint for the parish pastoral team as they move
toward greater teamwork and collaboration.

> Well, INSPIRE kept sending us invitations for an Advent Day, . . . [or] for a
> Spring Day, and those days, early on, helped us in the process of team building
> and reflecting. Then there was an invitation that came and [only] a couple
> people went. Then the next invitation came and we said, "I think we're
> okay." . . . When we would go to those meetings, we were hearing things that
> we had done. . . . We were hearing from other staffs [and saying], "Okay,
> we've been through that; we've done that. We've done that, [too]." . . . We
> were kind of hearing the same things over and over again. And we decided, I
> think we've run the course.

This endpoint is as important as the starting point. Programs to enhance the
effectiveness of parish pastoral staffs would do well to work with an understanding of how vision and outcomes can motivate collaboration, and how a
new phase is entered when influential voices declare that the initial vision
has been realized.

EXTERNAL RESOURCES

INSPIRE provided a number of resources to parish teams that they could not
obtain themselves. While the commitment of the pastor and the pastoral
vision was essential, it was the provision of these external resources that
facilitated the building of more-effective parish pastoral teams. The three
most critical external resources, in order of importance as indicated by the
majority of the interviewees, are consultants, networks, and funds.

Consultants

The consultants who worked on-site in enrolled parishes contributed the
single greatest influence on parish staffs. As professional service providers,
they brought outside expertise and offered a certain critical distance between
parish relationships and diocesan structures. INSPIRE consultants tended to
serve over relatively long durations, allowing them to develop a personal feel
for the needs and aptitudes of their clients. Consultants were highly regarded

by parish staff and particularly important for dealing with conflict, helping in times of grief, or modeling new tools and behaviors for effective collaborative ministry. This included expressing a certain confidence in pastoral ministry, as each consultant established a unique form of ministerial presence. Women in ministry were particularly likely to refer to women consultants as providing excellent models of being a strong, confident minister.

> I think a lot of it was the initial partner meetings we had with [the INSPIRE consultant]; the ones that focused around on, "How do you work as a team already?" "Where are your strengths?" "Where are your weaknesses?" . . . I think a part of it was targeting what our goals were. Like I said, the overarching mission of bringing [parishioners] closer to God is there, but what are the goals that support that? What are we going to do? . . . Could you do without the consultant? No. . . . [I]t really targeted for us things that we can't do for ourselves.

This was due in part to the consultants' considerable talents. Many of them had worked on parish staffs or in some similar function, and so understood the challenges as an insider, which gave them strong credibility. The consultants modeled appreciative inquiry styles, something some interviewees noted specifically, and commonly remarked on the affirming stances taken by the consultants.

> [The consultant] had a way . . . that was so very nice with people. [The consultant] was able [to] ask a question or give us an idea, but put it in such a way that you almost think it's your own. Pushy? [The consultant] wasn't pushy. [The consultant] had a good way . . . in working with people, I believe. I believe if you ask them directly questions about that, I bet you'd get people saying, yeah, [the consultant] was very good. . . . [The consultant] was prepared for it. [S]ometimes people don't want you to go one step away from what they have on their agenda, but [the consultant] listened.
>
> [The consultant] really had a good way of helping us get to the core of things and how we could improve ourselves as a parish staff. I did feel that [the consultant] really was good at getting to the core of it; helping us identify it; and then when [the consultant] stepped away, we had a momentum and then you see it fade a little bit.

As someone from outside the staff, the consultant could see and say things that staff members cannot.

> I think that [the consultant] was also a third eye [who] could see things that we couldn't . . . the trees through the forest (whatever the saying is). Like [the consultant] listened to all of our stories and [would] say, "Oh my gosh, the repeating theme is lack of appreciation; or burnout," or whatever the case was; [the consultant] could see it. [The consultant] could help us name it and then we would know what to do with it once we named it.

So part of what I think INSPIRE was about was helping our staff to look at
how they had been operating as a staff and how we wanted to operate as a staff
and kind of balance that with what were the needs of the parish. [The consul-
tant] uncovered some . . . of the ghosts or some of the elephants in the room
that nobody was talking about. [The consultant] helped us to name some of the
things that hadn't been talked about for some time.

Part of the consultants' effectiveness is due to their being located outside
diocesan structures.

I think [having a consultant who is not part of the archdiocesan structure] is a
huge plus. I think whenever you are sitting there with somebody who is going
to judge your work, it's hard to be free.

By enjoying consultation from persons external to the parish and diocesan
structures, staffs were free to take ownership of transitions. The "third party"
identification removed the institutionalized threat and consequent behavioral
deference typically afforded to visitors with official status somewhere in the
archdiocesan hierarchy.

Again, just being a third party, listening to us, then [the consultant] could write
down what we were saying we needed and what we wanted. Then again, it was
up to us to implement it. . . . We're still working on that, but it's having very
much improved through INSPIRE.

The role of the consultant, however, is far more than that of a disinter-
ested observer. Parish pastoral team members gave considerable trust to the
consultant, who played an important role in decision making as the pastoral
team moved forward in its goals. Though outside of "vertical" parish and
archdiocesan accountability structures, they were part of an alternative "horizontal" accountability structure which INSPIRE participants freely and mutually accepted (and about which more will be said shortly). In this sense, the
consultants functioned as "spiritual directors" for the staff and were even
referred to as such by some interviewees. This role gave the consultants wide
latitude for the effective exercise of remarkable personal authority.

Well, you need the consultant for the mission purpose. I think what [the
consultant does is that]—we had our mission, but [the consultant] really
guided us to our action steps. So I think that does need to come first. . . . You
have no idea how many times [the consultant] reviewed our . . . plans [and]
kept saying, "No!"

Consultants facilitated team-building exercises that helped move beyond
conflict and fragmentation toward mutual respect and collaboration. This

modeled behaviors that the team could later implement themselves, while launching them on a pathway to greater team effectiveness.

> [The consultant] got all of us to talk about the ugly stuff [together with the consultant], but more importantly . . . had us do exercises that you write down one gift that you see of each person around the table, and we shared that then with each other, once all that got written down. So we began acknowledging the good that was there, began to create some common ground for working together, more cross referencing of ministries, instead of the kind of "protecting my turf." So I think [the consultant] was very helpful with that.

Many referred back to tools shared and modeled by the consultants, such as "Strengths Finder"[4] or the Myers-Briggs inventory. The consultants clearly transferred many important tools and techniques to parish staffs. However, the most critical aspect of the work of the consultant was not about specific techniques but rather initiating a process and modeling relationship.

> It intrigued me that it wasn't about doing a project. It was about the process and not the project. The project was important. They held you accountable for the expenditure of funds for the project, but it was the process of what happened while you were doing the project [that was the real focus].

Networking Across Parishes

INSPIRE created a new opportunity to network parish staff as learning organizations, linked one to the other, horizontally.[5] Dioceses naturally relate to parishes in a vertical manner—diocesan offices push things "down" to the parish level, and parishes take things "up" with downtown. However, vertical relationships are often not the best means to foster the networking capacities that most pastoral staffs lack.

INSPIRE did something different. It built horizontal forms of relationship to which parishes freely committed and in which they could learn from other parish staffs committed to enhancing staff effectiveness. These networks were highly valued, even when parish staff members could not always attend meetings convened some distance from their parishes. The INSPIRE-created networking opportunities, including large-scale gatherings, as well as archdiocese-sponsored events identified in some personal development plans prepared for INSPIRE by individual staff members, were deeply valued and highly praised by the participants.

However, these voluntary networks had a certain "organic" quality by which commitment could not be enforced in the way it might be in a top-down organization. Not all participated as INSPIRE leaders envisioned or as these staff members themselves would have hoped. Further evidence of this organic element is that interviews revealed that the pastoral staffs and their individual members, including the pastor and key INSPIRE coordinators, had no precise idea of exactly when they started or ended INSPIRE. This suggests that the life of INSPIRE melded into parish life. Moreover, not all successful INSPIRE parishes, including the three where the interviews took place for this study, regularly reported and analyzed their goals. When they did, however, they almost always focused on how learning was becoming part of staff culture and the parish in general. Learning was central, and the building of learning networks was key.

> You need something to bring together people from parishes because, depending on what's been successful at a parish, it's great to get some new ideas. . . . So relationships could be set up between people to go help.

Networking is seen as a critically important need that helped enhance the effectiveness of parish staffs.

> [It was so important] to be able to network early on here with other parishes who have gone through their own struggles, similar or different, and dealing with their own successes and how did they get there. So that network of conversation . . . there's still a great need for it. Bringing parishes together, bring staffs together, lay and clerical, to look at staffing, look at mission, look at physical realities of declining numbers and rising costs and all that stuff. . . . So I think INSPIRE certainly nurtured those kind of things.

These networks did more than share ideas: they helped inspire staff with new possibilities. (Many references were made to the name "INSPIRE" as being particularly appropriate, and simply feeling "inspired" through INSPIRE.)

> I think for me, there's another dimension to it, other than just learning. To be in those meetings, it was not difficult to be inspired, no pun intended. That's an important part of being a staff, being leadership, is that we continue to be inspired by their stories and how they move through things and celebrate successes and grieve over failures and some of that kind of stuff. So . . . to listen to other people in that kind of a forum, was very helpful. Again, it's nothing the diocese normally provides.

INSPIRE did more than simply network parishes during occasional large-scale meetings. It helped parish staff resource each other on an everyday basis.

> It put us in touch with other . . . parishes that were working on similar things. . . . So that just to kind of bring them together into a room with some focus questions, or a theme to deal with, was very helpful. To listen to each other's experience was very helpful. Presenters, sometimes they were very good, sometimes missed the mark, but they became the platform for discussion to take place in the larger group itself and that became very helpful. And

there's no other forum like that in the diocese that puts parishes in touch with parishes. Deanery meetings . . . are all reports from offices downtown. We don't engage one another and we don't work on things together that are within our competency and with our abilities.

Funds

Along with the consultants and networking services, INSPIRE provided funds to participating parishes for a collective project and personal development for each staff member. The common parish project became an opportunity for the staff to model collaboration, and the individual personal development piece helped staff members to feel valued and special, giving them opportunities to do something outside of ministry they would not otherwise do.

Overall, INSPIRE funding helped develop a sense of accountability or stewardship. This was particularly the case for those who had personally applied for INSPIRE, signed the papers, acknowledged receipt of the funds, kept the INSPIRE-related files, and made sure that the INSPIRE-required reports were submitted on time, especially pastors and, secondarily, those who served as INSPIRE coordinators.

> Well, I do think we felt accountable. . . . I would say, too, . . . that I was invested. I was invested. I wanted it to—I saw a need and I wanted it to happen. I wanted to improve what was going on in our staff. I saw potential and I wanted to improve it.
> INSPIRE gave us money, so we felt accountable to them. . . . If there is money involved, there has to be accountability to them.

In two of the three parishes where interviews were conducted, the funding INSPIRE provided was specifically mentioned as not crucial for their participation or central to what INSPIRE meant to them, as valuable as it was. The core gain for these parishes was in the consultation and learning networks, though the funding facilitated this to some extent. In the case of one of the parishes, however, it was different. The parish has particularly limited finances. In this parish, INSPIRE helped to make possible growth experiences otherwise unattainable.

> [T]he inner city parishes, they just don't have it. I've been in a number of parishes and they just don't have the funds to do something like that. They just don't have it. . . . And it just can uplift them. Sometimes when they're trying to do something and there's no way they can afford it and you have to let things like that go, . . . but if they can have something that can help them to be inspired, I think that makes life so much better.

In these three areas—consultants, networks, and funding—INSPIRE provided resources that are at least in short supply for parish ministers.

CRITICAL ELEMENTS CATALYZED BY INSPIRE

Three major internal changes were critical for the external interventions offered by INSPIRE to take root. The most important was developing effective, regular meetings as a staff. The second had to do with mutual respect and affirmation across the staff, and the third was the identification and adoption of collaborative practices appropriate to particular parish contexts and challenges.

Staff Meetings

Many parishes do not have regular staff meetings, and when they do, the meetings are often not effective or are even counterproductive. This was the case for all three parishes where interviews were conducted. The intervention of the consultants was critical in modeling how good meetings can be conducted, but the staff had to actually begin meeting regularly and doing so in a way that was productive.

Effective meetings have to involve putting everything on the table rather than holding back and then having "side meetings" or gripe sessions. Effective meetings allow the development of a shared vision and practice of a shared spirituality. By building unity within the staff, positive meetings can help the parish as a whole—and model effective meetings that may be replicated in other parish groups.

INSPIRE parishes seem to have discovered that three elements of effective meetings enhance staff effectiveness. First, such meetings are oriented toward goals and priorities. Rather than simply receiving a report, staff members have an opportunity to engage common goals together. Second, such meetings must involve scheduling. Parish life runs around specific events, and the degree to which those events are known and discussed in advance, within the entire staff, is the degree to which communication will be effective and collaboration possible. Third, good meetings involve an opportunity for all to collaborate in planning and initiatives as appropriate, given each person's role, gifts, and experience.

> Our weekly staff meetings have helped us in many ways; what it is to incorporate another person into our group; or to share ideas; or it's a matter of, I got this in the mail and what do you think about this idea? . . . It opens up that dialogue on a regular basis for all of us to share new ideas, new thoughts. I think that opening and dialogue has made, I think—altered the relationships I

think, a lot of us have with each other and made it more collegial, more family, versus structure.

Good meetings allow for good communication, which includes breaking down of "silos."

> Sometimes, my thought back then was . . . we weren't working together. Not in competition with each other, but just not moving in the same direction. So I think that's where some of this came from. Everybody was kind of dealing in their own silo and a lot of the times the problems come from . . . lack of communication. . . . I know we changed the structure of the staff meetings in order to better communicate and have since changed them again.

Through INSPIRE, particularly its consultants, parish staff came to see that new ways of conducting meetings were helpful. Though they might take an investment of time, the benefit they yielded in creating efficiencies and in building a sense of unity and mutual support was remarkable.

> We really looked at each other's strengths. So if I was having something for [my ministry area], but I, my strength is not music, then I would know that [I could turn to] the music director. . . . Like with the food, I knew who to go to for that. So it really helped us to reach out to other staff to find what their strength was and know that they could help us in our ministry. We went from saying—and I know I personally tried to get us to do different language—it's like [my ministry] was not "my" ministry, it's "our" ministry. . . . So even just changing our language and how we looked at ourselves.

Mutual Respect

The meetings built up a sense of mutual respect and affirmation between staff, but the meetings themselves were not the only sources for such reciprocation. In consultant-led reflections the consultants opened up conversations during which team members affirmed one another and named how they each could rely on the other. Encouraging each staff person to understand that they are valued was particularly facilitated for some by the INSPIRE funds allocated for personal development goals. For others, it came from the sense of trust that developed over time, and a growing willingness to be vulnerable in staff meetings and interactions. Individual members came to be recognized for their gifts and talents, the new skills and self-assurance they developed, and the wide range of gifts that they could offer. Leadership moved from expectations of a top-down approach to one that embraced initiative, mutual support, and teamwork. Without the staff doing these things, the meetings themselves could not have become as successful as they did.

Pastoral staffs who participated in INSPIRE tend to associate significant peak experiences of staff mutual support with INSPIRE, as well as collaborative aspects of staff culture in general.

> I think what INSPIRE did was it offered us an opportunity to name the strengths, the weaknesses, the growth areas of our staff and our team and our parish. . . . If we wouldn't have had that time, that money, that personnel that provided us assistance, we would not have been able to take time to look at ourselves; to look at the parish.

Staffs who participated in INSPIRE commonly exuded mutual respect, increasing both staff morale, investment in a shared mission, and personal self-esteem.

> I can tell you, because of INSPIRE, I started my [advanced academic program] . . . because they really inspired me to do something. Because of this program, I started to believe I can do something.
> [W]e all listen to each other. We all support each other and we all understand that we are together, working together towards one goal. We are—we feel—I feel free to express any opinion I have; or new idea I have. I know it will be listened to and then taken into account and I think that's very important.
> [T]he staff previous to that did not have that trust on every level. Many of us on the staff had long relationships and trust levels, but just to kind of throw it all out there in the room and say, we are a staff. We have to trust each other. The assignment was to say one positive thing about everyone and you had to take your Post-It and put it on that person's chart and explain it to the group. It was a very emotional thing for some people. . . . It's a technique that Father has used continually as our staffs have evolved.

In developing this sense of mutual respect, a kind of virtuous cycle was created whereby staff came to relate to each other and communicate more effectively, and in more meaningful ways.

> [I]n telling our stories, sharing our stories and then working together, I think we felt stronger personally. Maybe some of them looked stronger because they were doing their personal plan too. I don't know this, but I think we all had a little bit more—we would bless each other and these different things were powerful, I think. Writing down a kind note to someone else about how much you love what they do for you and for the parish. I think I still have these things at home. The positive words, affirmation words on a sheet of paper. I think those things all made us each feel more valued and more critical to the parish growth and the staff. . . . We aren't just there, out in space. We are [each important] and we are a team and we need to know each other.

Staff members found the experience of coming to new levels of mutual respect for each other as transformative. Just like the consultants, staff members modeled good listening when they listened to parishioners and volunteers, and modeled new techniques as they used those techniques.

> We sat in a room and actually I still have the paper in my folder. . . . The staff sat around in comfortable chairs. [Our consultant] had us take a few moments to sit down and jot down a note for every person in the circle; a note about what their gifts were or what they appreciated. We were to take those then and then went around the circle and took the time to address those to [whom] we wrote it. The sharing was very good. It was very confirming and that got people talking to one another with kind of a different level of trust that hadn't been there before.

This experience of mutual respect developed a sense of teamwork and relationship among the staff. When asked to give a few key words about the spirit of the parish that emerged through INSPIRE, one said, "Engaged, committed, connected." Further, mutual respect led to collaborative action.

Other Collaborative Practices

Conducting regular, effective meetings and affirming the gifts of fellow staff members are specific practices of collaboration. These two practices are critical in every context. The third internal element is also about collaborative practices, but has to do with specific self- and team-reinforced expectations as each member contributes to specific efforts and ministerial services.

Some staff members used "Strengths Finder." Others used the MBTI. Regardless, these practices fit the context and helped the staff grow in critically important ways and to move gradually toward routine collaborative practices. As such, they had a common goal—helping staff to break out of a default mode of separate, specialized ministering "for the sake of ministering" rather than for a common mission.

> I think everybody on this staff is very competent in their own areas and they do a great job of running what their responsibilities are, but put that group together around the table and there's going to be some fireworks. It's just the nature of the beast. It's just some of the personalities involved. . . . There's still too much turf protection and not enough "we" rather than "my" or "I."

Some collaborative practices were specifically spiritual in nature, and participants reported learning a great deal from the consultant's sensitivity to spirituality. Some pastoral team members, for example, report having learned to use meditative music in their prayers and reflections as a result of a consultant's modeling of such a practice. One staff member said of INSPIRE-organized days of recollection, "It was prayer for the . . . parishes to be together as one and pray as one and share as one."

Individual staff members report growing personally through INSPIRE as leaders and as persons, even as the pastoral staff was developing as a team. As one mused about "the wisdom of INSPIRE": "[H]aving both a personal goal and a team goal or a group goal—yes, I have grown, I think." Getting to know themselves and their personal gifts led staff to make choices about the kinds of collaborative practices that were appropriate for them.

> So I just think we got to know each other, became more comfortable with one another and that just, again, the depth to which people went, I think depended on their personality, but I think just that cohesiveness, all the teamwork that we had done led to that, our having those discussions.

These three elements that depended on the actions of the team itself—effective regular meetings, cultivating mutual respect and affirming each other, and additional collaborative practices appropriate to the ministerial context and person—were critical to INSPIRE. By themselves, neither a context nor an engaged pastor was sufficient, nor were the three major INSPIRE interventions of consultant, networks, and funds. The team itself had to engage in simple but critically important practices of meetings, affirmation, and other appropriate collaborative practices.

Healthy Staff, Healthy Parish

There appeared to be a direct relationship between INSPIRE's effect on the staff, and the subsequent effect of the staff on the parish. In short, respondents indicated that INSPIRE made for a more healthy and effective staff, which in turn made for a healthier parish. Transformation in one part of the system connected to transformation in other parts.

OVERALL IMPACT OF INSPIRE ON THE PARISH PASTORAL STAFF

The greatest net effect of INSPIRE was the building up of more effective, collaborative parish pastoral teams.

> So about the most—the best benefits what we received is helping us to work together like a team. I can tell you, we have a very good team, very good. . . . So I'm so happy. . . . It's better.
> I really think that is the fruit of the INSPIRE program, bringing us together in doing teamwork.

Pastoral teams developed a new and deeper appreciation for collaboration.

> This way of being collaborative is highly valued. I just think the need to be collaborative . . . to work with parish staffs, because I just think as church continues to evolve, it's just going to be so important.

They also came to see strongly the value of bringing in outside help. As one team member declared, "I have no hesitation today because I know what getting a facilitator can do for us."

INSPIRE was a remarkable catalyst for so many parishes. Members of parish pastoral teams saw this very clearly.

> I think the seeds are planted in INSPIRE about bringing people together to look at gifts, address our issues and envision a better future. I think that's moved us along that path.

As staff members looked back, remembering the time before INSPIRE and after, the gift that was INSPIRE came readily to mind.

> Well, in regard to meetings, the staff told me here that they had not had a staff meeting in ten months [prior to INSPIRE]. So there was no regularity with the last person that administered the place. It was such a battle royal and shouting matches would occur; they just quit meeting. So there had not been a meeting for almost a year. So we then set up a calendar for meetings. We took turns running the meetings or facilitating the meetings. We all contributed to the agenda of the meeting; took turns leading prayer. So those kinds of skill sets; we did not do shouting matches.

The impact was clear for all to see within the parish. Parishioners noticed and appreciated the change within the pastoral team.

> I do feel like our parishioners are very thankful for our staff because they do see a team. They aren't just like, "I deal with this person and that's what I do at that parish." I think they really do see us as a team. They see us together a lot in different things and they see us overlapping more. We had these just separate ministries; we do overlap a little more. . . . So I feel INSPIRE brought us together and the parish noticed it. The parishioners really could identify a change and knew a little more of the overall parish staff, not just individual people.

OVERALL IMPACT OF INSPIRE ON THE PARISH

The effect of INSPIRE on the parish team was just the beginning, however. The goal of the grant behind INSPIRE was not simply to have the staff feel like a team, but to foster excellence in the parish as a whole. As it happened, one clear result was the transfer of INSPIRE-related learnings from the staff to the whole parish.

> [I]t came out in different ways, but I think one of the most helpful things we did, first as a staff and then, I believe, . . . took . . . to parish council and then to the school, the faculty, staff and administration . . . was a thing called Strength Finders. Again, this is, I think, all the fruits of INSPIRE.

No matter the particular element, INSPIRE went well beyond the staff. It became a crucial means of transforming the parish. Many participants noted that the move of the staff toward mutual respect, collaboration, and team-work led the parish as a whole down the same road. Each of the parishes has its own particular context, but all note a community transformed.

> But INSPIRE also impacted our parish council; INSPIRE gave structure and some rationale to our parish council. So it impacted that.
> Just from that experience, the importance of creating an interdependent team. I think as parishes grow, whatever the future looks like, understanding [not only] what are the gifts of the parish, but what are the individual gifts that each of the staff members brings and how can that go about transforming a parish [is crucial].

Opportunities for the Future

The transformative effect of the work of INSPIRE on parish staffs and parishes as a whole both make a strong case for carrying on the work of consultation and intentionally growing parish staffs into pastoral leadership teams. The need for a network that can replicate the most critical aspects of INSPIRE's service to the Church is strong.

It is also clear that parish pastors and parish staffs as a whole have massive pent-up demand for the kind of work done by INSPIRE. As such, work like that of INSPIRE, no matter how it is carried on, offers considerable opportunities for all those who would be involved, as well as academic institutions, dioceses, and parishes interested in partnering with each other. These opportunities in turn suggest new ways to cultivate networks of potential students, consultants, and thought leaders.

> [INSPIRE] brought something that very few people in this country can have and I would love to see it go forward because [of] the dynamics of trying to be a group that ministers with the needs that we have; and a couple times its come up, well, if we could have [our consultant] come back. It's something that's ongoing. I'd love to see it be an agency for people to tap into.

Demand for Training and Consultation

While some parish staff members prepare in formal training programs with extensive field supervision and advanced training, this is not true for many. Moreover, with or without formal initial training, staff members will continue to be formed through on-the-job training even while being overwhelmed with the day-to-day task orientation of parish ministry. This deficiency is no less strong for priests than for lay ecclesial ministers. In the minimum of six years of seminary training that each newly ordained priest has typically experienced, very little time has been spent on the actual everyday skills of conducting meetings, dealing with staff conflicts, and effective management and communications.

Such challenges as these are built into the reality of ministry and parish structures today. Precisely because the needs are chronic and cyclical, diminishing and then reappearing, they are an ongoing problem that needs to be addressed sometimes directly with considerable energy, and sometimes over a long term. In this sense, the work of leadership and pastoral team development is a matter for all parishes, all pastors, and all parish staffs.

Those who completed INSPIRE are sensitized to the benefit of this sort of work and therefore express their desire for ongoing and long-term continuance of the work.

> Great investment for the results we got. I definitely feel it really helped us through difficult times, it really pumped us up. I really—I would say a little stronger investment would be a revisit after a year. . . . "How you guys doing? Where are you? Remember those goals we talked about?" A little poke in the arm is never a bad thing. So I think maybe a little further investment would be a recheck. I think a recheck could go a long way.

Opportunities for Institutions of Higher Education

INSPIRE's experience of partnership between a university and an archdiocese suggests clear opportunities for any university or institution of higher education that can deliver the kind of expertise with which the Institute of Pastoral Studies and Loyola Chicago have become associated. This could include assistance of faculty, staff, graduate students, and related persons in facilitation and consultation. It could also include offering a steady cycle of seminars, including webinars, along with other well-timed offerings and events, so as to regularly recruit students in degree and certificate programs.

> That's why I went to school at Loyola [Institute of Pastoral Studies], because the question was asked, "Do you have the skill set for what you're doing?" Well, no one really cared about that before. So you could just see this whole new sense of taking pride in what you do and just asking if you have what you need to do your job well. . . . Just the asking of the question was huge for all of us. Like what we did was validated.

Many on parish staff are bewildered by the lack of investment that Chicago-area institutions of higher education make in offering resources that meet the needs of parishes. They are astonished by the lack of fit between the demand they perceive and what these institutions actually offer.

> Hello? How many Catholic universities do we have in the diocese? Geez Louise! . . . What kind of resources could be available to our school and religious ed [education] program? [Why don't] we . . . have a relationship with DePaul University or with Loyola University? . . . Programs of formation exist in religious communities. They exist in colleges. They exist in seminaries. What about formation for lay leaders? Is the [archdiocesan] Lay Ecclesial Ministry program the only thing that we've got to offer?

Parish staffs are very aware of the emerging patterns in ministry and parish life, but have few resources to respond beyond with the everyday, task-oriented reality of ministry. Institutions of higher education, particularly universities that can mobilize offerings, specialists, practical expertise, and conversation across disciplines, may have a strong opportunity here.

Opportunities for Building Networks

The evident demand for new networks across parishes presents an opportunity for organizational entrepreneurs even outside a university context. INSPIRE networked committed and relatively high-performing parishes across geographies and cultural groups, facilitating a learning process across parish staffs. This is the basis of good innovation—learning and adapting lessons from other contexts. While future programming will do well to connect excellent consultants and parish needs (see the following section), a core part of the work of any network that would carry on the vision of INSPIRE would link parishes desiring to learn and grow with each other, that they might share with each other and learn together.

> Well . . . the beauty of INSPIRE was meeting with other parishes and listening to the challenges and the successes that they had and how we could help them and what we could learn from them. So it wasn't just the speakers and the tools from INSPIRE itself, but it was really meeting, having days where we would gather in the city and meet with other parishes in INSPIRE and hear from their staff. That was really helpful for us. . . . So not only did we learn from others, but we were also mentor and a guide for the new parish teams coming [into the project].

Opportunities for Consultants

Whether Catholic or other universities will make an effort to serve the needs of the church in this way, and in doing so add to their student base, is hard to predict. It is equally hard to predict if an organizational entrepreneur will respond to the need by crafting a network of parishes. In both cases, there are clear incentives, both financial and mission-focused.

There are no less clear incentives, however, and perhaps even stronger ones, for connecting consultants to parishes in need of them. The key for any organization that attempts to further leadership development is to connect parish staffs with excellent external consultants who would serve for a limited time and at sufficient fee structures that would make such expertise feasible for both parishes and consultants.

> Well, I think that we were all leaders, but we needed someone to lead us. So [the consultant], independent third party coming in, that we could confidentially share . . . any problems that we had, but you really just bring us together and provide an environment where we could list what are the issues we have, or what are our priorities. So just to gather in a room and have a big board [on which] we wrote our priorities or our strengths or things that we wanted to do and just have that done.

External consultants can be particularly helpful to new pastors who want to be agents of change. Outside consultants who do not report to supervisory Church authorities are positioned to introduce new ideas in neutral open-ended ways, without conveying a sense of imposition. The external consultant allows a team to freely choose its future, and to therefore become that much more committed to it. Organizational consultants with understanding of church cultures and systems bring skills very similar to those of a well-trained pastoral counselor. There may even be a role for retired pastors, among others, in providing the kind of external consulting outside of formal archdiocesan structures that parishes need.

However, a successful match between a pastoral staff and consultant requires more than the consultant's technical knowledge. Equally important are the personal relational skills, experience, and cultural sensitivities that fit with the parish history and circumstances. The fit between the consultant's personal qualities and the profile of the staff and its needs is critical. Interviewees were readily able to name these qualities.

> Oh, [the consultant's] sense of laughter! [The consultant would] laugh at us. [The consultant's] sense of enthusiasm for everything we were doing. When you're warmly encouraged, you want to do more. When you're feeling successful. [The consultant really helped us in] seeing ourselves in relation to the team and seeing the team by itself, as a necessary thing for the success of the parish to function.

Opportunities for Managing Value: Funding and Financing

Parish staff involvement in any successor to INSPIRE depends not only on creating means of instilling interest and commitment, but on viable, sustainable financial models. Such models depend on controlling costs but even more so on institutional and organizational leaders with the vision to make the strategic investments, however modest.

The critical importance of investing in something such as INSPIRE was clearly understood by the participants. Such an investment was seen not only as a critical means of building up the future of the Church, but also as a means of improving efficiency: reducing costs of time and money in parish life while meeting critical ministry goals more effectively. Taken together, these relatively small gains could add up to significant increases in building up the Church.

> Fund it . . . I think certainly the archdiocese would have to fund part of it. I think parishes [should fund] as needed like when we would pay [a consultant] for that. People manage to pay the cable bills. . . . One of the things I've always appreciated and more places are doing it now, Loyola [Institute of Pastoral Studies] pays a third; we pay a third; [the staff person enrolled] pays a third, to help get these degrees. I think things like that . . . , you need to look at. I think if the archdiocese is committed to having successful parishes, they should be committed to doing part of this. I think it would actually cut down on some of their overhead, in terms of trying to fix things.

Building Collaboration, Building Church

Transformation in one part of the system does indeed connect to transformation in other parts. Pastoral teams developed a new, much deeper value for collaboration. They came to see the value of bringing in outside help. Parishioners noticed and appreciated the change within the pastoral team. INSPIRE became a crucial means of transforming the parish. Many participants noted that the move of the staff toward mutual respect, collaboration, and teamwork led the parish as a whole down the same road. Each of the parishes has its own particular context, but all became transformed.

Ultimately, INSPIRE is not simply about organizational development techniques, but self-understanding organizationally and personally. In a Christian religious context, this means theology. The transformation of which INSPIRE is a part was thus regularly rooted within an understanding of God's action and plan, as understood by theological concepts such as the working of the Holy Spirit and the nature of church itself. The critical importance of investing in something such as INSPIRE was clearly understood by the participants. Such an investment was seen not only as a critical means of building up both organizational effectiveness and self-understanding simultaneously. It reduced costs of time and money in parish life while meeting critical ministry goals more effectively. Taken together, this added to significant increases in building up the local church. In short, INSPIRE demonstrates that building collaboration truly builds church.

NOTES

1. See http://www.archchicago.org/strategicpastoralplan (accessed May 2016).

2. This phrasing reflects wording in an interim presentation for project stakeholders (unpublished and not dated), created by Dr. Brett Hoover, the project's first research professor. He identifies the cultivation of practices for "fostering interdependent leadership and promoting parish mission." His findings emphasize a typical parish staff context of an overriding task focus, ministerial isolation, intercultural challenges, and disruption caused by personnel transitions, among others. Hoover concluded that INSPIRE parishes tended to respond most effectively to these realities with practices such as cultivating a common pastoral vision, going on team retreats, sharing responsibility, conducting regular meetings well, and using instruments such as the Myers-Briggs Type Indicator (MBTI) to know each other's gifts better. Though this study is quite different from Hoover's, findings generally mirror his. (Editor's note: Dr. Hoover later prepared a report on pastoral task orientation, "When Work Culture and Ministry Collide," later printed in the project's 2011 Annual Report.)

3. For a complete description of research methodology, design, and survey documents, see Bryan Froehle and Mary Froehle, *Building Collaboration, Building Church?* INSPIRE Milestone Conference Report (October 2013), from which this chapter is drawn.

4. The Clifton Strengths Finder is a personal inventory that helps persons identify particular aptitudes and talents for thinking, responding, and acting. Teams in several community and corporate sectors use the inventory to better communicate, or to leverage individual skills and contributions. More than one parish team reported keeping the notes from a facilitated sharing on the strengths of persons on their parish staffs. They often kept the documents in a prominent place in their offices or homes. Other comparable resources like Myers-Briggs Type Indicator (MBTI) were similarly valued.

5. "Learning organization" is a reference to the work of Peter Senge, among others. See, for example, Peter Senge, *The Fifth Discipline: The Art and Practice of the Learning Organization* (New York: Doubleday, 2006/1990), 3–4.

Chapter Four

Toward a Culture of Dynamic Community

Parish Consolidation and Collaborative Leadership

William A. Clark, SJ

EDITORS' NOTE

As associate professor of religious studies at the College of the Holy Cross, Fr. Bill Clark has been engaged in the study of parishes and parish leadership for many years. (See note to chapter 1 for further career details.) While serving as the second visiting research professor for Project INSPIRE (2011–2013), he studied two parish clusters that enrolled in the project but realized different outcomes. With added material, this chapter is a revision of the paper he produced after that research and presented at INSPIRE's Milestone Conference in 2013.

INTRODUCTION: STUDYING "MERGED PARISHES"

After a century and a half of steady expansion, Catholic parishes in the United States have entered an era of restructuring and consolidation. In view of dramatic changes in demographics, material resources, and leadership, some of the most commonly shared experiences among active Catholics in certain parts of the country have come to include resource sharing, cooperation, and outright merging of previously separate communities. As of the arrival of its ninth archbishop, Blase Cupich, in November 2014, the Archdiocese of Chicago had not yet undergone a systematic process of parish reorganization of the type already implemented in many dioceses in the northeastern United States and elsewhere. Then in early 2016 after much preparation and consultation, Cupich issued a long anticipated public announcement, "inviting everyone in the Archdiocese of Chicago to join me in a multi-year planning process" that would bring about renewal, though not without restructuring including the likely closing of some parishes.[1] However, in recent decades Chicago parishes have been suppressed or more often merged in response to local circumstances. As part of an ongoing search for better pastoral and ecclesiological foundations for contemporary parish ministry throughout the Church, this chapter presents and compares two such cases. I will reflect on the results of a variety of research activities conducted as part of Project INSPIRE, a parish leadership initiative described elsewhere in this volume.

Clearly, restructuring is a major transition event in a parish. It presents a series of occasions for careful pastoral discernment and collaborative decision making. There is much to learn from such moments in the lives of parish staffs and communities. On the other hand, parish mergers present serious challenges to the collaborative pastoral teamwork examined in this volume. Mergers are fraught with now-familiar problems including community identity and loyalties, turf battles, staff redundancies, and changing clerical leadership roles, the very sorts of problems that can encourage suspicion and even the direct undermining of collaborative efforts. Further, for some theologians and parishioners alike, the experience of parish mergers has called into question the entire concept of "parish" as the organizing principle for local Catholic communities. When ominous restructuring announcements challenge our very understanding of local church communities and their leadership, "the merged parish" becomes an essential object for study.

THE METHOD OF THE STUDY

I conducted the field research that is the basis for this chapter while serving as a visiting research professor for Project INSPIRE at Loyola University Chicago between 2011 and 2013. Two clusters of communities recently merged into new canonical parishes—"Resurrection" and "Corpus Christi"[2] —were then available as case studies. They had several striking similarities, as well as very clear contrasts, and so promised to evoke a rich variety of questions and issues. Since both new parishes had received extended enrollments in INSPIRE, they were being actively discussed by the project staff and its parish consultants. My own study made use of information already collected for the project, as well as additional literature, on-site visits and observations, and interviews. The result is intended to be a pastoral theological analysis of two specific merged parishes in the Chicago area that I hope not only draws from but can also contribute to a much broader discussion about local church communities in many different contexts.

It is important to note, however, that my descriptions of the two newly merged parishes are not intended in any way to be complete characterizations, nor predictions of the ultimate success or failure of any given parish model. Rather, I hope that the descriptions will provide a set of evocative "snapshots" that can serve to stimulate discussion of the many factors, values, and potential outcomes involved in the process of merging several once-separate local church communities. Ideally, this discussion, in turn, will point toward certain fundamental issues in the theological understanding of the Church in its most local manifestations. (The methodology of the study is further detailed in an appendix at the end of this chapter.)

TWO STYLES OF PARISH CONSOLIDATION

The two cases examined here present great similarities in context, yet many differences both in procedures and results. Examined against the background of experiences of parish consolidation in other places, the differences suggest varying "styles" in the merger process. It may be useful to take note of some general characteristics of two such styles before considering specific details of the two Chicago cases. Such categorization has its hazards, of course. In the first place, distinguishing among styles of parish mergers should not be mistaken for making *legal* distinctions among them. From a canonical point of view merged parishes are simply parishes, functioning like all others (except for duties such as retaining the records of former parishes whose territories they may have absorbed). Rather, I use "style" to refer to the pastoral and administrative *strategies* used to bring together several previously distinct communities. Examined in detail, these strategies are as numerous as the communities and leaders that apply them, but broad patterns do emerge from the many examples. Paying attention to the patterns can help us understand the pastoral goals and underlying assumptions that may have been operating in particular cases.

What could be called an "administrative style" focuses largely on issues such as efficiency, cost-effectiveness, and the availability of personnel (especially priests). This approach is often adopted in the face of various external pressures (lack of priests, aging infrastructure, financial struggles, dwindling membership, etc.) or even certain theological preferences (for example, emphasizing the understanding of "local church" as identified with a bishop and a diocese, and correspondingly deemphasizing the status of parish *communities*). With this approach, decisions about both the merger and the subsequent organization of the new parish are likely to be made centrally and enacted quickly. Community input is not necessarily excluded; sometimes its importance is very well grasped. Generally, however, opportunities for that input will be quite carefully structured, limited, and controlled.

A "community style," by contrast, focuses on acknowledging and engaging the distinct community identity of each group within the merging parishes. The process begins by developing a deeper understanding of the strengths and weaknesses of these groups and subgroups, and allows local circumstances to shape the ultimate strategy. If new forms of cooperation are determined to be beneficial they will be developed, as far as possible, with the active involvement of the communities themselves, in ways that allow for reaction and adjustment. It is a bit of a paradox that this openness to community input may be less formal and less easily identifiable than the procedures constructed in the administrative style. This is because the community style works best when it unfolds slowly and becomes a general part of the local culture of the communities involved. The same external pressures and preferences that stand behind the choice of an administrative style might well be present here, too. The ecclesiology of the community style, however, responds to those pressures by retaining its high value on the local community, either as an essential resource for the diocesan church, or as a manifestation of church in its own right, or both.

TWO SIMILAR PARISHES

Although "Resurrection" and "Corpus Christi" parishes are located in quite different regions of the archdiocese, there are striking similarities between them. The merger processes in both cases were completed at about the same time, and brought together three formerly separate parishes, each rooted in a different ethnic European community. Each of the two new parishes operates with three worship sites, but with a single set of parish offices located at one of the former rectories. In both cases, the first pastor of the merged parish was a member of a religious order, and lived in another of the available rectory buildings with a small community of priests who provided assistance in the parish. Many of the other parish buildings came to be repurposed as social service centers. Most significantly, the large majority of each parish population is now made up of Spanish-speaking Catholics. Masses are offered in both Spanish and English, with some accommodation to a dwindling Polish-speaking population in both cases. Despite these outward similarities, however, the differences between the two parishes are also quite stark. The merging process at Corpus Christi can be easily identified with the community style, and that at Resurrection with the administrative approach.

Corpus Christi

Corpus Christi, which now includes both urban and suburban neighborhoods, was formed from the territory of what had once been six separate parishes. An earlier round of closures in that area of the archdiocese had reduced five of these parishes to two. The three parishes that then remained—"Assumption," "Holy Apostles," and "St. Mary"—shared a consolidated school. Eventually, all three parishes came to share a single pastor. "Father M" had had already been pastor of Holy Apostles for ten years, and had helped lead that parish through its own difficult merger and onto a spacious new campus. He had also either established or strengthened several highly visible social ministry projects, using buildings made available by the earlier mergers. He had worked closely for several years with another priest, "Father G," who like himself had extensive experience with pastoral work in Latin America and used that experience to connect with the rapidly growing Latino population of the area.

After three years of operating as what was called a "united Catholic community,"[3] all three parishes were officially merged as Corpus Christi, a single parish with three worship sites. Offices were located in the former rectory at Holy Apostles and the priests' residence was established at Assumption, where the school is also located. A new pastor, "Father T," was appointed, a member of a religious congregation who also arrived with a great deal of pastoral experience in Latin America. Although this change of leadership required adjustments and administrative changes that were sometimes difficult, the new pastor did not redirect parish energies so much as build on what had already been accomplished. He was replaced as pastor by an archdiocesan priest three years later.

Resurrection

The merger process at Resurrection was much less protracted. Three parishes originally built within a few blocks of each other by different ethnic European communities in the same urban neighborhood faced pastor transitions at about the same time. "St. Christopher" had recently received a resident pastor after a long period without one. The pastor at "Mary Immaculate," who had also assumed responsibility for "SS. Simon and Jude" when its pastor departed, was nearing the end of his second six-year term. The regional bishop opened the discussion of a possible merger in meetings that over the course of a year came to include five representatives of each parish. During that year, a small community of priests and students from a religious congregation arrived to live and work at SS. Simon and Jude. One of them, "Father D," was asked to serve as pastor for the merged parish, and took over that position the following year. At the end of six years in the neighborhood, Father D and his congregation left the parish and were replaced by two archdiocesan priests.

Despite significant maintenance and fund-raising issues, all three churches at Resurrection remained opened. The rectories at both SS. Simon and Jude and St. Christopher served as residences for priests, and the one at

Mary Immaculate was used as the combined parish office. The convents and school buildings had largely been leased to outside agencies providing educational and social services for the neighborhood. Despite this repurposing of physical plants, and a great many changes in schedules and personnel, the former parishes retained many of the marks of separate church communities. Each developed a somewhat different relationship to the now dominant Latino population of the neighborhood, while SS. Simon and Jude retained important ties to a rapidly diminishing Polish-speaking group. Events and projects that were important to the individual parishes are now advertised and opened to the whole community, but there remains a tendency for people to stay close to their former parishes. A number of formerly regular parishioners now quite pointedly attend Mass outside the neighborhood, while continuing to think of themselves as parishioners of one of the previous parishes.[4]

EVALUATING THE CASES: FOUR SALIENT FACTORS

Although my own preferences among the various approaches taken in these two cases will become clear, evaluating them is not a matter of choosing one to be an exclusive model for the future. Two constants of local ecclesiology dictate against that approach. First, each local community has its characteristic identity within the larger reality of the Church. As many similarities as these two new parishes have, they remain particular communities with unique combinations of strengths and weaknesses, opportunities and challenges. Responses proven pastorally useful in one location would not necessarily transfer successfully to the other. Second, their characteristic identities each have a "narrative" quality. Because the story of each parish is always unfolding, there is every reason to believe that the realization of "success" in both stories will continue to ebb and flow. What appear at this point as particularly dynamic features of one community may stall for lack of leadership or resources, or may develop in less favorable ways in the future. Likewise, positive aspects of parish life once obscured by perceived flaws may emerge as circumstances change and communities mature. The point of the analysis, therefore, cannot be to identify any one "key" factor or any single approach as the best. Yet the stories of these two mergers can help us reflect profitably on the nature of crucial elements in the life of parish communities, on the ways they might be affected by different pastoral approaches, and on how we understand parish communities in general.

There are many ways, of course, to discuss the differences between the two parishes, but my observations suggest that four factors are particularly important for distinguishing the different strategies used at Resurrection and Corpus Christi. They are process, pastoral leadership, community identity, and social ministry. Together, these four areas go a long way toward explaining the very different perceptions of the consolidation experience in the two parishes.

Process

The most striking differences between the procedures used in the two cases are the timelines they followed and their ways of engaging the laity. In these areas, the two approaches continue to demonstrate the community style on the one hand, and the administrative style on the other.

The changes in the parishes that would become Corpus Christi began to unfold slowly as much as twenty years before the official merger. As early as the mid-1980s, five of the six original parishes were sharing sponsorship of a regional Catholic elementary school. By 1991, three of those five parishes merged as St. Mary, and the other two, while retaining the joint name "SS. John and Matthias" and continuing to use both church buildings, also became a single canonical parish. In 1996, Father M took over as pastor at SS. John and Matthias, and soon led them in the process of choosing a new name, Holy Apostles. Not until 2002 was the unification of this parish completed, with the move to new and larger worship space. In the meantime, cooperation across the remaining parish lines continued to grow, including the relocation of the consolidated school to Assumption Parish. By 2006, the simultaneous vacancy of two of the three pastorates allowed another move toward full consolidation: Father M assumed leadership of all three parishes. Only with his departure in 2009 did the fully merged Corpus Christi Parish finally come into existence, eighteen years after the mergers that created St. Mary and Holy Apostles.

This slow, organic growth toward a new community organization usually afforded little formal engagement of the parishioners in planning, deliberations, and decision making. Father M reports that the parish councils of St. John and St. Matthias had met together about the merger of their two parishes only once in 1991—for the coin toss by which the unremarkable name "SS. John and Matthias" was chosen. But formal consultation is only one approach to lay engagement. As pastor at Holy Apostles, Father M was deeply "inspired" by a predecessor's "love for the people," and his own efforts to connect with them brought him, over time, an extraordinary degree of recognition and support, in both the parish and the wider community. To strengthen those relationships, he made use of existing councils and committees, parish social gatherings of all sorts, and numerous social ministry projects. He was also very supportive of the new "small Christian communities" (*communidades de base*) developed by Father G's "area ministry" across several parishes. This outreach helped many Spanish-speaking immigrants find a genuine and ongoing relationship with the church in their new home.

Father M became pastor of all three still-separate parishes via an administrative procedure that he describes as "continuing to do what I was doing all along." Mostly, that meant continuing to engage people in his attentive pastoral way. Even while moving toward ever-greater integration of the parishes' activities and services, he was careful to make use, as much as possible, of all three campuses, including many of the buildings of the older closed parishes. Fr. M's successor in 2009, Father T, paid considerably more attention to structures and procedures. Yet he continued Father M's priority of keeping all the parishioners engaged and connected in an optimistic atmosphere, and this approach continued to bear fruit.

In contrast to all of this, the administrative style employed in the second cluster, which became Resurrection Parish, simply did not leave time to cultivate the kinds of strong parish relationships from which Corpus Christi benefited. When the merger took place in 2008, with only a bit more than a year of public preparation, St. Christopher, SS. Simon and Jude, and Mary Immaculate had no previous history of cooperation, and all three were in the midst of important pastor transitions. St. Christopher did have about two years to get acquainted with, and respond very positively to, their first pastor in eight years (coincidentally, the same Father G who had worked with the Latino community at Corpus Christi). SS. Simon and Jude, on the other hand, after sharing Mary Immaculate's pastor for a time, had only a few months to negotiate the transition from a single diocesan priest to a community of religious before their new pastor took the reins of the whole merged parish. Mary Immaculate had to say farewell to its long-time pastor just when a familiar face might have been most helpful.

Procedurally, on the other hand, Resurrection had a somewhat clearer experience than Corpus Christi. The initiative for the merger came from the episcopal vicar, the regional auxiliary bishop who saw the potential for a unified pastoral approach to the growing Latino population. The process that he began in 2006 had several phases. Initially, the bishop met with the priests and deacons to consider the possibility of consolidation. The second phase, in early 2007, saw the inclusion of staff members and other active parishioners in the discussion. Later that year, when it was generally known that a merger was being planned, each of the three communities sent a delegation of five persons to discuss the practical implementation. Meanwhile, the archdiocese reached a staffing agreement with Father D's religious congregation, who arrived at SS. Simon and Jude that summer of 2007. After attending only the last few planning meetings, Father D was asked to take on the pastorate of the merged parish, which he did in July 2008. During the subsequent five years, Father D worked with staff members and representative councils to find practical ways of making the merged parish function as a unified community.

It is significant that those with whom I have discussed this process all locate responsibility for it outside of their own place in the structure. The cardinal, the regional bishop, the departing pastor of Mary Immaculate, and Father D's provincial have all been mentioned as "part authors" of the plan. Staff persons and parishioners actually present at Resurrection during my research, however, seemed reluctant to own the process, regardless of how they had come to view the eventual outcome.

It is also important that the initial discussions took place exclusively among the clergy. In addition to reflecting a particular underlying ecclesiology, this limited initial consultation may also have been viewed as a practical necessity, in order to lessen the likelihood of immediate conflict among parishioners and produce a plan that could then be more widely discussed. In fact, the experience of other mergers suggests that forums created with the announced—or poorly concealed—purpose of leading toward structural change in parishes tend to bring people together in a highly defensive mood. This was certainly borne out at Resurrection in the later stages of the process, even with open discussion limited to a committee of five from each parish.

Resurrection's more formal administrative process facilitated both the decision to merge the three parishes and the canonical implementation of that decision. However, it left virtually all of the deeper work of pastoral integration undone, and even largely undiscussed. Father D thus faced the task of trying to secure the trust and cooperation of three communities who were not used to working together, each of whom were experiencing loss. Simultaneously, he still had to work out many unavoidably contentious practical issues, such as the rescheduling of Masses and the restructuring of the parish staff. Though there had clearly been some progress toward a parish-wide identity in the years following the consolidation, there remained a prevailing sense of fragmentation at Resurrection. It was difficult to get a clear and consistent overview of the current life of the parish from key informants. Parish bulletins and web pages seemed self-consciously preoccupied with the theme of parish unity in a way that would be unnecessary if it were already a part of the culture of the communities. In sum, the formal process was not designed to keep the people deeply engaged in an ongoing process of community building, and subsequent results continued to confirm this.

At Corpus Christi, the community style of consolidation allowed parishioners and parish leaders alike the time to accustom themselves to the very idea of a merged parish, and they could wrestle with its concrete implications a little bit at a time. This helped form an atmosphere of optimism and confidence in the parish—the sense that the change experienced in the community is a kind of continuous progress. At Resurrection, meanwhile, after the merger became fact, parishioners and their leaders confronted the full range of problems all at once, and have often since expressed the feeling that the change they face is a sort of onslaught that needs to be battled. A defensive attitude prevailed.

Pastoral Leadership

Differences in process may be as much a matter of shifting circumstances as they are of deliberate strategy. Nevertheless, these same circumstances bring to light another crucial factor: approaches to and systems of leadership. These reveal consequential differences between styles of consolidation that the two cases make quite clear.

Far from operating as facilitators seeking only to build consensus, the archdiocesan and local clerical leaders were very active in the development of Corpus Christi Parish. To some parishioners at various points in the long evolution of that merger, leadership undoubtedly seemed "arbitrary" and "dictatorial" (common accusations in the emotionally laden process of parish consolidation under almost any circumstances). Yet, throughout the long process, there were also many deliberate and effective efforts at community development. The extensive and continually expanded social ministries in the parish, along with the formation of basic Christian communities, contributed considerably to these efforts. These initiatives were inspired and sustained largely by the extensive Latin American pastoral experience of Father M, Father G, and Father T. Community development, however, could only be truly successful in an atmosphere of general collaboration among the several parishes and their pastors, staffs, parishioners, volunteers, and donors. When the final consolidation of Corpus Christi took place, therefore, the merged parish inherited assets nurtured in the whole parochial cluster over the previous twenty years. Broadly respected and participated in, this heritage was neither abandoned as part of the past, nor left to be fiercely defended by an embattled faction of parishioners.

The story of leadership at Resurrection, on the other hand, often seems to collapse into the story of one person, Father D. A likely reason for this is that the administrative decision to merge the parishes came from the outside, before the building of any of the collaborative structures and habits that would be needed to make the merger successful. Parishioners were largely absent from real participation at this stage. Meanwhile, Father D faced pressure to take on the pastorate, despite his lack of both parish experience and facility in Spanish. He had already been assigned another full-time job by his religious congregation: to oversee formation of the Order's theology students and to serve as spokesman and promoter of vocations. This assignment was not rescinded. It is no surprise that he reported a constant sense of being overwhelmed by urgent demands, and was rarely able to take advantage of the resources and assistance that were in fact available for building a collaborative team ministry. As a result, a sense of fragmentation persisted at Resurrection, in the staff and in the parish as a whole. Only as the time approached for him to step down after five years did some staff members comment that their relationship with Father D had "begun to gel."

These enormous differences in approach to leadership, which play out on both the individual and the systemic levels, can also be seen in the handling of certain key issues that are unavoidably contentious when parishes are merged. Changes in liturgical schedules, for example, are almost always problematic. For many parishioners, Mass times, locations, and styles are not just matters of convenience and taste but also highly charged symbols of connection to the physical space and of relationships between faith and work, family and community, and other essential elements of life. Clergy tend to speak of such issues as if they arise solely from parishioners' unreasonable attachment to their preferences and routines. Yet, often enough, it is the preferences and routines of the *clergy* that parishioners see as being given the most weight.

At Resurrection, the Mass schedule remained in flux for some time after the merger, in part because of the temporary availability of additional priests (a former pastor, resident students, etc.) to preside at certain Masses. Some early changes, such as the replacement of a Spanish Mass at Mary Immaculate with an evening "youth Mass" in English, seemed based on the pastor's vague hopes for the future rather than on careful public consideration of the community's needs. The result was a Mass schedule that changed unevenly—more at one church than at the other two, retaining accommodations to a much-diminished Polish-speaking minority, continuing to underrepresent the Spanish-speaking majority, and so forth. It was not surprising that some interviewees spoke suspiciously about the unfair influence of certain favored parishioners and staff members. Such whisperings further demonstrate the inability of Resurrection's administrative style to generate an effective level of communication among various subgroups in the parish.

Even at what became Corpus Christi Parish, with its community-style merger, there were, to be sure, dwindling ethnic groups who were not at all happy with the slow erosion of their influence as the communities gradually consolidated. In that parish, however, a sense of forward movement toward a new community identity took hold during the much longer unfolding of the consolidation process. That optimism seems to have encouraged a charitable willingness on the parts of many of the subcommunities, parishioners and clergy alike, to adjust to one another's needs. The result was a three-site parish with a worship schedule that preserved a particular, though evolving, character for each church site, appropriately balanced between Spanish and English liturgies, with a calendar that nevertheless continued to accommodate the small Polish community with a monthly liturgy.

Staff reorganization is another typical point of contention in parish mergers. As the arriving pastor at the newly created Corpus Christi parish, Father

T set as his top priority a more efficient operation of the increasingly complex administration. This new focus precipitated a crisis when Father T asked
for the resignation of a staff member who had been Father M's "right hand."
This move caused a great deal of insecurity in the remaining staff. As an
INSPIRE consultant described it, "They were concerned for their jobs." Yet,
with help from the consultant and the overall INSPIRE process, Father T and
his reshaped staff were able to settle into a more productive relationship. As
he became more convinced that an atmosphere of cooperative trust was
worth the time and discomfort involved in building habits of communication,
Father T became more available to the process.

At Resurrection, ironically, the quick and "efficient" creation of the
merged parish led to some serious administrative problems. Father D seemed
intent on avoiding confrontation, and had difficulty sorting through the conflicting reactions of staff members to one another. Consequently, for a long
time the staff remained a patchwork from the previous parishes, and various
factions tended to "protect their own." Substantive changes in staff positions
went unrealized until tensions reached serious breaking points, and then the
changes brought even more conflict. In one instance, when some staff members objected to another staffer's lack of training for the job she held, her title
was changed (to another area in which she had little experience), but she
continued to do more or less the same work she had been doing. In another
instance, one staff member reportedly wrote and delivered a long and scath-
ing letter of dismissal to another staffer when the pastor "could not find the
time to do it." No sustained attempt was made to address the dire need for
improved communication and collaboration on the staff. Unfortunately, at
Resurrection, INSPIRE was viewed as a "luxury" for which the urgent
circumstances allowed no time, even though the new parish was officially
part of the leadership project.

Community Identity

If encouraging collaboration is an important measure of leadership in a
merged parish, we are also pointed toward the role of the community itself.
How do the parishioners' own local culture, assets, and patterns of association, their expectations and concerns, contribute to the process? To do justice
to such a question would, of course, require a thorough sociological analysis
far beyond the scope or intentions of this chapter. We can, however, find a
starting point for further thought and discussion in the two cases at hand. We
might begin by recognizing the limits of our ordinary ideas about "parish
community."

The original parishes in the neighborhoods now served by Corpus Christi
and Resurrection were of the ethnic European type that flourished in the
United States especially in the century between 1850 and 1950. However, for

over fifty years a different parish model has been asserting itself in much of US Catholicism, shaped in a world of suburbs and of less coherent urban neighborhoods. The suburban model has encouraged a general habit of thinking in terms of "worship communities" that form around a parish and rely heavily on parish leadership and programming for their unity and purpose.[5] This approach can cause us to lose track of an important dimension of the earlier model: it was not parish ministry that created the old ethnic communities. Rather, the parishes were created *for* (and in many ways *by*) those immigrant communities for their spiritual wellbeing. In many instances, ethnic communities that were gradually assimilated into the new suburban reality left behind small remnants in the old neighborhoods that often found one of their last cultural refuges in the parish churches. It is often challenging for remnant communities to welcome new neighbors into their urban parish, especially when their presence heralds the arrival of a new dominant ethnic group in the neighborhood. Even more difficult, however, may be the balance a parish institution must achieve between its own responsibility for building a worship community and its humble recognition of the communities that already exist all around and within the parish.

Pastoral leaders at Corpus Christi recognized the shifting demographics of their neighborhoods as a direct concern of the parish, and responded accordingly. At SS. John and Matthias, before the full parish merger took place, Father M knew that he had to meet the various subcommunities of the parish where they actually were—socially, economically, and in their attitudes toward church in general and the local church community in particular. As already noted, the parish enthusiastically took up the advocacy and assistance work so greatly needed among the new immigrants. It was tremendously important, as well, that all the parishes of what became Corpus Christi joined together in hosting Father G's base communities among Latino parishioners. This effort contributed not only to the strengthening of participants' ties to the church in the area, but to the vitality of the Latino community in general and to that community's shared identity across all the neighborhoods and territories of the original parishes.

Father M's consistent aim, nonetheless, was to encourage cooperation among *all* the ethnic groups. He worked diligently to bring together in his combined parish the different English-speaking communities and the growing Spanish-speaking community at St. John. At St. Matthias, a diminishing Lithuanian community had continued attending a Mass in their mother tongue for a long time after the merger with St. John. Father M tried, not entirely successfully, to prepare them for what he saw as the inevitable end of that tradition, as parishioners aged and Lithuanian-speaking priests became less and less available. He reminded them of their own immigrant roots, and tried to help them see the similarities between that history and the situation of the arriving Latino population. On the other hand, he also spoke to the active

Spanish speakers about managing their own, and their children's, assimilation into American culture. He emphasized the need to be careful not to
equate the practice of faith entirely with the speaking of Spanish, in order to
avoid the fate of some earlier ethnic communities who managed to make an
almost self-fulfilling prophecy of the adage, "Those who lose their language
lose their faith."

The search for a workable equilibrium among the ethnic groups was
given ritual expression when it was recognized that the double parish had
grown beyond the two small and aging churches (St. Matthias and St. John)
that the Holy Apostles community had been using. A newer and larger facility was purchased from an evangelical church in a nearby but more suburban
neighborhood. The move to the new space was accompanied by community
discussions, and then commemorated through a ritual of leave-taking from
the two older buildings. The subcommunities who identified with each of
those churches formed separate processions toward the new one, and were
met there by a third group of more recently arrived parishioners—mostly
Latinos—who preferred to identify only with the new unified community.
The new location included a rectory, office space, and parish center, but the
older campuses were, for the most part, retained for use by the parish's social
ministry projects.

By the time of the final merger at Corpus Christi, the painful transitions
away from earlier ethnic customs and languages toward new ones had largely
been completed. Most of the several Eastern European communities of the
original parishes had faded, including even the Lithuanians. The Poles at St.
Mary were the lone survivors of that earlier era, still able to celebrate a Mass
in their own language once a month in the church their families built. Meanwhile, many years after Father G's multiparish work with *communidades de
base*, the dynamic Spanish-speaking majority had shaped a self-sustaining
community that in important ways preceded the parish that had become its
spiritual home. The Latino community in the neighborhoods served by Corpus Christi had a definite character and recognizable identity, of which many
of its own members, as well as outside observers, were well aware. This
identity was based on many elements, of course, but among them would be
shared ethnic culture (the Spanish speakers being largely of Mexican descent, as at Resurrection), the experience of recent immigration, ongoing
economic challenges, and certainly a foundation of cultural Catholicism.
Although such a community did not need to be invented and held in existence by the parish as an institution, it had formed a vital link to the ministry
that nourished its spiritual coherence and advanced its material wellbeing.

Resurrection Parish was hampered by the circumstances of its merger
from taking the same kind of approach to community development as had
been taken at Corpus Christi. At the time of their consolidation, the three
parishes at Resurrection each seem to have been in a certain state of flux with

regard to their community identities, hesitating between former ethnic ties and the realities of a changing neighborhood. St. Christopher, founded by German immigrants whose descendants had long since assimilated into the English-speaking mainstream, was in the early stages of another sort of "merger," with the goal of bringing English and Spanish-speaking communities into a shared parish identity. Father G had arrived after the long period without a resident priest, and began immediately to make use of the base community strategy that he had used so effectively at Corpus Christi.

Mary Immaculate Parish, originally predominantly Irish, was perhaps a few steps back in a similar process, having a separate Spanish Mass and a youth ministry that reached out to Latino teens, but not yet the Anglo-Latino cooperation that Father G was introducing at St. Christopher. SS. Simon and Jude was facing a more complex situation; traditionally Polish, it had a considerable but clearly diminishing number of members (themselves now primarily English-speaking) who actively defended old parish traditions. Several years after the merger, the main Sunday morning Mass there still featured Polish for one reading, at least one hymn, and various prayers, including the Lord's Prayer. Nonetheless, a "Spanish Mass community" had formed at SS. Simon and Jude before the merger as well.

So it was that, in all three of the original parishes that would become Resurrection, the European communities were just beginning, in quite different ways, to accept that they were no longer the majority group, nor even the most active. The mostly Mexican Latino majority had not yet begun to recognize itself as a single community across the territory of all three parishes. There were thus not merely three but as many as seven separate subcommunities, including the Polish group, identifying themselves by language and original parish. None of them yet had a realistic appreciation of their own situations and interrelationships, let alone a vision of a united, cooperative parish community. The only notes of collaboration among them prior to the announcement of the merger had come in Father G's fruitful but incomplete efforts at St. Christopher, in the brief experience of shared pastorate between Mary Immaculate and SS. Simon and Jude, and in the substantial (if not total) overlap of the English and Polish-speaking groups there.

When the merger took place, a palpably defensive mood prevailed throughout the new parish, and Father D, the beleaguered first pastor, did what he could to "keep the peace." He did not, by any means, ignore the issue of community development, however. He invited the continuation of Project INSPIRE (which had begun at St. Christopher before the merger). He allowed the spread of Father G's base communities to other parts of the new parish. He was enthusiastic about a Chicago-based program in leadership for Latino Catholics, and about Resurrection being chosen for the first round of the archdiocese's "Parish Transformation" project. All of these efforts offered, with greater or lesser effectiveness, tools for community development and provided a series of very positive gatherings and workshops remembered with approval by key informants. Therein, however, lies both the value and the difficulty: leadership and community building were reported by Resurrection parishioners as a series of distinct events sponsored by the parish or the Archdiocese, rather than as a continuous movement toward a strategy for understanding, supporting, and working within the neighborhood and its constituent communities.

Taken together, these contrasting cases suggest that Resurrection and Corpus Christi diverged significantly in their ability to engage the social realities of their constituent communities rather than focus more exclusively on internal issues of the parish institution. Engagement of the type that Corpus Christi developed offered the church an important place in the thick web of institutions, patterns, relationships, and services that strengthen the community at large and in that way build a stronger foundation for the parish itself. An internal focus, on the other hand, even one intended to calm fears and bring about cooperation as at Resurrection, can have the effect of keeping the community focused on old perceptions and issues of little relevance to parishioners' ordinary lives. With all its attention focused inward, the parish is distracted from the real needs of its people. Real shared community becomes an ever-more elusive goal.

Social Ministry

The "real needs" of parishioners, of course, are many and varied, and also very much a matter of perspective. Nonetheless, recognizing that parish communities are shaped by their social context, and that this context can greatly affect the way parishioners understand the Church and its role in their lives, also points us toward the works of charity and justice as a fourth key factor for evaluating the Corpus Christi and Resurrection mergers. The US Bishops' 1993 statement on the social mission of the parish, "Communities of Salt and Light" (CSL), stated, "In responding to the Scriptures and the principles of Catholic social teaching, parishes are not called to an extra or added dimension of our faith, but to a central demand of Catholic life and evangelization."[6] Charles Curran's more recent discussion of the topic goes further to describe the parish as "the central place to carry out the social mission of the church."[7] Such statements suggest that attention to social ministry in merged parishes is not only a strategy for strengthening a parish's presence to the community at large, but also an important marker of the vitality of the parish itself as a Christian community. CSL cautioned that "social ministry not genuinely rooted in prayer can easily burn itself out. On the other hand, worship that does not reflect the Lord's call to conversion, service, and justice can become pious ritual and empty of the gospel."[8] The bishops write of "a strategy of integration and collaboration,"[9] encouraging all members of the parish to think in terms of the centrality of the social mission to the life of the parish as a community of faith. When such an approach is present, leaders in a merged parish get a positive indication of the gains already achieved, as well as support for the ongoing development of a shared identity in the new parish.

This outcome could be seen at Corpus Christi. Its network of community services was inherited largely, but not entirely, from the work done by numerous donors and enthusiastic volunteers encouraged by Father M at Holy Apostles in the ten years before he assumed the shared pastorate. Each aspect of the work had its own particular beginnings, advocates, sponsors, and target clientele, but every project responded to an evident need in the poor and largely immigrant population of the parish. Among the projects were traditional charitable offerings of direct assistance, including a soup kitchen, a food pantry, and a clothes closet. Substantial funding, management skills, goods, and labor were provided by dedicated parishioners, members of other "sharing parishes" linked to Holy Apostles through a regular archdiocesan program, and concerned individuals from nearby affluent communities. When Holy Apostles moved to its new suburban location, most of the buildings of the former St. Matthias parish were converted for use by the community services. The former St. John parish campus was turned over to a new high school, independent of the parish but serving the immigrant population under broad Catholic sponsorship. Former members of these communities could see that many of their well-loved parish buildings were still playing important roles in a dynamically expanding ministry.

In the meantime, Father M grew more and more involved in advocacy for the immigrant community across an increasing array of problems and issues, and so attended to enhancing the long-term prospects of immigrant families. An Immigration Center emerged to provide services such as legal aid, assistance with residency applications, and classes in English as a second language. The growing number of services and clients attracted attention from other agencies and even local government, seeking various cooperative arrangements with the parish. Through such collaborations, an overnight shelter in a former parish school was established by a regional agency that runs a number of such facilities.

Development of the programs continued after the final merger, under Father T. The jointly-run Catholic grade school, already relocated to Assumption, became a major focus of the new pastor's attention. Additional grants were obtained and new administrators hired to bolster other programs. The continuing interconnection of community, parish, and social ministry was demonstrated by the inauguration of new longer term emergency shelter projects. Discussion began about the possibility of moving the new high school from the former St. John site to open land adjacent to the relocated Holy Apostles church. Despite fears raised by the overhaul of staff and administrative policies (including the departure of Father M's business manager and the careful separation of parish finances from community service accounts), Father T remained fully engaged in Corpus Christi's commitments to the community. The social mission still commanded a huge share of staff time, financial resources, parish web pages, and Sunday bulletins, and was seen by many as one of the primary reasons for the parish's very existence. This understanding aided a very tight connection between the liturgical and diaconal (service-oriented) aspects of church life that could be seen both in the style of the liturgies and in the content of the preaching at all three of Corpus Christi's worship sites.

As I made my observations, Resurrection Parish had not yet articulated anything comparable to the shared mission of service that had become so central to Corpus Christi. The prior lack of any formal collaboration among the merged parishes, and the circumstances of the merger itself, made difficult any sense of parish identity or mission beyond the immediate demands of physical plant, finances, and administration. Suddenly faced with three aging campuses, Father D tended to see the several unused buildings less with an eye toward ministry and more as potential sources of rental income, or maintenance headaches, or both. At least one, the SS. Simon and Jude convent, was allowed to stand empty. The St. Christopher convent housed a community of post-college volunteers, nearly all of whom worked in projects elsewhere in the city. The schools at St. Christopher and SS. Simon and Jude were leased to external educational programs with no Catholic affiliation. The "new" school at Mary Immaculate (a 1970s-era structure), used in part by the parish religious education classes, also housed an externally sponsored literacy program.

Two parish-sponsored social ministries, both located at Mary Immaculate, did get regular positive mention by key informants in the parish. A neighborhood youth ministry was housed in a portion of the original school, which once occupied the upper floors of the church building (a typical early-twentieth-century arrangement in Chicago). The youth center was an outreach directed for many years by a Mary Immaculate parishioner who became something of a local legend for his knowledge of the neighborhood and care for the young people. The only one of the young adult volunteers from the community at St. Christopher's who actually did work at Resurrection became an assistant to this director. The center offered an ongoing schedule of activities, which drew a modest group of "regulars," as well as special events that attracted a larger group of neighborhood youth, and programs such as retreats and field trips away from the neighborhood. The other often-mentioned ministry was a modest food pantry, run from the parish offices in the former Mary Immaculate rectory. The office staff was responsible for responding to incoming food requests; a group of volunteers replenished the stock and gained access for the parish to a local food bank by participating in the volunteer rotation there as well. In these ways, steps were taken toward connecting the parish with some of the day-to-day needs and ordinary problems of the community at large.

Still, there was no project at Resurrection that was able to bridge the communities at all three worship sites in the way that outreach to Latino parishioners and other recent immigrants did at Corpus Christi. Each group tended to defend its former sense of identity and its traditional activities. These attitudes contributed to a strong impression of Resurrection as a number of separate "islands" of ministry, with participants trying to salvage those bits of activity with which they had been most familiar before the merger. Such preoccupations interfered with the ability to keep pace with changes in the neighborhood (even including the predominant presence of the Latino community), or to cope with consequences of the merger. For example, the dangers to young people of crossing gang-related boundaries that the merged parish now straddles seemed to be downplayed in the youth ministry centered at Mary Immaculate. Such fragmentation and inattention may have contributed to the greater sense of distance and relative lack of enthusiasm I experienced as a visitor to some of the ordinary liturgical celebrations at Resurrection. In many ways, the parish gave the impression of having yet to understand its concrete situation and its need for a shared sense of purpose.

COLLABORATIVE MINISTRY AND THE MERGED PARISH

The fact that both of these merged clusters of parishes had connections, before and after their consolidation, with the leadership team-building work of Project INSPIRE offers an opportunity to ask what these cases suggest about the strengths and weaknesses of collaborative parish ministry. INSPIRE's original mandate was to work with "excellent" parish staffs and help them develop team cultures that would carry their strengths into the future. But parish merger situations clearly provide a "limit case" for this type of collaborative work. The established team chemistry is significantly altered as the purpose, mission, and function of the staff undergo serious transformation, all in the midst and on behalf of a parish community that is also experiencing massive change in its composition and identity. Prior to the merger, staffs at the separate parishes may or may not have achieved the sort of collaborative interaction that would allow them to call themselves "pastoral teams." Regardless of past accomplishments, though, the tough circumstances of parish consolidation will make the persistent and demanding nature of collaborative team building all the more obvious.

The staffs at Holy Apostles (who would later join Assumption and St. Mary to form Corpus Christi) and at St. Christopher (who became part of Resurrection) were both members of INSPIRE cohorts that were assigned a consultant, developed team and individual learning plans, and received a share of INSPIRE's Lilly Endowment grant to realize those plans. Holy Apostles actually completed its INSPIRE process, with Corpus Christi being enrolled again after the completion of the merger. St. Christopher folded its team-building efforts, still in process when its merger was announced, into the activities of the new Resurrection Parish. Consultants, pastors, and staff members were in agreement about the success and value of the initial contact with Project INSPIRE in both cases. Holy Apostles was able to establish a team rapport and an expectation of collaboration within its growing staff of parish and community service administrators, while St. Christopher made strides toward the integration of its Anglo and Hispanic communities. Such results were quite typical of what INSPIRE was able to accomplish in many of the scores of parishes whose pastoral staffs participated in the project in the course of some ten years.

The more distinctive feature in the case of the merged parishes, however, lies in the stories of what happened after the original INSPIRE parish became part of a larger parish community. It is not surprising that the results reflect the relative strengths and weaknesses of Corpus Christi and Resurrection parishes, and of Project INSPIRE itself. The project did not offer a packaged "program" but was very successful, instead, in assisting the development of specific, contextualized leadership communities. If that process were disrupted by some major transition, particularly if the staff membership changed substantially and suddenly, there would be great danger of losing many of the gains that were tied to previous relationships and expectations. In both the cases I have presented, the strength of the staff culture in the one parish that had already participated in INSPIRE was a source of tension for some of their new colleagues.

At Corpus Christi, Father T's initially cool reaction to the INSPIRE process gave the consultant the impression that the new pastor was struggling to see its relevance in the face of what he considered to be significant administrative problems. Staff members, on the other hand, especially those who had worked with INSPIRE at Holy Apostles before the merger, confided in the consultant about their discomfort with the new pastor. Father T, in turn, wondered whether the consultant was not "stirring up trouble" where there had been none. In the end, however, the consulting process ended up playing an important role in helping both pastor and staff move beyond the initial distrust. The successful conclusion of the earlier learning plans at Holy Apostles, the strong parish identity and culture that the three parishes at Corpus Christi had already established during the shared pastorate of Father M, and Father T's own pastoral experience undoubtedly all contributed to this outcome. INSPIRE had helped to build the staff's expectation of collaborative forms of pastoral leadership in the first place. Eventually, carefully facilitated group process fostered a significant decrease in tension, and the staff's initial perception of not being heard by their new pastor gradually diminished. By the end of his short, three-year tenure, Father T was able to speak enthusiastically and in detail about INSPIRE's contribution to the staff culture at Corpus Christi and to his own ability to work within it.

Unfortunately, the collaborative work of Project INSPIRE was far less successful in addressing the transition issues at Resurrection. Some of the conflicts reported from the early meetings about the merger process suggest that the self-confidence of some of the St. Christopher team members (who had been learning group process through INSPIRE) may have led others on the planning committee to regard them as overbearing. Furthermore, the gains made at St. Christopher in integrating English and Spanish-speaking parishioners seem to have worried some representatives of the other churches, who became defensive about their own communities. Ultimately, the administrative nature of the merger shifted the process away from the kind of community-building concerns that had been the focus of Father G's two-year pastorate at St. Christopher. Attention moved instead to obtaining basic (though reluctant) agreement to the merger, working out initial practical arrangements, and receiving a pastor. Father D took on that role even before this minimal group process was really completed.

As a result, the new parish staff found itself turned toward urgent practical needs with no cooperative structure for addressing them. Father D was caught up in responding to a continuous series of crises and in trying to "keep the peace" among factions in the new parish, leaving him with few resources of vision and energy for cooperating with the INSPIRE process. In any event, perhaps because that process was seen by some as "belonging" to St. Christopher, interest and participation were slow to come from other sectors. A habit developed, also seen in relation to the several other programs in which Resurrection participated, of drawing a temporary "energy boost" for the parish from some special event or gathering, only to let the momentum ebb quickly away.

Project INSPIRE clearly relied heavily on the goodwill, talents, and enthusiasm of its participants. Its successes were built on general initial acceptance of its basic vision of collaborative pastoral team leadership, and of its foundation in attentive personal interaction and relationship. When that basic acceptance was in place, methods shared by the consultants proved to be capable tools for getting through very difficult transitions. The determination to collaborate, however, is not itself a resource that can be injected from outside the parish staff itself, even when consultants can strongly encourage it. If the groundwork has not been laid, or is actually disrupted by structural and attitudinal barriers, a collaborative process like INSPIRE will have no place to take root in the local culture. It is not too surprising to find that it made a stronger contribution in the merger situation that was more clearly based on a community-building model than on an administrative model.

PASTORAL AND THEOLOGICAL CONCLUSIONS

In telling something of the stories of Corpus Christi and Resurrection parishes, I have not attempted to hide my preference for the community style of parish consolidation. This approach seems to me rooted in the attention to human realities and interpersonal relationships that characterize Jesus's own presence to both his disciples and the crowds. No process can ever be entirely faithful to that heritage, of course, and motives will always be complex and mixed, but the primary driver of a merger like the one experienced at Corpus Christi appears again and again to be the strength and welfare of persons and communities.

What I have called the administrative style is not, however, simply the opposite of the community style. There are many instances to be cited in which a quick and efficient joining of two formerly distinct parish organizations under one administration is the only reasonable response to a true emergency. In many cases, probably most, such a process could also legitimately claim to be motivated primarily by "the strength and welfare of persons and communities." Regardless of the chosen style, the Resurrection merger was no doubt sincerely undertaken for those ends. The difficulty arises in that the administrative style, with its emphasis on organizational structures and leadership, makes its underlying pastoral motivations far less transparent, regardless of the rhetoric or formal procedures that may be used. Parishioners will likely experience an acute sense of distance and powerlessness, which will deeply affect their attitudes and actions within the new parish.

One important qualitative difference between the two cases here lies in the existence of a kind of viable community across parish boundaries even before the merger at Corpus Christi, whereas no such community yet existed at Resurrection. This community was not simply a matter of shared space, or even of ethnic and economic similarity, but also of self-understanding and mutual cooperation. If the merger of parishes becomes, on the other hand, an engineered attempt to create a "community" where none has been fostered before, it is likely to succeed only by driving away those groups and individuals who cannot imagine themselves as members of the one consolidated community. Some amount of this alienation seems inevitable, as indeed it proved to be even at Corpus Christi. The questions are, Is the possibility of disaffiliation taken seriously within the process, what efforts are made to avoid it, and what sort of pastoral care is provided to those who nonetheless fall victim to it? Certainly as well, there is another important question that must not be ignored: whom might we be *willing* to see leave our faith communities (and what are we ready to learn about ourselves from the answer)?

The Corpus Christi experience also suggests the importance of a genuine symbiosis between the leadership and the communities in merged parishes, by which they draw life and strength from each other. While this may seem to be nothing more than a truism, it was not applied to the merger that took place at Resurrection. There, circumstances that were allowed to dictate the entire shape of the merger process were almost completely defined by the disposition of clerical personnel, not by the communities and staff persons involved. If not for undue haste, it might have been possible at Resurrection, just as it was at Corpus Christi, to prepare the communities and potential leaders by establishing some common ground ahead of time.

To put it very starkly, a combination of too little regard for the communities and staffs and too great regard for the clerical leadership cannot result in a happy situation for the leaders, nor for the staffs, nor for the communities. A successful merger cannot result from a process that unfolds as if the very existence of the communities and staffs were already something of an inconvenience, or as if any ordained person could effectively lead any combination of communities by virtue of his ordination alone.

When, on the other hand, the whole leadership recognizes the special character of each subcommunity, and the ways they are interrelated, and makes efforts to acknowledge, reverence, and nurture those subcommunities, all sorts of creative solutions become possible. There can be attention to the fears of loss stirred up by announced consolidation plans (whether with "good reason" or not). Taking seriously such values as neighborhood intimacy and security, ethnic and family tradition, identity, and stability can strengthen an atmosphere of cooperation and a desire for unity. Alternatives that overlook such values—nostalgic parochialism that looks only to preserve older communities unchanged, or inflexible clericalism that only wants an efficient distribution of priests, or aloof bureaucracy that sees only its own task list—are not based on a workable understanding of the parish as an essential dimension of the whole Church.

Pope Francis, quoting his predecessor St. John Paul II, has written, "[I]f the parish proves capable of self-renewal and constant adaptivity, it continues to be 'the Church living in the midst of the homes of her sons and daughters.'"[10] The need for a renewed ecclesiology of the parish might be addressed if the Church could learn to look upon the now common experience of parish consolidation as an invitation to a culture of *dynamic community*. A parish community that could not only survive consolidation but actually thrive in its wake would be the local manifestation of the "pilgrim church,"[11] the church of "continual reformation,"[12] described by the Second Vatican Council. It would be characterized by attentiveness, openness, mutual appreciation, and ongoing development.

The "treasures" it would store and share with newcomers and with new generations would be more than a prescribed way of seeing the world with fixed rules for responding to its challenges and needs. Rather, the tradition of the dynamic local community would be a set of tools for an ongoing encounter in faith with the constantly changing world, and for maintaining the community's coherence in the midst of that continuous change. Such a community would draw particular strength from the ancient spiritual images of *charism*[13] and *pilgrimage*[14] which speak to the "flexibility" praised by Pope Francis. Because they complete and temper equally traditional images such as "*immovable rock,*"[15] such inspirations would be less likely to encourage lack of charity toward the wider world (and even toward other Catholics) under the guise of "fidelity" or "identity." Not to grow in these directions is to risk continual conflict rather than continual growth. The taproot anchoring and nourishing successful community transformations, the case studies here would seem to suggest, is an organic and resilient understanding of parish as a hybrid of dynamic community, authentic leadership, and empowered, mission.

APPENDIX—THE METHOD OF THE STUDY

As mentioned at the beginning of the chapter, the two parish clusters chosen for this study were selected for their striking similarities and differences. Furthermore, their previous connection to Project INSPIRE meant that initial contacts were already established and various kinds of background information were readily available to me as the INSPIRE visiting research professor.

That background information was provided through discussions with INSPIRE staff members and consultants (some of which were recorded and transcribed, or reviewed in field notes). I also conducted a review of project documents concerning both the new parishes and, in each case, one predecessor parish which had been involved in the INSPIRE process separately. As was the case with every parish in the overall project, the available documents included application forms, initial learning plans for each team and its individual members, periodic progress reports (both team and individual), periodic consultant reports, and a variety of notes and transcripts of occasional interviews with staff members and consultants.

I also engaged in a series of observations of public worship services (usually Mass) at the three active sites in each parish. My approach was to make these public observations without announcement or self-identification (although pastors and some staff members at both parishes knew who I was and why I was observing). In the course of about eighteen months, I attended at least two Masses or other services in each of the six worship sites at various times and seasons. I supplemented my field notes of these visits with printed materials that I collected at each site—weekly bulletins and occasional printed fliers for special parish, archdiocesan, or neighborhood programs, as well as the websites of each parish.

As I developed a basic sense of the situation in each parish, I arranged scheduled interviews with a number of staff people. With permission, some of these conversations were digitally recorded and transcribed, and others were reviewed in field notes. Questions were not standardized, but flowed from the conversations, in which I allowed interviewees to elaborate on particular topics as they saw fit. (This approach provided some additional indications of local perceptions and priorities.) The interviewees included then-current pastors of both merged parishes and two other priests who had been closely involved in the mergers, as well as a deacon, a business manager, a social service team, several visiting volunteers, and an external researcher familiar with social services in one of the parishes.

All of the reports, field notes, and transcripts mentioned here were entered into NVivo research software and coded, in order to assist the management and achieve the comprehensive intelligibility of such diverse materials.[16] Interpretation proceeded within a framework of relevant pastoral and theological issues suggested by the Chicago materials themselves, but also by my previous and ongoing observation of consolidated parishes in New England,[17] Germany,[18] and Australia.[19] Further perspectives are contributed by a growing national and international literature on the topic.[20]

Citations of specific research documents such as field notes and interview transcripts have not been included in this chapter because the sources are not publicly available. (The documents themselves are listed in the Works Cited section below.) The citations may be viewed in the original version of the research, presented at the INSPIRE Milestone Conference at the Water Tower Campus of Loyola University Chicago, October 25, 2013. The original paper and research materials, as well as many other materials pertaining to Project INSPIRE, are held at the McNamara Center for the Social Study of Religion at Loyola University Chicago.

SOURCES

Transcripts and Field Notes

October 23, 2011. Field Notes. Observation of liturgy at "Mary Immaculate."
October 30, 2011. Field Notes. Observation of liturgy at "Holy Apostles."
October 30, 2011. Field Notes. Meeting with "Father T."
November 6, 2011. Field Notes. Observation of liturgy at "St. Christopher."
November 13, 2011. Field Notes. Observation of liturgy at "SS. Simon and Jude."
November 13, 2011. Field Notes. Meeting with "Father D."
November 27, 2011. Field Notes. Observation of liturgy at "St. Christopher."
December 4, 2011. Field Notes. Observation of liturgy at "Assumption."
December 10, 2011. Field Notes. Observation of liturgy at "SS. Simon and Jude."
December 11, 2011. Field Notes. Observation of liturgy at "St. Mary."
December 16, 2011. Field Notes. Meeting with "Deacon C."
January 26, 2012. Field Notes. Meeting with "Volunteers 1, 2, and 3."
February 5, 2012. Field Notes. Observation of liturgy at "SS. Simon and Jude."

February 12, 2012. Field Notes. Observation of liturgy at "Mary Immaculate."
March 14, 2012. Field Notes. Meeting with "Researcher."
March 14, 2012. Field Notes. Meeting with "Volunteer 5."
March 19, 2012. Transcript. Interview with "Father G."
March 22, 2012. Transcript. Interview with "Consultant 1."
March 22, 2012. Transcript. Interview with "Consultant 2."
March 26, 2012. Transcript. Meeting with "Corpus Christi Community Services Staff."
March 28, 2012. Field Notes. Meeting with "Administrator 1."
April 1, 2012. Field Notes. Observation of liturgy at "Mary Immaculate."
April 20, 2012. Field Notes. Meeting with "Father M."
December 6, 2012. Transcript. Interview with "Father T."
April 28, 2013. Field Notes. Observation of liturgy at "Mary Immaculate."
May 18, 2013. Field Notes. Observation of liturgy at "Assumption."
May 18, 2013. Field Notes. Observation of liturgy at "Holy Apostles."
May 18, 2013. Field Notes. Observation of liturgy at "St. Mary."
July 31, 2013. Field Notes. Conversation with "Consultant 1."

Other Works Cited

Coriden, James A. *The Parish in Catholic Tradition: History, Theology and Canon Law.* Mahwah, NJ: Paulist, 1996.

Curran, Charles. *The Social Mission of the U.S. Catholic Church: A Theological Perspective.* Moral Traditions Series. Washington, DC: Georgetown University Press, 2010.

Dolan, Jay P., et al. *Transforming Parish Ministry: The Changing Roles of Catholic Clergy, Laity, and Women Religious.* New York: Crossroad, 1989.

National Conference of Catholic Bishops. "Communities of Salt and Light: Reflections on the Social Mission of the Parish." Washington, DC: NCCB, 1993.

Vatican Council II. *Lumen Gentium*, Dogmatic Constitution on the Church. November 21, 1964. http://www.vatican.va/archive/hist_councils/ii_vatican_council/documents/vat-ii_const_19641121_lumen-gentium_en.html.

Vatican Council II. *Unitatis Redintegratio*, Decree on Ecumenism. November 21, 1964. http://www.vatican.va/archive/hist_councils/ii_vatican_council/documents/vat-ii_decree_19641121_unitatis-redintegratio_en.html.

Other Works by the Author

Clark, William A. "Ark, Fueling Station, or Engaged Community? The Parish in U.S. Catholic Experience." In *Gemeinde unter Druck—Suchbewegungen im weltkirchlichen Vergleich: Deutschland und die USA/Parish Under Pressure—Quests for Meaning from a Global Perspective: Germany and the USA in Comparison*, edited by Andreas Henkelmann and Matthias Sellmann, 83–96. Münster: Aschendorff Verlag, 2012.

———. "'Save Our Church!'—Resistance to Parish Restructuring as Practical Ecclesiology." In *Catholic Identity and the Laity*. College Theology Society Annual Volume 54, edited by Tim Muldoon, 182–196. Maryknoll, NY: Orbis, 2009.

———. "Church and Authenticity in the Reconfigured Parish." Presentation to the Roman Catholic Studies section, American Academy of Religion Annual Convention. Chicago, IL. November 1, 2008.

———. "When the Church Goes to Court: What Do Recent Public Disputes Imply for the Life of the Local Church?" Presentation to the American Catholic Life and Thought section, College Theology Society Annual Convention. Dayton, OH. June 1, 2007.

———. *A Voice of Their Own: The Authority of the Local Parish.* Collegeville, MN: Liturgical Press, 2005.

Related Works

Baima, Thomas A., ed. *What Is a Parish? Canonical, Pastoral, and Theological Perspectives.* Chicago: Hillenbrand, 2011.

Ganim, Carole. *Shaping Catholic Parishes: Pastoral Leaders in the Twenty-First Century.* Emerging Models of Pastoral Leadership. Chicago: Loyola Press, 2008.

Jewell, Marti R., and David A. Ramey. *The Changing Face of Church: Emerging Models of Parish Leadership.* Emerging Models of Pastoral Leadership. Chicago: Loyola Press, 2010.

Mogilka, Mark, and Kate Wiskus. *Pastoring Multiple Parishes: An Emerging Model of Pastoral Leadership.* Emerging Models of Pastoral Leadership. Chicago: Loyola Press, 2009.

Rouet, Msgr. Albert (Archbishop of Poitiers, France), et al. *Un nouveau visage d'Eglise: L'expérience des communautés locales à Poitiers.* Etudes et Essais. Paris: Bayard, 2005.

Seitz, John C. *No Closure: Catholic Practice and Boston's Parish Shutdowns.* Cambridge, MA: Harvard University Press, 2011.

NOTES

1. Archbishop Blase Cupich, "Renew My Church: Dreaming Big about the Archdiocese of Chicago," *Catholic New World*, February 7–20, 2016, http://www.catholicnewworld.com/column/archbishop-cupich/2016/02/07/renew-my-church.

2. All names of communities and persons used in this chapter have been changed.

3. "Corpus Christi School" website, July 2013 (text from 2009; no longer accessible).

4. This group is estimated by one deacon to number between fifty and seventy-five persons, certainly not a large percentage of the membership.

5. The history of US parish development is presented in many well-known volumes, such as Jay P. Dolan et al., *Transforming Parish Ministry* (Crossroad, 1989); and James Coriden, *The Parish in Catholic Tradition* (Paulist, 1996).

6. National Conference of Catholic Bishops (NCCB), "Communities of Salt and Light: Reflections on the Social Mission of the Parish," Statement of the National Conference of Catholic Bishops (Washington, DC: USCC, 1994), heading 3, section 1, accessed August 9, 2013, at http://www.usccb.org/beliefs-and-teachings/what-we-believe/catholic-social-teaching/communities-of-salt-and-light-reflections-on-the-social-mission-of-the-parish.cfm#integration.

7. Charles Curran, *The Social Mission of the U.S. Catholic Church: A Theological Perspective* (Washington, DC: Georgetown University Press, 2010), 134.

8. NCCB, "Salt and Light," heading 3, section 2.

9. Ibid.

10. Pope Francis, *Evangelii Gaudium* (Apostolic Exhortation on the Proclamation of the Gospel in Today's World), November 24, 2013, #28; quoting Pope John Paul II, *Christifideles Laici*, September 30, 1988, #26.

11. Second Vatican Council, *Lumen Gentium* (Dogmatic Constitution on the Church), November 21, 1964, #48–51.

12. Second Vatican Council, *Unitatis Redintegratio* (Decree on Ecumenism), November 21, 1964, #6.

13. See, for example, 1 Corinthians 12–13.

14. In addition to the chapter from *Lumen Gentium* cited above, see examples in Psalms 122, 126, and 132.

15. See, for example, Psalm 125:1, and some of the figures mentioned in *Lumen Gentium*, #6: "Often the Church has also been called the building of God."

16. NVivo software is developed and sold by QSR International. See www.qsrinternational.com/product.

17. Research in New England has included participant observation, interviews, and public presentations in the Archdiocese of Boston, the Diocese of Worcester, Massachusetts, the Diocese of Springfield, Massachusetts, the Diocese of Manchester, New Hampshire, and the Diocese of Portland, Maine, between 2004 and 2013.

18. Research in Germany, in connection with the CrossingOver program (an exchange program of pastoral ministers between the Archdiocese of Chicago and several German dioceses) and the Ruhr Universität Bochum, has included observation and interviews in the Dioceses of Essen, Münster, and Hildesheim, in January 2012 and July 2013.

19. Research in Australia has included participant observation and interviews in the "Western Mission" of the Archdiocese of Canberra and Goulburn in May 2009.

20. See the "Sources: Related Works" section at the end of this paper for references to these works.

Chapter Five

No Favoritism

*Effective Collaborative Leadership
Practices in Multicultural Parishes*

Brett Hoover

EDITORS' NOTE

The multicultural context of much US parish pastoral ministry is suggested by the study presented in the previous chapter, in which both parish clusters included not only the remnants of several older European immigrant cultures but also the energy of much more recent Latino immigrant cultures. Using current literature and a further pair of case studies, the following chapter looks more closely at this multiethnic, multiracial experience *per se*. How is it unfolding in the United States, and are there any collaborative leadership models that can be effective in these challenging environments?

Dr. Brett Hoover is assistant professor of pastoral theology at Loyola Marymount University in Los Angeles. He has spent the past decade involved in qualitative research in Catholic parishes. He is the author of *The Shared Parish: Latinos and the Future of U.S. Catholicism* (NYU Press, 2014). He has written and spoken on parish life and various other topics. Dr. Hoover co-founded *BustedHalo*, an Internet ministry for young seekers. He served as INSPIRE's first visiting professor at Loyola University Chicago's Institute of Pastoral Studies, where he organized and laid out the foundations for the project's research and reporting mission.

INTRODUCTION

Because of the historical dominance of white men in corporations and business schools, much of the literature on leadership in the United States bears the cultural assumptions of a white, Euro-American context. This is so much the case that some pastoral theologians in the Hispanic context eschew the word "leadership" altogether, suggesting it carries hierarchical and individualistic connotations inappropriate for Hispanic pastoral ministry.[1] At the same time, newer business fields like organizational development (OD) question older, power-centered "great man" theories of leadership and advocate for a style of leadership that sees human beings as social beings and sees business and other activities as necessarily cooperative and mission-driven. In this volume, this is generally what the authors have meant by "collaborative leadership." In these pages, I would like to raise the question of how such an approach to leadership might practically work in the context of multicultural Catholic parishes.

Multicultural parishes have become such a part of the fabric of US Catholicism today that in many parts of the United States, one would be hard-pressed to find a Catholic who had never had an experience of worship or parish life touched by another language or culture. Despite this fact, we know surprisingly little about how such parishes work in practice and what kind of leadership is most effective within them.[2] To address such a lacuna, this chapter examines the *how* of effective, collaborative pastoral leadership in a multicultural parish. How does collaborative leadership work in such contexts and why? After some preliminary remarks about multicultural parishes, I pursue this vexing question through a presentation of two parish case studies, both multicultural, both led by pastors seen as successful by their parishioners, one parish in Chicago (and part of the INSPIRE project mentioned throughout this book) and another in Los Angeles. Although the parishes are quite different, in both cases, parishioners highlighted certain consistent leadership practices of the pastors. These practices not only "worked" but they also helped to shape the parish as a cooperative community of faith attempting to respond to the Gospel for the particular context. The pastors understood their leadership as primarily about shaping the corporate identity and culture of the parish. In the words of congregational studies scholar Jackson Carroll, "As producers of congregational culture, clergy give shape to a congregation's particular way of being a congregation—that is, to the beliefs and practices characteristic of a particular community's life and ministry."[3]

UNDERSTANDING MULTICULTURAL PARISHES

Despite my confident use of the term *multicultural parish* here, it is not clear, in fact, that scholars agree on what a *multicultural parish* is. For some, *multicultural* is a means of measuring or highlighting the presence and influence of groups other than Euro-Americans or whites. According to this approach, a multicultural parish would be any parish where people besides Euro-American Catholics have some influence on parish life.[4] Instead, I hold to a more literal interpretation of the word as describing a parish with multiple cultures. Many (though not all) sociologists of religion use it thus, along with terms like *multiracial* or *multiethnic congregation*.[5] All serve as barometers of how much people from different cultural, ethnic, or racial groups are willing and able to coexist in a single religious organization. Thus, in this chapter, I speak of a multicultural parish as a Catholic parish where a significant proportion of parishioners (at least 20 percent) come from a single ethnic, racial, or cultural group *other than that of the majority or plurality group*. To envision this, it might help to think about what is *not* a multicultural parish, that is, a monocultural parish where more than 80 percent of the parishioners come from a single group, whatever that group may be. Thus, my definition would exclude not only "mainstream Anglo" or dominant culture parishes but also parishes formerly known as *ethnic* or *national* parishes, those that overwhelmingly cater to a single ethnic or linguistic group.

Multicultural parishes are no recent innovation, despite a not uncommon perception that *multicultural* equates to something new. American Catholicism has nearly always boasted a significant number of parishes with multiple cultures. In 1785, the pastor of the first Catholic parish in New York City, Charles Whelan, described his parish as home to English, Irish, French, Spanish, Dutch, and Portuguese speaking people.[6] The first priest assigned to Chicago, Fr. John Mary St. Cyr, wrote in 1833 about preaching and teaching in English and French, and about ministry among the Potawatomi.[7] Of course, the monocultural national parish dominated much of nineteenth-century Catholicism, and the long lull in immigration from the 1920s into the postwar period translated to a more Americanized or assimilated parochial landscape. Nevertheless, multicultural parishes never completely disappeared, and the late-twentieth-century surge in immigration from Latin America and Asia has created more than ever.

Some statistics may be helpful. The National Study of Catholic Parishes with Hispanic Ministry found that 43 percent of parishioners at parishes with Hispanic ministry are actually non-Hispanic whites.[8] In my own research from 2013 to 2014, I looked at various dioceses to discern how many parishes in each have mass in more than one language. I found a great deal of regional variation, as indicated in Figure 5.1.

In the study of Chicago parishes on which much of the work discussed in this book is based, 47.5 percent of the parishes involved were multicultural parishes, and 45 percent had mass in more than one language. Reading between the lines, of course, this means that a narrow majority of these parishes were monocultural and had mass in only one language—usually English but sometimes Spanish. This pattern turns out to be something of a national trend. Hosffman Ospino found that, although some 40 percent of Catholics are Hispanic, 25 percent of Catholic parishes have at least some minimal form of Hispanic ministry.[9] The Center for Applied Research in the Aposto-

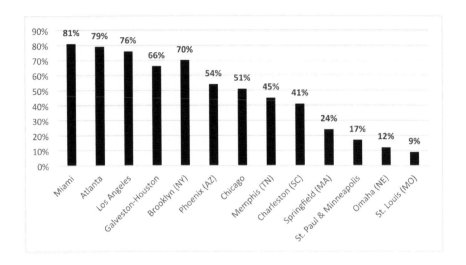

Figure 5.1.   Parishes with Mass in More than One Language

late (CARA) at Georgetown University found that 71 percent of parishes
have mass only in English, and 88 percent of the registered parishioners in
those parishes are white.[10] Tellingly, Black, Asian, and Hispanic parishioners are much more likely to pass by their local parish en route to attendance
at another parish.[11] All this confirms a national picture where a minority of
Catholic parishes do the heavy lifting in terms of addressing cultural diversity while others focus more or less exclusively on Catholics of European
descent.

At the same time, the Latino Catholic population continues to grow as the
white Catholic population shrinks, especially among the young. According to
the Pew Research Center, 47 percent of Catholics between 18 and 29 years of
age are Hispanic while 44 percent are white.[12] Most of us can see the outcome of such patterns; indeed, the pattern has already become visible in
many parishes. Crowded masses serve a young, mostly Latino and Asian
Catholic population in select parishes while other masses and other parishes
serve a very committed but aging white population. In Chicago, archdiocesan
figures show that while two-thirds of Catholics attend mass in English, over
three quarters of the masses are in English. While close to a quarter of
Chicago Catholics attend mass in Spanish, only 15 percent of the masses are
in that language.[13] The implications are clear. Parish life in this country will
increasingly require a shift of resources from Anglo to Latino and multicultural parishes, even as we try to find some way to honor the contributions of
Catholics of European descent as their influence wanes.

LEADERSHIP IN MULTICULTURAL PARISHES: GENERAL OBSERVATIONS

The focus of this chapter, however, is on *leadership* in multicultural parishes. Thus, before considering the data that emerged from case study parishes, a few general observations about leadership in multicultural parishes are in order. First, many urban parishes—including a large number of multicultural parishes—serve working-class or poor communities. Such parishes rarely employ several professional lay ecclesial ministers as staff members. Moreover, the people who understand these contexts best often do not possess the educational qualifications typically expected of those employed as lay ecclesial ministers. In other words, these parishes rarely have a parish staff in the way conventionally understood in more affluent parishes. Of course, poorer parishes still have pastoral leadership beyond the priest pastor. But most pastoral leaders are volunteers; others are part-time permanent deacons (often not compensated). We might say that such parishes have pastoral leadership teams with a variety of statuses rather than paid professionals.

Second, many US Catholics are under the impression that immigrant Catholics prefer what is sometimes described as a "pre-conciliar model of church leadership," that is, a more authoritarian and less participatory approach. They are seen as less likely to empower women. While there is evidence that some immigrant Catholics demonstrate more traditional respect for the clergy than do Euro-American Catholics, immigrant-serving parishes are often the most participatory of parishes. Because Hispanic communities often lack the professional leadership class of Anglo-dominant parishes, they depend on volunteers and local pastoral leaders for everything. Apostolic movements like the Catholic Charismatic Renewal and *Jovenes para Cristo* usually serve as parish-based schools of lay leadership and spirituality. The relative youth of the Hispanic community often translates to gigantic religious education and sacramental preparation programs, all staffed by volunteers. Socioeconomic need creates a need for more social services, also often run by volunteers. Finally, it bears mentioning that the majority of these volunteers and local pastoral leaders are women.

Third, a leadership issue that looms large in all multicultural parishes is managing the harmonious coexistence of distinct racial, cultural, and ethnic groups. My own research suggests that tensions almost inevitably erupt over language, room use, liturgy, parking, and attention from the pastor and other priests. Especially if there is a pronounced difference in power position between the groups, those tensions can feel to parishioners almost insurmountable. A history of racial or ethnic discrimination in the local or national context often plays out within the parish. In one parish I studied, Hispanic immigrant Catholics complained frequently about racism in the parish, describing their inferior resources within the parish and the way they were always blamed for problems on the physical plant. Euro-American Catholics, on the other hand, tended to see racism only in terms of overt bigotry, and institutionalized racism at the parish remained largely invisible to them.

Many multicultural parishes handle tensions between cultural groups by studied avoidance—keeping the groups away from one another as much as possible. For example, many parishioners at one multicultural parish chose to park on a nearby street when they came for mass, hoping to avoid having to negotiate their way through the church parking lot as the English mass let out and people began to gather for the Spanish mass. Intercultural communication theorists describe avoidance as a behavioral consequence of the anxiety and uncertainty naturally evoked by differences of language and culture.[14] This makes efforts to move beyond that avoidance all the more valuable and appreciated. People are shocked when someone at a bilingual liturgy offers them the sign of peace in a halting version of their own language. In our Chicago study, parishioners in two parishes rejoiced in their promotion of bilingualism to help build bridges between groups—either through habituating people to the use of two languages in worship and meetings, or through opportunities for people to learn one another's languages, at least in a rudimentary way.

But avoidance seems to carry the day much of the time, and it may be necessary as groups unfamiliar with one another begin to coexist in a multicultural parish. Anxiety thus remains lower and conflict stays rare. But the fewer resources a parish has, the more its facilities are at capacity, and the longer groups coexist, the less effective avoidance will be over the long term. And avoidance makes the inevitable tensions that occur seem more like unreasonable and heavy burdens and less like one of the normal challenges of life in a multicultural world. Though there is no firm data on this, it seems that most parishes find it difficult or impossible to move beyond avoidance. Some end up effectively organizing separate parishes in the same place. Other parishes react by moving toward the opposite extreme, coercive assimilation, forcing non-English speakers to attend mass in English and suppressing customs and habits not in accordance with Euro-American culture. This leads to the departure of non-English-speaking groups for other parishes, for Pentecostal or Evangelical churches (especially where no other Catholic parishes exist), or for nothing at all. Occasionally, something like the reverse occurs. Immigrant parishioners reach critical mass in the parish, and Euro-American Catholics depart as they find there are no longer groups or ministries addressing their needs.

In my experience as a researcher, only a few parishes manage to balance the real pastoral need for worship and ministry in distinct languages or for different cultural groups with a coherent common sense of parish and Church. That is, only a few parishes develop a collaborative experience of parish partnership where leaders in different communities know one another and occasionally cooperate in joint parish projects. In all of the cases of this sort of intercultural collaboration that I have known, an influential pastor (or other important pastoral leader) has provided the pastoral vision necessary to accomplish this. People do not naturally cooperate across cultural, racial, or ethnic lines. They have to be called to it. Must it be the pastor who calls them? It seems counterintuitive to focus so heavily on the role of the pastor in the midst of an examination of effective, collaborative leadership in a multicultural parish. Since *Lumen Gentium* reminded us that the Church is the gathering (*ekklesia*) of all the baptized, many of us have endeavored to get past the clerical hangovers of yesteryear and avoid exclusive focus on the clergy. I would hope that lay pastoral leadership in a parish might be just as effective in calling parishioners to an experience of partnership across cultures.

Yet one of the difficult but important findings of our research in Chicago was the near complete nature of a priest pastor's authority in Roman Catholic parishes. In the past, I have referred to this as the pastor's "canonical monopoly" on parish authority. After all, the 1983 Code of Canon Law implicates a pastor in the very definition of a parish: "A parish is a certain community of the Christian faithful stably constituted in a particular church, whose pastoral care is entrusted to a pastor (*parochus*) as its proper pastor (*pastor*) under the authority of the diocesan bishop" (canon 515 §1). Once a pastor is placed "in possession" of a parish by the diocesan bishop (canon 527), church law gives solely the pastor the function of governing the parish (canon 519). According to canon 532, the pastor has full responsibility for the administration and material goods of the parish. As canon law scholar John Renken puts it, "The pastor is not simply the delegate of the diocesan bishop. Within his parish, he functions with ordinary power, given him in law by reason of the office he holds. His power is proper [that is, belonging to him by right], exercised in his own name."[15]

In practice, this means that the involvement of other pastoral leadership team members in the shared governance of the parish community depends entirely on the pastor's permission and encouragement. Both parish employees and volunteers—even parochial vicars assigned by the bishop—effectively collaborate in pastoral leadership only as long as the pastor remains willing to encourage or countenance them doing so. For a variety of reasons, this is even more the case in multicultural parishes. Priesthood functions as an effective symbol of leadership in almost all Catholic cultures, and priest leadership will remain familiar even in a Catholic parish radically different from the one a person grew up in. Many poorer countries do not have the resources to support professional ministers other than the priest, and many immigrants are unfamiliar with lay ecclesial ministers. Also, more often than with lay leaders, priests are afforded the time and financial support necessary to learn new languages to minister to their people. Priests are often the only leaders able to communicate with all the distinct racial or ethnic groups in a parish.

A fourth point about leadership in multicultural parishes hinges on the way parish leaders in multicultural parishes—indeed, in all parishes across the board—envision their ministry. In the Chicago study we found that the dominant secular culture's attitudes regarding work heavily influence parish leadership. The sociologist Steve Derné argues that cultures shape human life by providing us with social frameworks that make some things imaginable and other things unimaginable.[16] In the United States, we find it difficult to imagine work as anything but a series of discrete tasks performed by individuals within a specified time frame. Intercultural communications theorists refer to this as operational thinking: "The American approach is functional and emphasizes solving problems and accomplishing tasks."[17] In Chicago, parish leadership teams had a hard time escaping thinking of their ministry exclusively in terms of tasks. Thus, they suffered because of this, with pastoral leadership teams feeling busy, burnt out, overworked, and often unable to make spiritual connections to their ministry or even remember why they were doing what they were doing in the first place.[18] This turned out to be as true for Latino and multicultural parishes as it was for Anglo parishes. Migration scholars and theologians have long noted that work patterns are one of the first things to be altered in immigrant cultures by the influence of the dominant culture.[19]

This acute case of task orientation in parish work cultures creates a strong need for more reflection on the deeper spiritual and pastoral reasons why pastoral leaders engage in the discrete tasks of parish ministry. What they need is a pastoral vision, by which I mean to describe 1) the way in which parishioners are invited to imagine the future of their community in the light of faith, 2) in order to inspire and guide today's activities and programs, 3) so that such activities and programs feel purposeful and consonant with the community's understanding of God's presence among them. Such a vision has to be a response to the questions and challenges experienced by a particular community in its particular social, cultural, and ecclesial context. As practical theologian Helen Cameron puts it, "Local churches that see mission as the essence of what they are are willing to be changing in response to their context, the surrounding culture and their dialogue with the Bible and tradition."[20]

Research suggests that successful parishes have strong pastoral visions, often expressed in guiding images and pithy phrases. Thus, in Chicago we heard talk of a parish "sharing Christ with love," a parish as a "people of the plaza," or a parish determined not to just be a spiritual service station. The way in which a pastor uncovered and communicated a pastoral vision also mattered a great deal. As was said of one parish in Chicago, "The pastor was outstanding. He was a tremendous leader, had a great vision for the parish.

The parish really grew and developed under his leadership." At another, pastoral leaders saw with the arrival of a new pastor "a willingness to be creative in finding new forms and styles of ministry for this community." They rejoiced in this "pastor with a vision who sees the pastoral team as important to overall parish development."

Thus, in general, research shows that effective, collaborative pastoral leadership depends on the pastor (or on an equivalent key leader, in some cases) and the pastoral vision he articulates for the parish. But what makes a pastor effective in uncovering a pastoral vision that speaks to a particular community, communicating that vision, and inspiring others to work with him on a team guiding the parish toward that vision? Our research in Chicago showed successful parishes almost always had a strong pastor with good interpersonal skills who shared power rather than hoarding it. Conversely, a pastor with weak interpersonal skills or one who guarded his authority jealously had great trouble leading a parish. But this is only the most superficial foundation necessary for good pastoral leadership. What specific skills and practices make pastoral leaders effective and collaborative leaders in multicultural parishes? Why are they effective? To answer these questions, we turn to two case studies, each a profile of a successful, collaborative pastoral leader in a multicultural parish.

ST. ROSE OF LIMA PARISH IN CHICAGO

One of these case studies was a Chicago parish involved in the INSPIRE project, an urban multicultural parish that I call St. Rose of Lima.[21] Father Paul was the pastor of St. Rose of Lima. A relatively small parish in what was originally a white working-class neighborhood, St. Rose transitioned demographically, and within a decade had become majority Hispanic, though its Anglo community remained committed and present. The pastor, Fr. Paul, who is Euro-American but speaks Spanish, came later on at a precarious time for the parish. Political and ecclesial winds blowing through Chicago persuaded some parishioners that the parish was on the archdiocesan chopping block, though no such decision had actually been made. In addition, the parish had lacked a pastor for an interval. In short, people were worried about the future of their parish and looked to their new pastor for help. Not unlike many poorer urban parishes, St. Rose did not have much of a professional staff. The pastoral team included Deacon Miguel and Sr. Donna, a Dominican nun, neither fulltime. When Fr. Paul came, however, he brought together an additional set of volunteers to work with in guiding the parish, including Mary, an older Anglo women who became a motherly bridge figure, and Juan Manuel, a thirty-something bilingual man.

Study of St. Rose during Father Paul's tenure confirmed the "vision matters" argument. Fr. Paul had spent time developing and promoting a pastoral vision for the parish centering on partnership between its two major cultural groups. As one parish report noted, "The future will be to have people work together experiencing both cultures and languages." Fr. Paul wanted parishioners to see cultural diversity as an opportunity rather than as a problem. [22] While this may sound rather obvious, such an imagining of the parish as a partnership between cultural communities reads as distinctive and creative to many American churchgoers. Given the history of racial and ethnic discrimination in the United States, we tend to expect what sociologists call *homophily*. Homophily is the social fact that in practice most people prefer the company of people who are like them. As a youth minister in my study of multicultural parishes in Southern California observed, "As humans we're drawn to a specific group of people. . . . I guess I've never understood why that's a factor, but we're human." Martin Luther King, Jr., famously noted that 11 a.m. on Sunday morning was the most segregated hour of the week. Because faith communities in a nation without an established religion are in some sense voluntarily chosen, homophily often translates to racially or culturally segregated faith communities. Thus, when Catholics "parish shop," that is, search for a parish that suits them, they are likely to choose a parish full of people like them. [23]

For this reason, a pastoral vision of multicultural partnership can seem fresh, even exciting. Such a vision also taps into Catholic ecclesiological principles. For example, communion or *koinonia*—historically experienced as the spiritual bonds between churches and their bishops across time—is translated into a local experience of connection between parishioners of distinct cultural communities. Catholicity, the universality of the Church, becomes locally visible in the many hues of people within a multicultural parish. Also, a pastoral vision of multicultural partnership can feel like a helpful tool for navigating an ever-more diverse society. In one parish I researched years ago, a young couple noted to me that the public schools were the only place in town other than the parish where people of different cultures related to one another. Where else might people go to learn how to become more culturally sensitive and competent in a society that increasing demands these skills?

Whether or not Fr. Paul's vision felt fresh, theologically appropriate, or relevant, it did prove persuasive to parishioners. This occurred in part simply because he showed parishioners how and why it could work. He did a number of things to put his pastoral vision of partnership between cultural communities into practice. First, he discussed this view of parish mission in pastoral leadership team meetings, carefully gathering their input. He and that team ran a series of town hall meetings for parishioners to do the same. This dynamic of structured and inclusive listening practices—setting times for gathering feedback at meetings in which all participants are invited to speak—seems to be particularly crucial to successful parish leadership in multicultural communities where worries about favoritism operate nearly all the time. Fr. Paul was good enough at it that other parish leaders would observe and imitate his approach, making a point to go around and make sure that all participants had a chance to speak, even if they were initially nervous to do so. Such an approach to listening persuades people that the pastor and other leaders are really interested in their perspectives. This is crucial when certain groups of parishioners feel invisible to the larger society in their daily lives. Even if people walk by them without recognition in their everyday service jobs, at church they are recognized and listened to.

In Fr. Paul's case, these listening strategies were accompanied by conscious efforts to ensure that the leadership team, originally mostly Anglos, reflected the actual demographic makeup of the parish (Anglo and Latino). This is sometimes referred to as *representation.* Representation demonstrates that leadership is listening, paying attention, and truly recognizing what sorts of people make up the parish community. Representation serves as almost a minimum requirement for making a common vision of partnership across diverse groups seem credible. Fr. Paul also pushed people toward bilingualism, that is, toward learning at least a little bit about one another's languages. He created and taught a bilingual Bible study for the pastoral leadership team. Next, he shepherded the creation of a network of small faith communities (or base communities) within the parish. The groups were language specific, but they gathered together periodically for bilingual backyard masses and potluck dinners. At these events, as one parishioner put it, "The divide between Hispanics and Anglos disappears."

Fr. Paul's story begins to help us see more clearly what makes a pastor an effective, collaborative leader at a multicultural parish. A leader, especially a pastor or administrator, has to present an inclusive vision for the parish, but he also has to make sure different cultural groups are all well represented on the parish leadership team. If they are not, his vision loses credibility. He has to find concrete ways of bringing the groups together periodically—not always—for a common experience of church. And he has to be seen as listening to people, even modeling listening for other parish leaders. If he cannot do these things, people go to their default cultural expectation that homophily and self-segregation reign as an unchallengeable norm. They wonder if the Christian vision of one Church for all people is idealistic but not functional, that it has no real way to involve, empower, and unite people across cultural, ethic, and racial boundaries.

QUEEN OF HEAVEN IN SOUTHERN CALIFORNIA

This collection of leadership practices tells us a great deal, but it requires confirmation and nuance if we are to really understand effective collaborative leadership in a multicultural parish. Otherwise, it is vulnerable to being dismissed as *sui generis*, the peculiar but nonreplicable practices of an extraordinary parish. So I turn to Queen of Heaven parish in Southern California to see if its story might confirm or nuance what we observed at St. Rose of Lima.

Queen of Heaven is very different from St. Rose of Lima.[24] It is what some call a megaparish.[25] Over seven thousand people attend eleven weekend masses in Spanish and English with Filipino music at one mass. Queen of Heaven lies in an inner suburb of Los Angeles made up of working- and middle-class families, and it is a majority Latino city. The parish attracts Spanish-speaking immigrants from Mexico and Central America, English-speaking US-born Latinos, Filipino immigrants and their children, and a very small number of elderly whites who have remained in the parish since the 1950s. The pastor, Fr. Joe, is a US-born Mexican American and a fast-talking, energetic priest in his early forties. He will be the first to tell you that he did not grow up speaking Spanish. Nevertheless, he is now fluent after many years of experience in Hispanic ministry and pastoring Hispanic-dominant parishes. The parish has several professional staff members, including Fathers Jordan and Benjie, two priests from the Philippines. Fr. Benjie is very energetic like the pastor and speaks excellent Spanish. The young Latina youth minister, Maripaz, grew up in the parish. A no-nonsense middle-aged white man, Kevin, runs the parish's social services.

As happened with Fr. Paul at St. Rose of Lima, at Queen of Heaven parish many people described Fr. Joe as a good pastor with a strong pastoral vision of the different cultural groups operating together in partnership. One of the parish secretaries at Queen of Heaven summed up Fr. Joe's vision in a way that suggests again how unique it seemed to many people, "Father's really good at inviting everyone. . . . He always wants all of us to be involved." But whether or not such a pastoral vision seems unique or compelling, again we have to ascertain why it becomes credible to parishioners. How do people know that a pastoral vision like that of Fr. Joe is something more than just pious words? Why should they trust him and his vision of cultural groups in partnership?

At least part of the reason people did trust Fr. Joe is that they perceived him as a pastor for all the groups of the parish. His youth minister said, "I think Father is really good at integrating himself into all cultures." She noted that before his tenure, there was a lot of perceived favoritism: "One priest favors that community better or one priest favors *this* community better." In part this perspective stemmed from reports, fair or unfair, that Fr. Joe's predecessor was mainly interested in the LifeTeen youth ministry program, and was thought to be particularly inattentive to the concerns of the Filipino community. "People didn't feel respected by him," said one Filipina parishioner. Fr. Joe admitted that, perhaps because he is a Latino, it took a while for the Filipino community to see him as, as he put it, "pro-Filipino." Nevertheless Fr. Joe managed to project just such an image, not only to the Filipinos but to many different groups. A parish secretary noted that now she never heard people complaining about him paying exclusive attention to any group. In other words, Fr. Joe succeeded in being seen as pastor to all groups because they could not identify him definitively with any particular faction or group. In fact, he told me that he consciously worked to confuse those who might want to pigeonhole him into a particular category.

When pastoral leaders like Fr. Joe and Fr. Paul succeed at authentically communicating leadership without favoritism, they surprise a flock accustomed to homophily, but they do something theologically more important. Suddenly, they are seen not as loving and serving God's people as a human being might do, preferring one's own, but loving and serving as God does, loving all. In the Sermon on the Mount, Jesus urges his listeners to love their enemies "so that you may be children of your Father in heaven; for he makes his sun rise on the evil and on the good, and sends rain on the righteous and on the unrighteous" (cf. Matthew 5:43–48). But the monumental story that illustrates the Christian calling to universal love occurs in the Acts of the Apostles. In Acts 10, God himself teaches Peter how to be a shepherd of all without favoritism or regard for human identity markers like race and ethnicity. First through a dream and then through the faith of the foreigner and Roman centurion Cornelius, Peter learns his lesson about God's favor: "I truly understand that God shows no partiality, but in every nation anyone who fears him and does what is right is acceptable to him" (cf. Acts 10:34–35). When Fr. Joe and Fr. Paul succeeded in convincing their parishioners that they loved and served all the groups, in the perspective of their parishioners at Queen of Heaven, they took on a theological credibility.

But how did they do this in practice? At Queen of Heaven how *exactly* did Fr. Joe project this image of a trustworthy person who truly served as pastor of all the cultural groups? Some of this impression emerged from his high energy level, informality and accessibility, and hands-on approach. He often dressed informally and wandered around. A Filipino parishioner noted how, the first time she met him, he was stacking bulletins in the church. Another related how people see him putting his own donation envelope into the collection on Sundays. An English-speaking Cuban-American parishioner talked about how his accessibility and energy brought people to church. Of course, such charismatic leadership can backfire. Research on charismatic leaders distinguishes between ethical or "socialized" leaders who push people toward the collective good and an ethical vision and unethical or "personalized" leaders who push people toward the leader's agenda and good.[26] But Fr. Joe did not use his charisma to ensure that parish events drew attention to him but to a vision of the parish where all members could participate and flourish. A Filipina parishioner noted, "You can feel how much he wants to unify both cultures."

His high energy also enabled him to go around authorizing and blessing the diverse events of the various groups and ministries. He made sure to attend events of all the different communities. He emphasized different kinds of ministries and groups, depending on the cultural group. For example, even though he himself was more progressive, Fr. Joe brought representatives of the more conservative Neo-Catechumenal Way apostolic movement to the parish.[27] A Spanish-speaking parishioner noted that when someone asked for permission to conduct an event or celebration at the parish, he almost always said yes. When members of the Filipino community wanted to erect a statue in honor of the Virgin Mary, he enthusiastically got behind their efforts. One man from Mexico noted how, when his group would scatter out to the neighborhoods to invite people to church, he would come and offer a blessing before they left. Fr. Joe *seemed* almost universally present to bless and authorize a proliferation of ministries and activities at Queen of Heaven. This sounds like a recipe for burnout. In reality, though he was a man of tremendous energy, Fr. Joe did much of this blessing and authorization in brief visits or vicariously through his pastoral staff. Fathers Jordan and Benjie did a lot of the actual blessing and authorizing. Regardless, as a result of these efforts, Queen of Heaven *felt* like a place where many things could happen for many different kinds of people.

And like Fr. Paul at St. Rose of Lima in Chicago, Fr. Joe was intentional about listening to parishioners and assessing the parish's needs based on what he heard. This program of listening, for example, persuaded him that he should start his work as pastor focusing on building up leadership among Spanish-speaking parishioners, since they were the largest group. Fr. Joe listened both informally and also in more disciplined and structured ways. Kevin, the parish's director of social services, described him as someone who was always out talking with people. A trio of Latino parishioners took my research assistant on a tour of the parish, and along the way one of them told her that Fr. Joe really wanted the good of the parish. Another chimed in that even when he was busy, he would always stop and take a few minutes to listen to you, and that in those few minutes he was fully present.

But Fr. Joe also conducted formal listening sessions and put together historical timelines with groups from the parish. A Filipino parishioner described how, upon his arrival, Fr. Joe had invited members of the Filipino community to a series of meetings in the parish hall. "He asked everybody, 'What are your concerns? What are your needs? And how do you want the parish to come along?'" Fr. Joe did not simply listen to people personally; he also insisted that other pastoral leaders listen in an intentional and structured way as well. For example, he required Kevin to keep detailed records on whom the parish's social services programs served and how.

Indeed, part of the dynamic of parish life in a megaparish like Queen of Heaven was that no one person—including the pastor—could conduct the lion's share of pastoral outreach. Fr. Joe frequently worked with what I call his lieutenants—his assistant priests, lay staff members, and other pastoral leaders in the parish. Upon arriving at the parish as a new pastor, after listening to the Filipino community, he set out to recruit a Filipino priest for the parish. He managed to recruit two, one of them Spanish-speaking, and he had another priest in residence, Fr. Justin, who was a hospital chaplain from Nigeria. Fr. Joe commented about his success getting these priests to act as a team: "It's not one of these houses where they try to play us off on each other." He contrasted this with parishes where each priest does his own thing, often at cross-purposes. But at Queen of Heaven, this team approach was also institutionalized. Each priest or lay ecclesial minister served as liaison for particular parish groups, and he or she had primary responsibility for communicating with the group. Parishioners could not easily, as Fr. Joe put it, play one staff member against another. The effect was that parishioners from all the different groups received consistent messages about the trajectory of parish life.

Consistency breeds trust, as the lack of it breaks down trust. Consistency also emerged in the way Fr. Joe or members of his team would intervene with parish leaders who failed to act in accordance with this pastoral vision of partnership between cultural groups. Often this involved parish leaders worried about losing their own power if the pastor's vision gained traction. They would never challenge the pastor or his team publicly, of course, but rather would start small, subtle rebellions. But, the parish secretary noted, Fr. Joe turned out to be pretty good at nipping those rebellions in the bud. Well-networked in the parish, he would hear about them and invite the person for a face-to-face meeting. Confronted directly, the person would usually give up on their rebellion fairly quickly. These interventions were not always conducted by Fr. Joe but often by other staff members. For example, Fr. Joe spoke of Fr. Jordan and Fr. Benjie performing the difficult and somewhat countercultural work of intervening with the elders in their own community.

All these practices—from authorizing and blessing meetings and activities to formal listening sessions to timely interventions—helped people perceive that their pastor and staff were shepherds for all cultural groups without favoritism. Yet even this perception is not enough for a vision of partnership between cultural groups to become a reality. Parishioners need an actual *experience* of that partnership. Thus, pastors have to find concrete ways of bringing members of different groups together for a common experience of parish life, even if only periodically or chiefly among parish leaders. At a shared parish, the majority of pastoral activity—worship, ministry, faith sharing, religious education—necessarily takes place in language-and-culture-specific groups. People need to pray in the language of their hearts, and parishioners can only share faith and make complex decisions together when they can communicate clearly and in considerable depth. This is why, for example, the small faith communities at St. Rose of Lima had to be language-specific. And this system of parallel worship and ministry ends up being both the strength and weakness of a shared parish. It creates safe space for different groups to live their faith. But coexistence in the same parish depends on some kind of common reference, a minimally common experience of parish life. Given the ordinary presence of language and culture barriers, such shared experiences have to be orchestrated and planned. People need ways and means of coming together for some common experience of parish life, and good pastors create and shape those opportunities.

In fact, creating such opportunities was the most frequently noted leadership practice of Fr. Joe at Queen of Heaven in Los Angeles, and the same practice received substantial attention in accounts at St. Rose of Lima. As already noted, at St. Rose Fr. Paul invited both English- and Spanish-speaking leadership team members to be part of a seven-month bilingual scripture study. He made a habit out of closing important parish events with a bilingual mass with alternating English and Spanish parts but where nothing was repeated to avoid prolonging people's worship experience. The small faith community program also held periodic bilingual masses and potluck dinners.

Also at Queen of Heaven, communal meals provided people from different cultural groups with the opportunity to share an experience even if they could not understand one another or communicate directly. Fr. Joe organized a Saturday morning breakfast each month, with food provided by different groups for everyone. But Fr. Joe's efforts at Queen of Heaven went far beyond that. He persuaded the Spanish- and English-speaking groups who carried out separate Divine Mercy devotions to combine their efforts under the leadership of his assistant priests. He invited families from all the communities to bring their Thanksgiving foods to the trilingual Thanksgiving mass (English-Spanish-Tagalog) to be blessed. His efforts went beyond just different language groups. When he found out that two groups were planning festivities for the Feast of Our Lady of Guadalupe—one young Latinas and the other older women—he pushed them to work together. And even as he pushed such joint practices, others in the parish seemed to catch on. For example, the separate language groups for the RCIA—Rite of Christian Initiation for Adults—decided to host a retreat together.

Even though Catholics often ultimately appreciate these common experiences of parish life across cultural (and language) groups, they generally do not seek them out. Neither leadership teams nor parishioners themselves are likely to collaborate in a multicultural parish simply because multiple groups are there. Indeed, intercultural communication theorists routinely note that mere contact between cultural groups does not necessarily lead to improved relationships.[28] Pastoral leaders have to create and structure opportunities for that contact to flower into collaborative relationships, both on the parish staff or leadership team and in the parish in general. Creating such opportunities is what you might call the capstone of leadership practices that form part of an effective portfolio for a collaboratively minded pastor of a multicultural parish. It is crucial in creating for multicultural faith communities what Jewell and Ramey call the "total ministering community":

> The ability to create a total ministering community calls for a mind-set in which pastor and pastoral leaders see the community working together as a whole to bring about the mission. Opportunities are created for leaders to work together. The pastor, staff, [parish pastoral] council, and parishioners work together for the sake of the parish community.[29]

CULTIVATING LEADERSHIP PRACTICES

Part of my argument here is that leadership practices really matter in initiating effective and collaborative pastoral leadership at a multicultural parish. Practices are, by definition, things that people do repeatedly until they become expected patterns of behavior that consistently convey a message. The two pastors and their pastoral leadership teams at St. Rose of Lima and Queen of Heaven had to engage in certain practices over and over again to keep alive their credibility promoting a Christian vision of partnership, that is, of communion of all the different cultural, ethnic, and racial groups. We have seen many of those practices in action in these pages:

- Active listening across cultural groups, including both informal listening practices—asking parishioners about parish activities and cultivating wisdom figures—and formal listening practices like listening sessions and town hall meetings;
- Articulating a pastoral vision of partnership across cultural groups rooted in that listening;
- Ensuring that parish leadership adequately *represents* the different cultural groups;
- Assembling a pastoral staff or "executive team" that operates together as one, both dividing up good pastoral practices but also offering consistent messaging in doing so;
- Blessing and authorizing groups, activities, and ministries in all cultural groups;

- Engaging in targeted interventions when parish leaders veer from the common vision of partnership between cultural groups;
- Creating space for distinct racial or ethnic communities to have common experiences of parish life and of Church.

These practices often matter more than factors often cited in conventional wisdom, such as the personality or personal charisma of the priest-pastor. In fact, I would argue that this chapter is not a tale of two charismatic priests whose leadership styles could never be emulated. On the contrary, while both men were generally well regarded by both pastoral leadership team members and parishioners, their personal styles were not universally effective nor welcomed by everyone. Fr. Paul sometimes lacked assertiveness, so much so that difficult people could hijack meetings. Fr. Joe spoke so quickly and so loudly that his intensity alienated people. In reality, there was no hidden genius here or unseen grace of ordination. The leadership practices I have described can be learned and replicated.

Furthermore, I have focused on these leadership practices as performed by priest-pastors because they remain firmly at the helm of most parishes in the United States. In a small but growing number of parishes across the country, there is no resident pastor. In a larger percentage, a single pastor ministers to several parishes, some separated by considerable distances. And not a few pastors and priests are working diligently to build a Church where effective and collaborative pastoral leadership does not depend so heavily on the priest-pastor's authorizing it and pressing for it. Yet as long as the pastor retains his "canonical monopoly" and all eyes look to him, we have to focus attention on how we train and equip the present and future pastors of multicultural parishes. Priests need to learn the leadership practices I have outlined here, practicing the skills that sustain them.

LEADERSHIP AS A PARTICIPATIVE PRACTICE

But the focus on pastors is ultimately a short-term solution. Already in the narrative about Fr. Joe at Queen of Heaven, we saw how crucial it was that his "lieutenants," the parochial vicars assigned to the parish and the lay ecclesial ministry staff, also performed the leadership practices mentioned— listening formally and informally, articulating a common pastoral vision, blessing and authorizing a variety of ministries, intervening, and finding spaces for a common experience of Church—and perform them not only in their own cultural group but across cultural groups. Ultimately, all pastoral leaders have to learn these skills and practices. In a multicultural parish, there is really no space for a lay ecclesial minister or priest who only wants to minister to his or her own people. At stake here is the "theological credibility" bestowed when people see that their parish leaders, like God, show no partiality or favoritism. Ultimately, good parish pastoral leadership in a multicultural setting is not just about "leadership practices," as if a parish were an ordinary business or nonprofit organization. These practices rather, embraced by all, function as a manifestation of a divine love intended for all without distinction. They are at least some of the contours of our participation in the Church as a sacrament of God's love in a divided world. As *Lumen Gentium* reminded us, "The Church is in Christ like a sacrament or as a sign and instrument both of a very closely knit union with God and of the unity of the whole human race."[30]

BIBLIOGRAPHY

Archdiocese of Chicago Office of Research and Planning. "Data Composite: Facts and Figures for the Year Ending 2009." Chicago: Archdiocese of Chicago, 2009.

Baggett, Jerome. *Sense of the Faithful.* New York: Oxford University Press, 2009.

Bennett, Milton J. "Toward Ethnorelativism: A Developmental Model of Intercultural Sensitivity." In *Education for the Intercultural Experience*, edited by R. Michael Paige. Yarmouth, ME: Intercultural Press, 1993.

Bird, Warren, and Scott Thumma. "A New Decade of Megachurches: 2011 Profile of Large Attendance Churches in the United States." Hartford, CT: Hartford Institute for Religion Research, 2011.

Cameron, Helen. *Resourcing for Mission: Practical Theology for Changing Churches.* London: SCM Press, 2010.

Carroll, Jackson. *God's Potters: Pastoral Leadership and the Shaping of Congregations.* Grand Rapids, MI: Wm. B. Eerdmans, 2006.

Derné, Steve. *Culture in Action: Family Life, Emotion, and Male Dominance in Banaras, India.* Albany, NY: State University of New York Press, 1994.

Edwards, Korie. *The Elusive Dream: The Power of Race in Interracial Churches.* New York: Oxford University Press, 2008.

Garces-Foley, Kathleen. "Comparing Catholic and Evangelical Integration Efforts." *Journal for the Scientific Study of Religion* 47, no. 1, 2008.

Garragha, Gilbert Joseph. *The Catholic Church in Chicago, 1673–1871: An Historical Sketch.* Chicago: Loyola University Press, 1921.

Gray, Mark M. "Special Report: Multicultural Findings." Washington, DC: Center for Applied Research in the Apostolate, 2012.

Gudykunst, William. "An Anxiety/Uncertainty Management Theory of Effective Communication." In *Theorizing Intercultural Communication*, edited by William B. Gudykunst. Thousand Oaks, CA: Sage, 2005.

Hennessey, James. *American Catholics: A History of the Roman Catholic Community in the United States.* New York: Oxford University Press, 1981.

Hoover, Brett. *The Shared Parish.* New York: NYU Press, 2014.

Jewell, Marti R., and David A. Ramey. *The Changing Face of Church: Emerging Models of Parish Leadership.* Chicago: Loyola Press, 2010.

Maines, David R., and Michael J. McCallion. "Evidence and Speculations on Catholic De Facto Congregationalism." *Review of Religious Research* 46, no. 1, 2004.

Mateo, Hilda. "Hispanic Ministry and Leadership: Developing Christian Discipleship *latinamente*." In *Hispanic Ministry in the Twenty-First Century: Urgent Issues.* Miami: Convivium Press, 2015.

O'Connor, Jennifer, et al. "Charismatic Leaders and Destructiveness: A Historiometric Study." *Leadership Quarterly* 6, no. 4, 1995.

Ospino, Hosffman. "Hispanic Ministry in Catholic Parishes: A Summary Report of Findings from the National Study on Catholic Parishes with Hispanic Ministry." Boston: Boston College: 2014.

Pew Research Center. "U.S. Catholics: Key Data from Pew Research." Washington, DC: Pew Research Center, 2013.

Putnam, Robert D. "*E Pluribus Unum*: Diversity and Community in the Twenty-First Century." The 2006 Johan Skye Prize Lecture. *Scandinavian Political Studies* 30, no. 2, 2007.

Renken, John A. "Parishes, Pastors, and Parochial Vicars." In *New Commentary on the Code of Canon Law*, edited by John P. Beal, James A. Coriden, and Thomas J. Green. Study edition. New York: Paulist Press, 2000.

Riebe-Estrella, SVD, Gary. "A Youthful Community: Theological and Ministerial Challenges." *Theological Studies* 65, 2004.

Stewart, Edward C., and Milton Bennett. *American Cultural Patterns: A Cross-Cultural Perspective.* Boston: Intercultural Press, 1991.

Thornhill, John. "Influential 'New Ecclesial Movements' Face the Challenge of Inculturation." *Australasian Catholic Record* 84, no. 1, January 2007.

US Conference of Catholic Bishops, Cultural Diversity Secretariat. *Best Practices for Shared Parishes: So That They May All Be One.* Washington, DC: USCCB Publishing, 2014.

Vatican Council II. *Lumen Gentium*, Dogmatic Constitution on the Church, November 21, 1964. www.vatican.va/vat-ii_const_19641121_lumen-gentium_en.html.

NOTES

1. Hilda Mateo, "Hispanic Ministry and Leadership: Developing Christian Discipleship *latinamente*," in *Hispanic Ministry in the Twenty-First Century: Urgent Issues* (Miami: Convivium Press, 2015).

2. My own book *The Shared Parish* (New York: New York University Press, 2014) has tried to bridge this gap, as has a document from the Cultural Diversity Secretariat of the US Conference of Catholic Bishops, *Best Practices for Shared Parishes: So That They May All Be One* (Washington, DC: USCCB, 2014). A number of social scientific studies that include multicultural parishes have also appeared, including Jerome Baggett, *Sense of the Faithful* (New York: Oxford University Press, 2009), and Kathleen Garces-Foley, "Comparing Catholic and Evangelical Integration Efforts," *Journal for the Scientific Study of Religion* 47, no. 1 (2008): 17–22.

3. Jackson Carroll, *God's Potters: Pastoral Leadership and the Shaping of Congregations* (Grand Rapids, MI: Wm. B. Eerdmans, 2006), 25.

4. See, for example, Mark M. Gray, "Special Report: Multicultural Findings" (Washington, DC: Center for Applied Research in the Apostolate, 2012).

5. See, for example, Kathleen Garces-Foley, *Crossing the Ethnic Divide: The Multiethnic Church on a Mission* (New York: Oxford University Press, 2007); Gerardo Marti, *A Mosaic of Believers: Diversity and Innovation in a Multiethnic Church* (Bloomington, IN: Indiana University Press, 2005); and Michael Emerson, *People of the Dream: Multiracial Congregations in the United States* (Princeton, NJ: Princeton University Press, 2006).

6. Charles M. Whelan to Papal Nuncio at Paris, New York, January 28, 1785, quoted in James Hennessey, *American Catholics: A History of the Roman Catholic Community in the United States* (New York: Oxford University Press, 1981), 75.

7. John Mary St. Cyr to Bishop Joseph Rosati of St. Louis, June 1833, quoted in Gilbert Joseph Garragha, *The Catholic Church in Chicago, 1673–1871: An Historical Sketch* (Chicago: Loyola University Press, 1921), 49–56.

8. Hosffman Ospino, "Hispanic Ministry in Catholic Parishes: A Summary Report of Findings from the National Study on Catholic Parishes with Hispanic Ministry" (Boston: Boston College, 2014), 14.

9. Ospino, "Hispanic Ministry in Catholic Parishes," 5.

10. Gray, "Special Report: Multicultural Findings," 6–10.

11. Ibid., 35–36.

12. Pew Research Center, "U.S. Catholics: Key Data from Pew Research" (Washington, DC: Pew Research Center, 2013).

13. Office of Research and Planning, "Data Composite: Facts and Figures for the Year Ending 2009" (Chicago: Archdiocese of Chicago, 2009), 68.

14. William Gudykunst, "An Anxiety/Uncertainty Management Theory of Effective Communication," in *Theorizing Intercultural Communication*, ed. William B. Gudykunst (Thousand Oaks, CA: Sage, 2005), 288.

15. John A. Renken, "Parishes, Pastors, and Parochial Vicars," in *New Commentary on the Code of Canon Law*, ed. John P. Beal, James A. Coriden, and Thomas J. Green, study ed. (Mahwah, NJ: Paulist Press, 2000), 690.

16. Steve Derné, *Culture in Action: Family Life, Emotion, and Male Dominance in Banaras, India* (Albany, NY: State University of New York Press, 1994), vii–viii.

17. Edward C. Stewart and Milton Bennett, *American Cultural Patterns: A Cross-Cultural Perspective* (Boston: Intercultural Press, 1991), 32.

18. This point was also made by the Emerging Models of Pastoral Leadership Project. See Marti R. Jewell and David A. Ramey, *The Changing Face of Church: Emerging Models of Parish Leadership* (Chicago: Loyola Press, 2010), 26.

19. Gary Riebe-Estrella, SVD, "A Youthful Community: Theological and Ministerial Challenges," *Theological Studies* 65 (2004): 302–304.

20. Helen Cameron, *Resourcing for Mission: Practical Theology for Changing Churches* (London: SCM Press, 2010), 1.

21. All of the parish and personal names are pseudonyms.

22. This observation was also made by subjects in the Emerging Models of Pastoral Leadership study. See Jewell and Ramey, *Changing Face*, 24.

23. On "parish shopping," see David R. Maines and Michael J. McCallion, "Evidence and Speculations on Catholic de facto Congregationalism," *Review of Religious Research* 46, no. 1 (2004): 92–101; and Hoover, *The Shared Parish*, 155–156. On homophily in American churches, see Korie Edwards, *The Elusive Dream: The Power of Race in Interracial Churches* (New York: Oxford University Press, 2008), 118–119.

24. Queen of Heaven was part of a different research project I supervised in Los Angeles, funded by a fellowship from the Congregational Studies Team and the Louisville Institute. A research assistant and I had the opportunity to tour Queen of Heaven with a representative from each of the three distinct cultural groups at the parish and then to interview a small group of parishioners from each group. We also interviewed Fr. Joe, two parish staff members, and a parish secretary.

25. There is no widely accepted definition of a megaparish. The term comes from *megachurch*, a mostly Evangelical phenomenon usually defined by churches that have more than 2,000 worshipers on a typical Sunday. See Warren Bird and Scott Thumma, "A New Decade of Megachurches: 2011 Profile of Large Attendance Churches in the United States" (Hartford, CT: Hartford Institute for Religion Research, 2011), 3.

26. Jennifer O'Connor et al., "Charismatic Leaders and Destructiveness: A Historiometric Study," *Leadership Quarterly* 6, no. 4 (1995): 529–555.

27. The Neo-Catechumenal Way is an ecclesial movement founded in Spain in the 1960s. In the United States, it is now largely Spanish-speaking and passionately devoted to evangelizing. It has sometimes been known for operating in tension with traditional parish structures. See John Thornhill, "Influential 'New Ecclesial Movements' Face the Challenge of Inculturation," *Australasian Catholic Record* 84, no. 1 (January 2007): 67–79.

28. See, for example, Robert D. Putnam, "E. Pluribus Unum: Diversity and Community in the Twenty-First Century," The 2006 Johan Skye Prize Lecture, *Scandinavian Political Studies* 30, no. 2 (2007): 141–142; and Milton J. Bennett, "Toward Ethnorelativism: A Developmental Model of Intercultural Sensitivity," in *Education for the Intercultural Experience*, ed. R. Michael Paige (Yarmouth, ME: Intercultural Press, 1993), 21.

29. Jewell and Ramey, *Changing Face*, 80.

30. Vatican Council II, *Lumen Gentium*, Dogmatic Constitution on the Church, November 21, 1964, §1. Accessed September 20, 2013, http://www.vatican.va/.../vat-ii_const_19641121_lumen-gentium_en.html.

Chapter Six

Reimagining the Urban Parish

Leadership Strategies in Mexico City and Chicago

Elfriede Wedam

EDITORS' NOTE

The discussion in this chapter grows out of the author's longstanding academic interest in urban ministry and current focus on community and globalization. She has been particularly interested in the challenges to people's sense of identity and security in an era increasingly defined by social forces that seem beyond the control of the individual. A resident of Chicago, she has in recent years pursued these interests through contacts with Roman Catholic leaders in Mexico City, a study of particular relevance because of the large Mexican immigration to the Chicago area. Her contribution here is an essay that uses her experiences in both cities to compare and contrast cultural settings as well as leadership approaches, theologies, and forms of religious participation, all viewed from the perspective of a sociologist of religion.

Dr. Elfriede Wedam is advanced lecturer in the Department of Sociology at Loyola University Chicago, and research associate at Loyola's McNamara Center for the Social Study of Religion. She is, at this writing, the principal investigator of Project INSPIRE, with oversight of the database of Chicago parishes compiled during the active years of the project. Her areas of research and publication include urban sociology and race and ethnic studies, and German sociology and cultural history.

NEW CHALLENGES FOR PARISH COMMUNITIES

In an examination of the Catholic parish model at Loyola University Chicago, some conferees suggested that territorial parishes no longer work as compelling forms of community. One emerging alternative may be the "ec-

clesial movement:" a fluid, open-ended, temporary, choice-driven set of relationships and activities where entry and exit are easy and frequent. Such
"loose connections," in sociologist Robert Wuthnow's pointed phrase, increasingly describe the ties among citizens of late modernity; they are people
who voluntarily choose the relationships they enter rather than be compelled
by obligations or ascriptive (intrinsic) bonds.[1] These forms of association
honor an individual's freedom to select their affiliations, but are vulnerable
to the fragmentation that results from the indeterminate conditions these
characteristics create. "Loose connections" satisfy but to a point. Nonetheless, what is that point and how does a parish create membership around
structured indeterminacy? What kind of membership does this signify for a
worshipping community?

These are among the challenging questions addressed in this volume, not
new questions, but made exigent under twenty-first-century conditions of
urban and social restructuring amid globalization stresses. As theologian
Robert Schreiter reminded the audience at Loyola that day, in the face of
fragmentation, people continue to search for wholeness.[2] The question of
how to engage in a sharing life is pressing. Consequently, I suggest we need
both a theology of Catholic participation and responsibility, and a theory of
community that addresses voluntarism and obligation.

Using comparisons among three Chicago parishes that have responded to
urban change in different ways, I begin to sketch how community is experienced through different forms of participation in Catholic life. These examples contrast with research from Mexico City where the context of parish life
has been challenged in ways different from the American cases and where
the search for ecclesial responses has also taken a different path. Yet both
settings offer reflections on new struggles and potential insights into the
nature of Catholic communalism. Chicago comparisons highlight three Catholic cases: St. Nicholas of Tolentine Church, a territorial parish (that is, a
parish with responsibility for all the residents of a clearly defined area around
it) on the city's Southwest side that transitioned from predominately European to Mexican ethnicity beginning in the mid-1990s, St. Jerome Church, a
territorial parish on the North side that also transitioned to predominately
Mexican but includes several Latino/a ethnicities as well as non-white ethnicities, and Old St. Patrick Church in the west Loop, also a territorial parish
but one in which a large percentage of active members have joined "intentionally," from outside the parish's official boundaries. It is predominately
European-white with a heavy concentration of American Irish.

The urban context in each of the Chicago parishes varies, suggesting how
areas within cities have different impacts on the institutions located in them.
The urban context of Mexico City is, of course, again considerably different
beginning with the sheer size of a region that contains over twenty-two
million people compared to Chicago's entire SMSA (Standard Metropolitan

Statistical Area) population count of seven million. Nonetheless, the cities share characteristics of density and heterogeneity as well as the creativity and stimulation that such characteristics attract.

MEXICO CITY PARISHES IN TRANSITION

In 2012, I was invited to the *Instituto Superior de Estudios Eclesiásticos*, since absorbed by the Universidad Católica Lumen Gentium (UCLG), in Mexico City to discuss new urban parish models which I investigated in Chicago as responses to the restructuring—social, economic, and religious— that was affecting religious life generally but especially parish participation in urban settings. Researchers from UCLG reported a series of trends that are evident in the United States as well, but the differences in the size of the overall as well as Catholic populations in the two countries obscures some of the urgency that is evident in the northern case. The Catholic population of Mexico City is 84 percent.[3] While there are no reliable figures on the proportion that is nominal, survey results have indicated that about half of the young adult Catholic population between the ages of 12 and 29 is not practicing.[4] The largest segment of this latter group is made up of educated Catholics. Of course, not all Mexican Catholics are looking for involvement in parishes, because they may live too far away from a parish church or for other reasons.

During the Mexico City conference, researchers from UCLG reported several concerns that revolve around the preparation (or lack of it) by the diocese for executing a pastoral ministry adequate for the twenty-first century.[5] Such a ministry is urgently needed, according to this view, because younger educated Catholics have been steadily drifting away from parish participation. But because there are still many younger Catholics attending church, most priests and bishops in Mexico are unaware of or avoid addressing this problem. Thus, as one researcher noted, "If young people have distanced themselves from belief, the church has also distanced itself from young people."

UCLG researchers claim that bishops and many pastors use the language of urban pastoral ministry but do not engage in it; that is, they evidence, in the words of the researchers, "no clue of urban culture." In the seminaries, there is generally a lack of preparation for addressing the needs of better-educated Catholics as well as an inability to address these Catholics in innovative or creative ways. Too many of the seminaries continue training in "traditionalist" (i.e., paternalistic, hierarchical, excessively clerical) modes of relating that hinder lay participation in decision making. Because seminaries offer insufficient pastoral training, little recognition is given to the contemporary social and cultural phenomena of changing urban landscapes. This paucity results in little training in dialogue with laity and insufficient initiatives for laypeople. The urban landscape is an increasingly difficult terrain for pastors in the traditional parish model to navigate, as some pastors estimated their parishes to have as many as 100,000 members and vast distances from one end of a parish to the other.[6]

In 2000, the Archdiocese of Mexico City responded to such problems by establishing a training program through the Center for Formation of Laity for Specific Actions (CEFALAE). Each vicariate housed an office, yet implementation has been incomplete for a variety of reasons and, in the words of one leader, the project was a "failed" initiative. While its purpose was to create education centers for the fostering of lay leadership, a major drawback was the low level of religious education among Mexican Catholics in general, including those who already worked in parishes. For this reason, the bishops wanted to offer these employees a means to improve their religious education, but were hampered by a lack of organization and an overabundance of centers that could not be competently staffed. For example, some parishes were obligated to send a specific number of persons to these centers for training, but these members were actually not much engaged in the parish in the first place. In other cases, pastors lacked pastoral skills, which meant they did not develop working projects for people who came to the CEFALAEs. Currently there are only a handful of CEFALAEs remaining in the diocese. One leader noted, "The diocese is really like a monster. It is almost impossible to adopt a general strategy."

Nevertheless, more than twenty manuals have been prepared to aid laity in pastoral roles, but after three years, no significant changes have been reported. This is despite the view of the researchers that the manuals were generally well done. They are sold in some Catholic bookstores but used in only "a few communities." Thus, those involved in parishes prior to the failed implementation are the same people today and not substantially moving this initiative forward.

In 2007, the Fifth General Conference of the Bishops of Latin America and the Caribbean (held at Aparecida, Brazil, in May of that year), in its concluding document (for which Jorge Cardinal Bergoglio served as chair of the drafting committee), recommended home visits as a missionary strategy. This approach was then implemented in a small number of Mexican parishes. As noted in paragraph 517 of the document, dioceses were directed to "promote the pastoral ministry of welcome to those who arrive in the city, and those already living in it, moving from passively waiting to actively seeking and reaching out to those who are distant, with new strategies such as home visits."[7]

Where it was tried, similar results were found. Gated communities blocked parish staff from gaining access. Aparecida noted the need for strategies that could reach "places in cities that are closed off, such as housing developments, condominiums, residential towers, or those located in so-called slums and *favelas*" (paragraph 518). Often skeptical neighbors were unhelpful because they wished to avoid solicitations by salespeople and evangelists. Because of high mobility among residents, identifying parishioners became difficult. Researchers noted that the diocese employs a variety of house visiting systems, including life- and faith-sharing groups and houses of prayer in which participants focus on prayer and faith formation. A more complex system involves creating "house communities," but these tend to be difficult to establish.[8] Instead practitioners reported that home visits only work as a communal practice when spaces of relevance and empathy are created. By this is meant a threshold of "well-receivedness" that must be met for visits to be turned into living communities.

The challenge is complicated by a concern for the loss of Catholic identity which life in Mexico City's sprawling urban mass promotes. Towns and rural areas anchored this identity in the past but the younger generation is losing it, as I learned from the students in the Urban Pastoral Master's program of UCLG. Some Catholics return to their towns of origin in search of roots, but can they truly recover "memories" they themselves never experienced?[9]

A major challenge reported by UCLG is what they describe as the loss of Catholic communalism. In a study of multifamily units in Mexico City, researchers identified several obstacles in the ability of local parishes to connect with new parishioners in particular. The outer gates to their homes now bar priests who once routinely made home visits to invite new residents to the parish. While this form of privacy can be off-putting to the longstanding practices of parish priests, the larger threat comes more directly from new choices Catholics have exercised, namely to opt for "intentional parishes" rather than territorial ones. For example, some Catholics join parishes near their work rather than their residence. Others select according to liturgical or aesthetic or preaching preferences, similar to what American parishioners increasingly do.[10] But given the more traditional expectations of Mexican priests, these choices are viewed skeptically. This seems to hinge on the question of who gets to decide what it means to belong to a parish or be a *parishioner*. Some priests critique laypeople claiming they are not ready to form community, accusing them of egoism and individualism. Are priests exercising a traditional (perhaps autocratic) form of authority that urban Catholics have learned to reject, or is there evidence that Catholics are rejecting community?

OLD ST. PATRICK: AN URBAN CHURCH

During my visit in 2012, the Mexican researchers became particularly interested in a model illustrated by the case of Old St. Patrick Church in Chicago's west Loop area.[11] While Old St. Patrick's remains a territorial parish (it has not been designated as a "personal parish" as permitted by Canon 518), it is an "intentional parish" by the actions of the majority of its parishioners. Founded in 1846 by Irish immigrants as the first English-speaking parish in Chicago, its recent parish history begins in the mid-1980s. At that time, deindustrialization had emptied the near-in city areas of once-plentiful industrial jobs; therefore, few residences remained within the parish boundaries. A young diocesan priest noted its central location along a major expressway interchange and developed a church survival strategy to reach professionals and others working in the central business district, the Loop, nearby. The new pastor, soon joined by an associate with a similar vision, eschewed the traditional model of service to members and instead asked that Catholics coming to the church immediately engage in some form of mission to others. Young adults were particularly attracted to this form of church, which then became the base for new membership growth.

Because the church is a historic landmark, having survived the Great Chicago Fire of 1871, it could not be razed, and because it was situated in the path of eventual gentrification stimulated by "return to the city" development in and around the loop, the pews were soon filled with middle-class and upper-middle-class members who brought interests and energy channeled into a variety of lay-initiated activities. An important concern of these new members, a host of workplace issues, spurred the parish's formation of the Crossroads Center for Work and Life, while other energies were directed toward service to poor and minority communities nearby. The two leading pastors were known for excellent homilies, good music and liturgies, and openness to the concerns of the laity in the world. Indeed, as members frequently reported, new ideas were typically met with "yes, do it" rather than resistance. For example, the Jewish-Catholic Dialogue Group is an innovative interfaith program entirely founded and run by lay members, including their religious education curriculum for children being raised in both faiths.[12] Territorial boundaries became irrelevant to the self-proclaimed mission of the church, and hence members came from all over the metropolitan region of Chicago, although predominately from the white middle-class areas on the north side and near northern suburbs.

Sociologist R. Stephen Warner has termed this type of church a "de facto" congregation, one to which members *choose* to belong, not because they *must* belong, according to territorial boundaries. American Catholics are increasingly (from about 40 percent to 60 percent, depending on the diocese) choosing their church rather than attending the one within whose boundaries they live.[13] The question that emerges is this: How does choosing change the nature of the relationships that parishes have historically fostered, relationships based in ascribed rather than voluntary community characteristics? In research on Catholic parishes in 1992, Philip Hammond showed that parishes in which the majority of parishioners attended by selection rather than adherence to territorial boundaries were a demonstration of personal autonomy and individual expression that led to low parish involvement compared to those parishes that retained the territorial model.[14] While this is a powerful argument for the value of "traditional" communities, the case of Old St. Patrick's challenged Hammond's findings. At Old St. Patrick's, the voluntary membership base led to the opposite, namely, high parish involvement. Nonetheless, Hammond points to a real concern: What is the consequence for community—and identity—when removed from territory? He argues that territory requires communal obligation and that identity—particularly Catholic identity—is a matter of "fulfilling one's destiny as a baptized Catholic," hence, not a choice. In a follow-up to his masterful study of Catholic parishes in the North after World War II, John McGreevy pointed out that there is a real danger that a religious consumerism based on individual autonomy offers "little resistance to 'absorption by business culture.'"[15]

In Mexico City, pastors claim authority to define parish belonging, resisting the desires of parishioners. As UCLG leaders have observed, while one can request to be registered at a parish of one's choice, it is not readily granted and "the majority of the people do not wait for this approval." Indeed, the critique of the territorial parish is that since it is based on a feudal model, it does not take into account the variety of conditions that have changed the needs of parishioners (including ways in which they experience community) vis-à-vis their parishes (for example, the evolution of the city or current economic pressures that weigh heavily on Mexican Catholics). The 1983 Revised Code of Canon Law, based on Vatican II, reflected an emphasis on parish as community rather than organization or institution.[16] While the 1917 Code Canon 216 tied people to the territorial parish, the 1983 Code Canon 518 provides for personal parishes under four particular conditions, including care of Eastern rite Catholics, language and national origin, and various groups requiring spiritual care such as university personnel, military forces, charismatic groups, and even experimental groups. The Code leaves open the conditions for a personal parish by stating "or even upon some other determining factor." To be sure, the cases in Mexico City on which I am reporting are not "personal" parishes; they are "intentional" parishes, without canonical recognition as such. The Code does not appear to anticipate people choosing their parishes based on their own personal criteria. Nonetheless, the point is, that loyal Mexican Catholics do not feel they have to be bound by a territory—that a sort of "de facto congregationalism" appears to be operating here.

Again the question is raised, can either "personal" or informally designated "intentional" parishes remain communal? Most Mexican pastors argue that the territorial parish provides security, identity, and is irreplaceable as a model for Catholic relationships. There is evidence to support this view. Philip Murnion wrote in 2000 that "the territorial parish brings people into relationships not of one's own choosing."[17] This particular insight identifies a communal potential of the parish that cannot be achieved under the voluntary model. Relationships of choice are vulnerable to the typical dynamics of individual preference, particularly the "homophily principle." Protestant congregations demonstrate these outcomes; they are more often divided by social class and race than are Catholic parishes.[18] Other sociological research has noted this tension, "During a time of unprecedented individualization there is a paradoxical upsurge of interest in the idea of community."[19]

AMERICAN PARISHES IN TRANSITION

Yet new conditions created by the different forms of restructuring facing Americans—economic, social, and religious—beg for amendments that permit Catholics to express their identity as Catholics while simultaneously adjusting to these broader societal demands. Hence, where else can we observe American territorial parishes seeking new forms of community under these conditions? And how do parishes that do not have the benefit of starting with a "clean slate" as Old St. Patrick's did make the transition that would meet the needs of their mobile population while also holding members accountable for each other? Two cases that I studied on opposite sides of the city of Chicago have had a historically tight membership base within their boundaries, yet have worked through some (though not all) of these restructuring challenges.[20]

St. Nicholas of Tolentine Church is located on the southwest side of Chicago in what had been a dense working-class, ethnic neighborhood dominated by Poles, Lithuanians, and Slovaks with some Irish and Italian mixed in. This was a "classic" territorial parish, although their cultural orientation tended to be more "cosmopolitan" in that several ethnicities were represented and active in the parish and Vatican II liturgical renewal was readily accepted. Once the children and grandchildren of the original parishioners began trekking to the suburbs, new immigrants arrived, following the invasion and succession model that Chicago School sociologists predicted in the 1920s.[21] Beginning in the 1960s, the neighborhoods to the east of St. Nick's witnessed the racial and ethnic changes whose responses marked these areas as the bigoted Southwest side. African Americans, Latinos, and Middle-Eastern residents began to move in "like a wave rolling off the lake," and changing, in the words of one pastor, the area's "emotional geography." In other words, the tight social and moral bonds of these predominately Catholic residents in a relatively isolated part of the city had to be reconstructed to include their new neighbors, fashioning relationships for which, until that time, there had been no models to guide them. [22] By the start of the 1990s, large numbers of immigrant Latinos/as moved into the parish and the members of St. Nick's were challenged to create internal community with "others" whose language, cultural habits, and use of the church and school were different from the moral and social order of the original residents. These characteristics were typical of a tight Catholic community that had often resulted in a "defensive Catholicism" vis-à-vis neighborhood changes. Tensions surrounded the institution of the Spanish liturgy. Among other complaints, Poles grumbled that "we didn't get a Polish mass when we asked for it."

A second wave of Euro-white outmigration began in the late 1980s, which stimulated some Catholic leaders to write a new *Theology of the Parish* to address these challenges. [23] Their aim was to explain how parishioners could reshape their Catholic identity from an exclusive one toward becoming inclusive instead. But an important ingredient in this new focus included not merely creating community with newcomers, but realistically acknowledging practical problems of the neighborhood, including needed economic investment and security concerns such as graffiti and increasing crime (whether perceived or real). The authors wrote that "self-interest in the context of the interests of others," is a central theme in Catholic social teaching, which more fully ensures both a moral and a practical foundation for viable community life."

Despite these parish efforts to connect with parishioners across racial and ethnic divides, increasing challenges of economic uncertainty and a second wave of "white flight" required new strategies. In 1994 St. Nick's parish joined the Southwest Organizing Project (SWOP), an affiliated community organization of the Industrial Areas Foundation, to help them understand what to do. Because the focus of SWOP was on institutional networking with both religious and secular organizations, St. Nick's quickly learned that remaining within the Catholic world, as they had done for many decades, was no longer an adequate response to the broader urban restructuring dynamics occurring around them. SWOP emphasized issues of economic development, assistance with housing foreclosures, education, security, and immigration rights. The organization's goal was to stabilize membership within the churches and, hence, the neighborhood. However, they were confronted with the reality that free-market individualism inhibits social justice efforts toward economic fairness, creating instead economic precarity. As James Capraro, the former executive director of the Greater Southwest Economic Development Corporation acknowledged at the time, Catholics are also subject to economic forces they cannot control while remaining seduced by the promise of individual reward. Some stability was achieved but Euro-whites continued moving to the suburbs and the parish grew beyond three-fourths Latino. In addition, parish leaders soon discovered that second-generation Latinos, too, seek their destiny in suburbs, making it difficult for the parish to reroot immigrants. Today, many see the parish as a stopping-off point on the way to greater prosperity away from the old city neighborhoods. At St. Nick's, a degree of economic and demographic stability was achieved over the preceding twenty years. Having survived the financial crisis of 2008, SWOP remains a viable institution. Its mission statement describes SWOP as a broad-based organization that includes churches, mosques, and other institutions.

I briefly summarize a second case, that of St. Jerome Catholic Church on Chicago's far Northwest side, because it offers several additional lessons for this challenge. Unlike St. Nick's with its history of relative isolation on the Southwest side, hampered by a lack of local rail transportation until the mid-1990s, for over thirty years St. Jerome has been part of a diverse and cosmopolitan neighborhood strongly connected to the city. This neighborhood (Rogers Park) maintains its ethnic and racial mix as the most diverse community area in Chicago with comparable proportions of blacks, whites, and Latinos, with a smaller proportion of Asians. Incorporating a Spanish liturgy at St. Jerome's was accomplished in the 1960s by Cuban immigrants and without undue conflict. But difficulties among various subgroups also mark this parish's membership over time. African immigrants/Haitians distinguish themselves from African American blacks; two different ethnic groups—Bosnians and East Africans—mix easily with (white) English speakers (and Africans more so than with other blacks); Mexicans, El Salvadorans, Cubans, and small numbers of other Latino nationalities continue to have tensions, although somewhat less today than twenty years earlier. Sharing a common religious culture helps overcome some differences, for example, through celebrations such as the Via Crucis street procession that enjoys participation from all ethnic groups.

This parish, too, is a transition point rather than a destination point as it was for earlier European immigrants, with high transiency among new immigrants, once again challenging the ability of the parish to reroot people in ways that were once effective. This is the contemporary urban parish dilemma: how to compel commitment on the shifting sands of the new metropolis.

SEEKING MODELS OF URBAN PARISH

Researchers at UCLG (Mexico City) reported that a generation ago, urban ministry efforts focused on rural to urban migration and the transition of agricultural workers to becoming "urbanized." These are no longer the current concerns; instead, urban ministry leaders have urged pastors and parishes to address the cultural and religious pluralism of the city, including the syncretic styles of indigenous religion, which are still popular. "The people separate themselves from parochial communities because these do not correspond to their expectations and real life conditions," reported members of UCLG. Therefore, the question remains of how to retain communal obligations when parish structures do not compel or effectively require them.

In the United States, Catholic parishes still have some of the structural resources (space, infrastructure, organization) that enable a rerooting of social relationships; that is, they are able to create new communities with members in new urban contexts. But rooting is continually challenged by new opportunities in the current urban era, particularly, class mobility and nonparochial school options in an environment that is no longer "defensive Catholicism," a condition that marked much of the history of Euro-ethnic immigration during the "classic," brick-and-mortar, period of American Catholicism. Between approximately 1880 and 1924, anti-immigrant and anti-Catholic sentiment among established Americans provoked a protective reaction among Catholic clergy and laity. Bishops encouraged the building of parochial elementary and high schools and a variety of social activities such as youth sports leagues, radio programs, singing and theater clubs, and other like programs. Increasingly, these Catholic communities built an inward-looking and boundary-drawing Catholic culture that supported the survival of Catholics treated as marginal by mainstream society but also excluded other Americans, particularly those who did not share their ethnicity or race.[24]

As modeled by the "theology of the neighborhood" on the Southwest side in the 1990s, a necessary theologizing of the new cultural experiences of diversity must address ways of overcoming racial and ethnic polarization and exclusion in the Catholic context like that heard in a chorus of concerns declaring, "The 'Spanish' are taking over *our* parish." American parishes are no longer viable independent operations, keen to avoid stepping on another pastor's "turf." Instead, to retain the Catholic presence in the absence of a sufficient number of clerics to lead parishes and, in many urban and rural areas, the absence of a sufficient number of laity to participate in a meaningful communal life requires collaboration between parishes and their pastors, rather than independence and competition. This includes collaboration with secular organizations that also have stakes in the welfare of their areas. A theology of the urban parish can also no longer ignore the economic realities around them, in which the securities once afforded blue-collar Catholics whose union jobs provided a modest but sustainable life and future have all but disappeared. Following James Capraro's lead, incorporating grassroots economic development is on the table for forward-looking parish councils. In current interrelated urban processes, religious structures must address economic ones. Urban sociologist Harvey Molotch recently recommended a "very old-fashioned idea" for helping cities succeed against the "development derby" juggernaut. [25] He counseled that "rather than figuring out how mayors can make their cities better competitors, we should concentrate . . . on how to improve, as directly as possible, the lives of these cities' inhabitants." While he listed parks, good schools, bike lanes, museum walls, and free Internet access as modest but important contributions while speaking to public policy makers, I would suggest that religious structures are interwoven with the urban scene as interdependent resources posing viable opportunities for community development.

CATHOLIC IDENTITY

What is the nature of Catholic communalism today? Given the voluntary nature of religion today, much depends on individual participation, even for cradle Catholics. Catholic identity can no longer be taken for granted. The US Catholic population remained stable since the 1970s due to Latin American immigration, without which Catholic numbers would have mirrored losses recorded among liberal Protestant denominations. Territorial parishes have limitations in size and authoritarian leadership, but voluntary affiliation reduces opportunities for engaging with difference as well as with developing stable relationships. Sociologists have observed the increasing turn toward "loose connections" as the preferred form of relating in many contexts. [26] The argument is that voluntary associations rather than obligatory ties fit better our late modern, upwardly mobile, autonomous, and urbanized population. [27] Electronic media and networking are regularly touted for their ability to connect individuals in new and reliable ways. [28] Social movement organizations, for example, have claimed increased effectiveness in achieving their goals due to better connectivity. Yet deeper emotional communication that results in shared understandings, as Ferdinand Toennies pointed out a century ago, seem to require face-to-face relationships despite the convenience of new media. As Craig Calhoun discovered, community without propinquity appears to result in indirect rather than direct relationships, playing a supportive rather than primary role in our lives. [29] We are still left with the earlier question of how to engage in a sharing life. [30] Sociologist E. Digby Baltzell put it this way, "How can a society institutionalize new social and legal relationships which will best promote a mature and responsible neighborliness appropriate to an urban, bureaucratized, and rational [rather than local and patriarchal] social order?" [31] In both the Chicago and Mexico City settings we noted how Catholic affiliations are strained by the massive social and economic changes of the current era. Catholics today exercise choices of attendance and affiliation unheard of prior to the Second Vatican Council. Membership attrition to evangelical churches and nonpracticing or disaffiliated status are well-documented. I suggest that religious institutions broaden the scope of their mission beyond spiritual goals to address the complex life circumstances (or in Habermas's meaningful phrase, "lifeworld") of current and potential members.

CONCLUSION

In her 2009 American Sociology of Religion presidential address, Mary Jo Neitz observed that rural megachurches (megachurches with low-commitment participation) "may leave some people, church members and not, nostalgic for ways of being together to which they do not wish to return."[32] As Zygmunt Bauman pointed out, we want the joy of belonging without the discomfort of being bound.[33] In this essay, the focus has been on how to anticipate and prepare for the changes occurring in American and Mexican urban parish life under the new circumstances of late modernity. Parishes in the twenty-first century can no longer meet the needs of residents whose everyday lives are lived independently rather than integrally (at least in part) with their Catholic affiliation.

One new model of urban parish is found in the case of Old St. Patrick's Church in Chicago's West Loop area. As an intentional parish, the church is thriving as measured by lay involvement and economic advantage. Its applicability to Mexico may be limited, but the change in church structures that appears to have the greatest potential for reimagining parish life in both nations is the ability of members to choose their affiliation and invest their volunteer time in flexible ways. Intentional or personal parishes are resisted in Mexico much more than in the United States, yet older structures seem no longer suitable to the current times. Authoritarian leadership and low lay involvement remain problematic for both locations, an unsustainable state of affairs. To be sure, personal parishes are not without limitations as voluntary affiliation reduces opportunities for difference. Meanwhile, a territorial designation defines responsibility for all living within its boundaries, hence, a greater likelihood for communalism emerges. Yet progressive change may only be successful in building on the past when current needs are not ignored.

REFERENCES

Bauman, Zygmunt. *Community: Seeking Safety in an Insecure World.* Cambridge, MA: Polity Press, 2001.

Bernard, Jessie, ed. *The Sociology of Community.* Glenview, IL: Scott Foresman, 1973.

Calhoun, Craig. "Community Without Propinquity Revisited: Communications Technology and the Transformation of the Urban Public Sphere." *Sociological Inquiry* 68, no. 3 (1998): 373–397.

Coriden, James A., Thomas J. Green, and Donald E. Heintschel, eds. *The Code of Canon Law: A Text and Commentary.* Mahwah, NJ: Paulist Press, 1985.

Day, Graham. *Community and Everyday Life.* London: Routledge, 2006.

Hammond, Phillip E. *Religion and Personal Autonomy: The Third Disestablishment in America*. Columbia: University of South Carolina Press, 1992.

Hervieu-Léger, Danièle. *Religion as a Chain of Memory*. New Brunswick, NJ: Rutgers University Press, 2000.

McGreevy, John. "Faith and Morals in the U.S., 1865-Present." *Reviews in American History* 26 (1998): 239–254.

———. *Parish Boundaries: The Catholic Encounter with Race in the Twentieth Century Urban North*. Chicago: University of Chicago Press, 1996.

Molotch, Harvey. "Zero-Sum Urbanism." Review of *The Metropolitan Revolution: How Cities and Metros Are Fixing Our Broken Politics and Fragile Economy*, by Bruce Katz and Jennifer Bradley, and *Keys to the City: How Economics, Institutions, Social Interaction, and Politics Shape Development*, by Michael Storper. Public Books, 2014. Accessed February 3, 2014. http://www.publicbooks.org/nonfiction/zero-sum-urbanism.

Murion, Philip. "Parishes and the Public Arena: An Exploration." Commonweal Fall 2000 Colloquium. Accessed October 2, 2014. http://www.esosys.net/pew/papers/fall2000commonweal/murnion/murnionpaper.htm.

Neitz, Mary Jo. "Encounters in the Heartland: What Studying Rural Churches Taught Me about Working across Differences." *Sociology of Religion* 70 (2009): 343–61.

Numrich, Paul D. and Elfriede Wedam. *Religion and Community in the New Urban America*. New York: Oxford University Press, 2015.

"Panorama de las religiones en México 2010." Aguascalientes, Mexico: Instituto Nacional de Estadística y Geografía, Secretaría de Gobernación, 2010.

Park, Robert E. "Community Organization and the Romantic Temper." In *The City*, edited by Robert E. Park, Ernest W. Burgess, and Roderick D. McKenzie, 113–122. Chicago: University of Chicago Press, 1925.

Serrano, Jesus, and Federico Altbach. "Report from Mexico City Research on Urban Pastoral Questions," Universidad Catolica Lumen Gentium, 2012.

Slattery, Michael, and William O. Droel. "Christians in Their Neighborhood." Southwest Catholic Cluster Project. Chicago: Archdiocese of Chicago Office of Peace and Justice, 1991.

Smith, Christian, and Michael O. Emerson. *Divided by Faith: Evangelical Religion and the Problem of Race in America*. New York: Oxford University Press, 2000.

Warner, R. Stephen. "The Place of the Congregation in the Contemporary American Religious Configuration." In *American Congregations, vol. 2: New Perspectives in the Study of Congregations*, edited by James P. Wind and James W. Lewis. Chicago: University of Chicago Press, 1994.

Wedam, Elfriede. "Catholic Spirituality in a New Urban Church." In *Public Religion and Urban Transformation: Faith in the City*, edited by Lowell W. Livezey. New York: New York University Press, 2000.

———. "'God Doesn't Ask What Language I Pray In': Community and Culture on Chicago's Southwest Side." In *Public Religion and Urban Transformation: Faith in the City*, edited by Lowell W. Livezey. New York: New York University Press, 2000.

Wellman, Barry. "Physical Place and Cyber Place: The Rise of Personalized Networking." *International Journal of Urban and Regional Research* 25 (2001). Special Issue on "Networks, Class and Place," edited by Talja Blokland and Mike Savage.

Wuthnow, Robert. *Loose Connections: Joining Together in America's Fragmented Communities*. Cambridge, MA: Harvard University Press, 2002.

NOTES

1. Cf. Robert Wuthnow, *Loose Connections: Joining Together in America's Fragmented Communities* (Cambridge, MA: Harvard University Press, 2002).

2. Education Panel, INSPIRE Milestone Conference at Loyola University Chicago, October 26, 2013.

3. Instituto Nacional de Estadística y Geografía, "Panorama de las Religiones en México 2010," accessed February 2, 2016. http://internet.contenidos.inegi.org.mx/contenidos/

productos//prod_serv/contenidos/espanol/bvinegi/productos/censos/poblacion/2010/panora_
religion/religiones_2010.pdf.

4. "Encuesta Nacional de Juventud, 2005" (Mexico City: Instituto Mexicano de la Juventud, 2006).

5. Jesus Serrano and Federico Altbach, "Report from Mexico City Research on Urban Pastoral Questions" (Mexico City: Universidad Catolica Lumen Gentium, 2012).

6. The archdiocese of Mexico City does not keep membership records. Pastors estimate the number of members through general government records and personal visits, together with laypeople, to those in their territory.

7. http://www.aecrc.org/documents/Aparecida-Concluding%20Document.pdf. Cardinal Bergoglio served as chair of the conference drafting committee. The closing document appears to anticipate language of Evangelii Gaudium, the first Apostolic Exhortation of Pope Francis.

8. Informal communication with Federico Altbach, April 4, 2016.

9. For a provocative view of the connection between tradition and loss of religious affiliation, see Hervieu-Léger, 2000.

10. "Intentional" is not a canonical category; it is defined by choices members make. "Personal" parishes are designated by bishops based on membership which is particular to a defined group such as ethnicity, language, or Newman Centers for college students, and permitted by Canon 518 in the 1983 Revised Code of Canon Law.

11. Elfriede Wedam, "Catholic Spirituality in a New Urban Church," in *Public Religion and Urban Transformation: Faith in the City*, ed. Lowell W. Livezey (New York: New York University Press, 2000).

12. Ibid.

13. R. Stephen Warner, "The Place of the Congregation in the Contemporary American Religious Configuration," in *American Congregations, vol. 2: New Perspectives in the Study of Congregations*, ed. James P. Wind and James W. Lewis (Chicago: University of Chicago Press, 1994).

14. Phillip E. Hammond, *Religion and Personal Autonomy: The Third Disestablishment in America* (Columbia: University of South Carolina Press, 1992), 62–87.

15. John McGreevy, "Faith and Morals in the U.S., 1865–Present," *Reviews in American History* 26 (1998): 248.

16. James A. Coriden, Thomas J. Green, and Donald E. Heintschel, eds., *The Code of Canon Law: A Text and Commentary* (Mahwah, NJ: Paulist Press, 1985), 415.

17. Philip Murnion, "Parishes and the Public Arena: An Exploration," Commonweal Fall 2000 Colloquium, accessed October 2, 2014. http://www.esosys.net/pew/papers/fall2000commonweal/murnion/murnionpaper.htm.

18. Christian Smith and Michael O. Emerson, *Divided by Faith: Evangelical Religion and the Problem of Race in America* (New York: Oxford University Press, 2000).

19. Graham Day, *Community and Everyday Life* (London: Routledge, 2006), 215.

20. Wedam, "Catholic Spirituality," and Elfriede Wedam and Paul D. Numrich, *Religion and Community in the New Urban America* (New York: Oxford University Press, 2015).

21. Robert E. Park, "Community Organization and the Romantic Temper," in *The City*, ed. Robert E. Park, Ernest W. Burgess, and Roderick D. McKenzie (Chicago: University of Chicago Press, 1925), 113–122.

22. Ibid.

23. Michael Slattery and William O. Droel, "Christians in Their Neighborhood," Southwest Catholic Cluster Project (Chicago: Archdiocese of Chicago Office of Peace and Justice, 1991).

24. McGreevy, "Faith and Morals."

25. Harvey Molotch, "Zero-Sum Urbanism," review of *The Metropolitan Revolution: How Cities and Metros Are Fixing Our Broken Politics and Fragile Economy*, by Bruce Katz and Jennifer Bradley, and *Keys to the City: How Economics, Institutions, Social Interaction, and Politics Shape Development*, by Michael Storper, Public Books, 2014, accessed February 3, 2014. http://www.publicbooks.org/nonfiction/zero-sum-urbanism.

26. Robert Wuthnow, *Loose Connections: Joining Together in America's Fragmented Communities* (Cambridge, MA: Harvard University Press, 2002).

27. Zygmunt Bauman, *Community: Seeking Safety in an Insecure World* (Cambridge: Polity Press, 2001).

28. Barry Wellman, "Physical Place and Cyber Place: The Rise of Personalized Networking," *International Journal of Urban and Regional Research* 25 (2001), special issue on "Networks, Class and Place," ed. Talja Blokland and Mike Savage.

29. Craig Calhoun, "Community Without Propinquity Revisited: Communications Technology and the Transformation of the Urban Public Sphere," *Sociological Inquiry* 68, no. 3 (1998): 373–397.

30. Cf. Bauman, *Community: Seeking Safety*.

31. E. Digby Baltzell, as quoted in *The Sociology of Community*, ed. Jesse Bernard (Glenview, IL: Scott Foresman, 1973), 189.

32. Mary Jo Neitz, "Encounters in the Heartland: What Studying Rural Churches Taught Me about Working across Differences," *Sociology of Religion* 70 (2009): 352.

33. Bauman, *Community: Seeking Safety*.

Chapter Seven

A Crisis of Trust, a Crisis of Credibility, a Crisis of Leadership

*The Catholic Church in Germany in
Quest of New Models*

Andreas Henkelmann and Graciela Sonntag,
Translated by Robert Schreiter, CPPS

EDITORS' NOTE

For more than a decade, the CrossingOver program has linked the Archdiocese of Chicago with several dioceses in northwestern Germany and became associated with Project INSPIRE early in the history of both programs. (See our Introduction for more information about CrossingOver.) The association introduced a number of the authors of this volume to both the similarities and differences between the situations of parishes in the two countries, and to the exciting possibilities for mutual learning. Strong collegial relationships have followed, among German and American theologians, sociologists, historians, and pastoral ministers. In this chapter, two of our German colleagues examine cases of parish reorganization and leadership initiatives in the dioceses of their area, raising both strong critique and grounds for great hope for the Church, in Germany and elsewhere.

Dr. Andreas Henkelmann served as research associate for CrossingOver (www.crossingover.de) from its origins in 2003 until 2016, and has also been managing director of the Zentrum für Angewandte Pastoralforschung, the Centre of Applied Pastoral Theology (ZAP) in Bochum (www.zap-bochum.de). He studied Catholic theology and history in Vienna, Münster, Tübingen, and Bochum. His current *habilitation* work focuses on the history of lay ecclesial ministers in Germany and the United States.

Ms. Graciela Sonntag has been a research associate for the CrossingOver program at Ruhr University of Bochum since 2011, also serving as a pastoral associate for the Diocese of Münster in Germany. She studied Catholic theology and mathematics in Münster. Her doctoral dissertation in pastoral theology offers a comparative study on the future of lay ecclesial ministry and its contribution to the pastoral work of the Church in the United States and in Germany.

Robert Schreiter, CPPS, is Vatican Council II professor of theology at Chicago Theological Union. He holds a theological doctorate from the University of Nijmegan. He is past president of the Catholic Theological Society and of the American Society of Missiology, and for twelve years served as theological consultant to Caritas Internationalis. He is the author of several books including *Constructing Local Theologies*, republished by Orbis Press in a thirtieth anniversary edition, 2015.

INTRODUCTION

On Friday February 20, 2015, a house tour occurred in a provincial German town that, if the scope of news reporting is any indication, the whole country had been waiting for. Officials guided fifty journalists in six groups, the first outsiders to view the private spaces of the residence of the Bishop of Limburg. The diocese's motivation for this unusual press conference was well known: the freestanding bathtub, the walk-in clothes closet, and the pond for the koi carp stood symbolically for a bishop who in the meantime had come to be known only as "Bishop Bling-Bling." The guided tour through the dwelling was supposed to demonstrate that the new diocesan leadership wanted to make a clean sweep in the hopes that with openness and transparency a fresh start would be possible.

Opening up the private quarters made clear that the scandal around Franz-Peter Tebartz-van Elst had not just done enormous economic damage to the diocese; the deeper problem was rather loss of authority and credibility. If one looks back over other cases, above all the 2010 resignation of Walter Mixa, the Bishop of Augsburg, and furthermore the sexual abuse scandals, the case of Tebartz-van Elst was just the most recent high point of an ever-more dramatic crisis of leadership for the entire ecclesiastic officialdom. This crisis has to do with the question of how to exercise credible Church leadership, be it at the diocesan, parish, or any other structural level.

In this chapter we present a thematically organized examination of the question from two different perspectives. In the first step, we offer an analysis of the Church crisis in order to identify, against this background, the leadership problems. The second section deals with two possible paths to resolve the leadership crisis at the level of the parish, paths that diverge diametrically. One is a model of the megaparish, called colloquially in Germany the "XXL-Parish." The other is a model of community leadership according to canon 517.2. Continuing the clothing-size metaphor, one might call the latter the "XXS-Parish." One thing is clear regarding these models: while there are no clear solutions, there is reason for hope.

ANATOMY OF THE CRISIS

"Church in Crisis: Diaspora Germany—Is Germany a Christian Country?"[1] "Even the Churches in Bavaria are in Crisis"[2]; "Commentary on the Crisis of the Churches: Scandals Are Not the Main Problem"[3]: headlines like these have marked reporting about the Catholic Church in Germany not just in recent years, but for decades. Already in the 1960s articles like "Church in Crisis: Faith in Fraternal Trust Remains" were the rule rather than the exception.[4] The current crisis therefore has a long pre-history and yet has another dimension from the one in the 1960s.

Let's begin with the prehistory. If one proceeds from a few statistics, there was as yet no crisis in sight at the beginning of the 1960s. Let us take as the beginning date the year 1963. Regular Church attendance of all Catholics was at 55 percent against 51 percent in 1952.[5] Likewise, the number of priestly ordinations or of those leaving the Church did not differ dramatically from the 1950s. But beneath the surface, there was already a social change under way in the first half of the 1960s that would completely change the character of the Church in Germany.

During the *Kulturkampf* struggles in the second half of the nineteenth century, when different liberal and nationalistic governments attempted to impose restrictions on the Catholic Church's influence on its faithful, a Catholic milieu pervaded many Catholic-majority regions of the country—a subculture with its own code of values and structures that shaped the lives of most Catholics from cradle to grave. But beginning in the 1950s a change of values overwhelmed all segments of society, including the Catholic milieu. After the Economic Miracle—a period of unprecedented economic growth and prosperity—and the consequences that flowed from it, there came a material saturation so that norms such as discipline, reliability, obedience, or subordination, especially among the younger generations, were repressed or overlaid with postmodern values of self-development such as emancipation, autonomy, or participation. The continued existence of distinct cultural segments of society was thus basically put into question, as these depended on individuals who, as a matter of course and without much deliberation, assimilated into them by way of the family, the neighborhood, the school, or the association. This taken-for-granted nature was already widely lost in the second half of the 1960s, as would become dramatically evident in two events during 1968.

Immediately after its appearance that July, the encyclical *Humanae Vitae* evoked a widespread storm of protest that would erupt in September at the

Catholic Congress in Essen. Among other things, the criticism coming from younger Catholics was directed not only at what they considered to be an obsolete sexual morality; it was also leading toward demands for a democratization of life within the Church. The year 1968 made clear that younger Catholics were no longer willing to follow Church leadership unconditionally, but rather wanted to see the norms and values of their generation anchored within the Church, or else they would leave the Church. They perceived the traditional leadership style, based purely on the hierarchy and the clergy, as alienating and off-putting. They felt encouraged in their wishes and conceptions by the Second Vatican Council. One could maintain that the ecclesiology of *Gaudium et Spes*,[6] ushered in theologically the demise of the self-contained Catholic milieu.

Much has been written about the Church's successes and failures after the Council, but from a historical perspective, there has been little research. To blame the Council for the miseries of our own time, as is often and eagerly done from a conservative point of view, comes up too short. The radical nature of the change in values is underestimated, and the significance of some of the standard indices of Catholic life mentioned above is misjudged. The numbers for Church attendance before and after the Council, for instance, can only be compared in a limited way, because the underlying motivations had changed in the meantime. Social as well as intra-Church pressure decreased. Those who go to Church now do so because they want to, not because it is expected of them by their spouse, neighbors, family or the parish priest, as was normal during the times of the Catholic milieu.

But it is also the fact that nearly all the indices have been sinking continually since the middle of the 1960s.[7] In the beginning of 2013, Church attendance was at 10.8 percent. Also, the total number of Catholics is declining. This is so for two reasons. First, we should note the high number of those leaving the Church, over 100,000 people per year since 1990. In 2010 and 2013, the number of departures reached nearly 180,000. Associations with the abuse scandals and the discussion around Bishop Bling-Bling are unmistakable. Second, the number of baptisms continues to plummet. In 1970 there were still 456,070 baptisms, outnumbering 369,852 funerals. In 2013 baptisms amounted to 164,664 in contrast to 230,000 funerals. The reasons for this development lie not only with the decline in the total number of children but also in the increasing disinterest in baptism itself even among parents who themselves had been baptized. Especially, couples who have not been married in the Church are often no longer inclined to present their children for baptism.

The precipitous decline in baptisms allows us to understand challenges the Catholic Church ultimately faces in the area of finances. Already in 2003, profound financial crises confronted most German dioceses. Clear declines in church tax (*Kirchensteuer*) revenues were primarily caused by the economic crisis, rather than by people leaving the Church.[8] Nearly all dioceses had to tighten their belts, lay off personnel, skimp on renewing infrastructure or even dismantle infrastructure by, for instance, closing church buildings. Such austerity measures are history, and thanks to the stabilized employment figures, church tax revenues are high. But the resurgent revenue levels are unlikely to last, even were the economic situation to remain secure, because the number of Catholics paying the church tax will continue to decline. Expenditures, therefore, must decrease in the middle term. Putting the right steps into place will be a complicated task, because nearly all German dioceses have hired a large number of lay ecclesial ministers[9] so that the total number of pastoral personnel has only decreased slightly despite the decline in number of priests. Furthermore, this decline has not begun slowing to a halt. The ranks of diocesan and religious clergy sank from 18,663 in 1995 to 14,490 in 2013. The number of priesthood ordinations is likewise declining when compared to the 1990s. In 2013 the number of newly ordained priests stood at 98.

The declining number of priests was cited as one of the most important reasons for a path-breaking decision announced in 2005. Felix Genn, then the Bishop of Essen, announced that, against the background of the economic problems with which nearly all dioceses had to struggle, there would be a fundamental restructuring of his diocese. In the period immediately following the announcement, the number of parishes was reduced from around 270 to 43. Many of the former parishes, though retaining their own church buildings, were classified as substructures of one of the 43 parishes. But in 96 cases, the former parishes completely vanished and the diocese decided that no further funds could be allocated for the church buildings.[10] The transformations throughout the Diocese of Essen started a trend. Up to the present time all dioceses have undertaken restructuring in a similar fashion; in many dioceses the process is incomplete or likely to begin again, given the further diminishing number of priests.

The restructuring processes continue to meet much resistance, but also have their supporters beyond the diocesan administrative offices, because these supporters see in them greater possibilities for pastoral ministry more suited to the present times than the old small-scale structures. Background to this can be found in, among other places, the so-called Sinus-Milieu Study.[11] In the study, social subcultures were classified according to their lifestyles and value orientations, and then related to the more classical ratings of lower, middle, and upper classes. The study has been conducted several times at irregular intervals, but in 2005 researchers structured it in reference to religion and church. The results revealed what many had intuited in their everyday experience: of the ten milieus studied, only three were classified as open to the Catholic Church. The study proved in this way that the parish communities were very narrow with regard to the social and cultural background of their members. The Sinus-Milieu Study was repeated in 2013 and came to the same conclusion, clearly revealing increases in the number of unchurched Catholics.

At the same time, in the face of so many studies showing a falling off of church affiliation, one should not get the impression that there are no indications of a turnaround or of continuity. While there may be encouraging signs, a single reliable model for the Church of the future is not yet discernible. Perhaps it is a sign of our times that there will not be such a model; rather, the Church must learn to live with a plurality of diverse models.

The problems we have raised indicate in any case that an essential challenge consists in finding a new style of leadership. This becomes especially clear in the face of the profound loss of credibility by the clergy due to the flood of scandals (which automatically puts in question the authority of all leaders in the Church, even when they are laypersons), compounded by the enormous challenges arising from the restructuring processes. How shall parishes at the scale of 20,000 Catholics be led? With what models of leadership should structures within the parish work?

If one wants to find credible and also realistic answers to these questions, one must consider two further background issues. For one, a distinctive co-responsibility of the laity has been further developed in the German Church since the Second Vatican Council. At the parish level, it is to be found in the *Pfarrgemeinderat*, the parish council.[12] Study and discernment are in order, as to whether such an entity can do effective work in a megaparish, and whether it can have a future as an elected body when voter participation in many dioceses is under 10 percent. However, it is certain that from a theological point of view there cannot be, in any case, a way around a distinctive participation of laity in leadership. This is compellingly indicated because— to raise the second issue—a purely hierarchically oriented model that places authority exclusively in the ordained ministry is no longer convincing in a society that puts strong value in personal development and self-determination, and places a very high value on democracy. Without pressing for relativizing the specific theology of ministry, it is nonetheless evident that church models of leadership will encounter serious obstacles to acceptance if they do not possess plausibility in the social and cultural context. We will now deepen these general observations.

STEPS TOWARD SOLUTIONS AT THE LEVEL OF THE PARISH

Since the 1990s German dioceses took different paths to guarantee the pastoral care of local churches in light of the ever-increasing shortage of priests. In essence, two sorts of solutions have been put forward. Both meet the requisites of canon law, albeit in different ways.

Many (arch-) dioceses (e.g., Essen, Münster, and Berlin) instituted structural reform, at first envisioned as cooperation among several parishes overseen by a so-called community of parishes or a pastoral care unit, which ultimately required a parish priest to lead the pastoral activities of the community and be responsible to the bishop. This widening of the territory for pastoral care, within which there could still be several quasi-independent communities, ended up in many places with decisions to merge originally freestanding parish communities into parishes that today may include up to 40,000 Catholics. For this reason they have been dubbed "XXL-Parishes."[13] The nearly arbitrary expansion of the territorial bounds of a parish is possible because canon law does not specify anything as to limitation of territorial size, let alone the appropriate number of members. Dioceses such as Limburg, Aachen, Munich, Mainz, and Freiburg tried going in another direction. They have deacons and laypersons participating in the leadership of parish communities by following canon 517.2, which makes provision for priestless parishes as an extraordinary and temporary measure.

From a legal point of view both steps are seen as "legitimate" solutions to managing a looming leadership crisis caused by a dearth of priests. Their effectiveness is measured above all by their pastoral theological conditions and also, alongside all the challenges they pose, the opportunities they open up. We shall illustrate by way of examples.

PARISH LEADERSHIP BY LAYPERSONS, FOLLOWING CANON 517.2 OF THE 1983 CODE OF CANON LAW

> If, because of lack of priests, the diocesan bishop has decided that participation in the exercise of the pastoral care of a parish is to be entrusted to a deacon, to another person who is not a priest, or to a community of persons, he is to appoint some priest who, provided with the powers and faculties of a pastor, is to direct the pastoral care. (canon 517.2)

Regarding the practical application of this canonical determination, it is not insignificant that the history of its origin exhibits clear parallels to an ecclesiastical praxis in Latin America during the 1960s. Even then, the bishops of Latin America were "in search of a new and more intensive presence of the Church in the current transformation of Latin America in light of the Second Vatican Council."[14] Very soon after the Council, creative processes of change were set in motion regarding the question of parish leadership. The priest shortage spurred rethinking of structures in Latin America, and later in Germany. In other words, the canon can be seen as the implementation of a concrete experienced praxis—not as a strategy that may in any way be taken for granted with regard to canon law.

The application of the new law in Germany can be deemed as rather cautious. It received a variety of interpretations. Confronted early on with the priest shortage because of its scattered population and far-flung communities, the Diocese of Limburg implemented a model of parish leadership according to canon 517.2 in about fifty parishes between 1995 and 2008. The responsible person was, as a rule, a full-time worker, most often a theologically studied and trained layperson (normally a professional lay ecclesial minister, in German a *"Pastoralreferent"* or a *"Gemeindereferent"*), installed alongside a moderator-priest.[15] As a bit of prehistory it should be mentioned that especially in the case of the Diocese of Limburg, but also in other dioceses since the 1970s, full-time laypersons, for all practical purposes, were already serving as actual parish leaders or were entrusted with central tasks of leading parishes. A different interpretation of canon 517.2 may be found in the Diocese of Aachen. There a whole team, entrusted for the pastoral care of a particular parish, carries out the canonical provision. The team consists, as a rule, of a lay ecclesial minister, a priest moderator, and volunteers elected from the parish community.

Behind these efforts lies the idea that for a viable parish (and that means in a narrower sense a parish unhindered in its fundamental characteristics as a local church community), there is no need to legally dissolve it just because, for the time being, no priest is available to entrust with the leadership. There is an explicit presupposition in this approach: a community should be maintained only if it is also able to function. So regarding parishes, the constructed social context meets the characteristics of what pastoral theologians call the Community Principle. In most instances what lies behind this Community Principle is an image of a lively community with a large number of groups and volunteers. The governing idea is "closeness."[16] The location of the parish in a certain village or a certain neighborhood in the city is essential to its identity. The principle, therefore, is only to be considered for parishes of several thousand Catholics at a maximum. It is plausible in contexts with clear social homogeneity and thus the desired closeness, more often the case in rural areas rather than large cities. In cases where physical closeness is marked by a highly diversified social range (for example in midsized and metropolitan areas), the pressing question becomes, To what extent are parishes of this type able at all to offer a pastoral program matched to a modern (or post-modern) society, in which distinctive social subgroups are no longer tied to particular neighborhoods? The Sinus-Milieu Study had previously noted this question.

That this parish leadership model is no panacea becomes evident with another problem. In places where the participation of the faithful is low and the Church performs its ministry as a service provided by full-time personnel, a model of leadership along the lines of canon 517.2 will not work because it requires many active volunteers who express a sense of ownership for their parish. The decision for a leadership according to canon 517.2 has to be supported by the parish itself. The path that seeks participation in pastoral care by non-full-time personnel, as chosen by the Diocese of Aachen, presents a hopeful option. It emphasizes that the Church is borne by the place, and on this basis all those baptized and confirmed have the capacity to be called upon to share the pastoral responsibility.

That this can be a very promising path to follow was demonstrated in the summer of 2008, when three such canon 517.2 parishes were surveyed in the Dioceses of Aachen and Limburg. There was clearly great satisfaction with these moves, among those in charge and those who were engaged in the ministry of their parish communities, as well as among parish members who did not participate in parish life or who experienced it "from outside." The wide endorsement reflected certain conceptions and expectations of Church, reflected in how pastoral ministry was shaped.

These expectations confirm the picture, sketched above, of a parish where the canon 517.2 model could fit. It portrays a Church that is present to a place and because of that can be part of people's lives. Such a leadership model can be experienced insofar as the Church strives to take seriously its location in a given place and its commitment to that place. Opinion surveys in the parish communities revealed that people expected the Church to provide a personal presence as well as a flexible and continuous temporal presence. The attraction of this parish leadership model lies in its potential to help the Church realize "closeness" to the people, "because it lives in social proximity with the people."[17] The problem stated above remains. It is questionable whether such an image of a parish community fits everywhere and at all times, thus whether all people want to live in social proximity, or whether there is not a danger here of glorifying a golden past with the Church at the center of the city neighborhood or the village.

It is important to continue to consider how canon 517.2 may hold open the possibility of thinking about the Church community in a more comprehensive way, rather than just as represented by the clergy or full-time professionals. This view permits, precisely, a better understanding of whom to entrust with participation in pastoral care without putting essential qualities of ordained ministry into question. As indicated, the Diocese of Aachen has already moved in this direction by entrusting leadership in such parishes, not to a single deacon or full-time layperson, but rather to a team, one that to a significant degree may also be composed of volunteers delegated by the parish community.[18]

Up to now, however, this is more vision than reality. Applications of canon 517.2 have come from initiatives of single bishops and tend to be implemented rather controversially as emergency responses to the priest shortage. To date there appears to be no consensus within the German Bishops' Conference, where not all bishops express openness to the practice. It contradicts the theological conviction of some individual bishops that the application of canon 517.2 undermines the constitutive and non-negotiable meaning of the priestly office. It is notable that not even a general discourse on experiences with alternative leadership models has been taken up within the Bishops' Conference. The necessary engagement requires a great deal of courage, but today's German bishops have an example they could follow from the Latin American bishops at Medellin in 1968. The occasion for them was entirely in the sense of the Council, the effort "to renew and to create new structures in the Church that make possible an ongoing dialogue and ways for cooperation of bishops, priests, religious, and laity." [19]

MERGER INTO AN XXL-PARISH

Other German dioceses have embarked on an alternative resolution of parish leadership in light of the priest shortage: merger. Several freestanding parishes (in the Diocese of Essen, the highest number was eight), each with its own pastor, are brought together in a new megaparish and the diocesan bishop names a single priest as pastor. The territorial principle of a parish, which served as the guiding principle in the previously discussed case of parishes led according to canon 517.2, gets due recognition and so formally stays in place. But it is strongly relativized, if not even undermined, as a principle. For the bigger the territory, the more impossible it becomes to understand it as homogeneous and to generate comprehensive modes of pastoral care for the whole territory that cover all the needs that the older kind of parish tried to address. As a matter of fact, in an XXL-Parish territorial boundaries extend out to such an extent (with up to 40,000 Catholics, as for example in the Diocese of Essen) that many of those involved keep questioning whether the Church can be understood as a "Church in this place" ("*Kirche vor Ort*"), a Church that lives the lives of people in their immediate environment. In the sense of a parish family that is shepherded by a pastor, the Community Principle no longer applies.

For some the XXL-Parish is unacceptable from the perspective of a theology of community. For others it carries with it a challenge in a positive sense. For the expansion of the territorial (and social) boundaries offers an opportunity often not fully appreciated: a merger process can also lead to breaking up starkly parochial community structures that have been constricting in nature or, in other words, tendencies toward petrifaction. [20] The new possibilities offer pathways that can lead out of the narrowing milieu of the Church, which we have already described. In the new and larger space of the XXL-Parish, closeness or, rather, presence of the Church could be realized by the Church being inserted in distinctive life-spaces where human beings may be found, and not by asking people to come to church because it is "so centrally located and just around the corner." "Decentralized" is a key term in the new kind of parish. And in this idea there is another opportunity: being decentered in its best sense promotes networking and stronger participation on everyone's part. However, this requires a new leadership style and a pastoral policy of cooperative facilitation.

Following this line of thinking, the parish can be conceived as a network in which the individual nodes of Church presence (such as a daycare center, a hospital, a small Christian community, or a youth group) are seen as fundamentally equal in rank. Church happens where the baptized and confirmed present the Christian message on their own initiative in local and personal modes of expression, connecting with other people and enabling them to enter into other nodes in the network. The task of XXL-Parish pastoral teams is to coordinate this networking of initiatives and new structures of participation. Full-time leadership is charged with facilitation and promotion of such short- and longer-term networking structures within the territory of the XXL-Parish.

Of course as a rule, mergers come with a reduction of resources (real estate and finances) and paring back of personnel. But it also can be shown that pastoral teams consisting of the parish priest, lay ecclesial ministers, and deacons (directors of Church music and social workers may be counted into this as well) become larger teams with multiple competencies. The networking activity of such a team presumes, on the one hand, large measures of cooperation, communication, and transparency. On the other hand, the larger team makes possible a sorting out of responsibilities according to strengths and weaknesses. Not everyone has to be a "jack of all trades," as was previously the case in very small parishes where one person had to cover all the areas of pastoral endeavor. "Points of concentration become possible and a charism-oriented deployment of personnel comes into the realm of the possible."[21]

SUMMING UP

It should have become clear that neither model of leadership—a parish led according to canon 517.2 or the XXL-Parish—represents a real solution as long as it is understood as a way to "manage" a shortage of parish priests or as an emergency solution with the intention of continuing the Church in the old way. Conversely, the two paths that German dioceses have blazed each open new opportunities, if they are taken seriously, to consider a new way of being Church—a way that is oriented by the Conciliar theology of the People of God and thus values the responsibility and participation of all the baptized and confirmed in Church mission. Both approaches toward leadership must prove themselves against this background. Such a legitimacy problem is also a quest for a new leadership style less founded upon a functional sense of leadership than it is, above all, upon two decisive criteria that return to the renewing Church a perceptible, credible form. One criterion for such a leadership style is the multiplicity of individual strengths resulting from cooperative leadership that consequently also makes the participation of many people possible. The second and possibly even more decisive criterion consists in understanding leadership as a leadership of service. Those who lead with a servant attitude pursue development of the potential they see in others. A Church led in this twofold manner would be a serving Church that acknowledges multiplicity that would then be aligned with its original mission.

Against this background neither of the two approaches to an alternative leadership of the local Church is ultimately better than the other. Each has its justification and certain potential for realization from place to place. And each must be measured against the message of Jesus. They are, to be sure, an instrument for carrying out the missionary task of the Church, namely to go out to all people and bring them the Good News. This is well described in the words of a parish priest of a merged parish in Recklinghausen (Diocese of Münster). In his letter about the merger to the parish community, he wrote: "We bear responsibility—in these changing times—that God will be present also in the coming generations in this city, in the way Jesus Christ spoke of Him. And this parish community presents itself to meet this responsibility of carrying out this biblical task."[22] What is valid for a merged parish community (in Recklinghausen) also holds true, of course, for a parish led according to canon 517.2. What remains, however, is the question of the creativity of the German dioceses as they work with both instruments.

RECOMMENDED LITERATURE

Böhnke, Michael, and Thomas Schüller, eds. *Gemeindeleitung durch Laien? Internationale Erfahrungen und Erkenntnisse.* Regensburg, 2011.
Gabriel, Karl. *Christentum zwischen Tradition und Postmoderne.* Freiburg in Breisgau, 2000.
Warode, Markus, Bernd Schmies, and Thomas M. Schimmel, eds. *Veränderung als Chance begreifen. Fusionsprozesse in Orden, Kirche und Gesellschaft.* Band 2: *Erfahrungsgeschichteaus Orden und Kirche.* Münster, 2013.
Unfried, Andres, et al. *XXL Pfarrei. Monster oder Werk des Heiligen Geistes?* Würzburg, 2012.
Vatican Council II. Pastoral Constitution on the Church in the Modern World, *Gaudium et Spes.* December 7, 1965. http://www.vatican.va/archive/hist_councils/ii_vatican_council/documents/vat-ii_const_19651207_gaudium-et-spes_en.html.

NOTES

1. *Frankfurter Allgemeine Zeitung*, December 29, 2014, http://www.faz.net/aktuell/politik/inland/krise-der-kirche-ist-deutschland-noch-ein-chrisliches-land-13342759.html.
2. *Die Welt*, February 28, 2015, http://www.welt.de/regionales/bayern/article135704083/Selbst-die-Kirchen-in-Bayern-sind-in-der-Krise.html.

3. *Die Welt*, April 26, 2010, http://www.welt.de/debatte/kommentare/article7328706/Skandale-sind-nicht-das-Hauptproblem-der-Kirche.html.

4. *Die Zeit*, March 11, 1966, http://www.zeit.de/1966/11/die-kirche-in-der-Krise.

5. All the statistics given here are from http://dbk.de/zahlen-fakten/kirchliche-statistik.

6. The Second Vatican Council's Pastoral Constitution on the Church in the Modern World, *Gaudium et Spes* was promulgated by Pope Paul VI on December 7, 1965.

7. All the statistics given here are from http://dbk.de/zahlen-fakten/kirchliche-statistik.

8. The term *Kirchensteuer*, "church tax," is easy to misunderstand. It refers not specifically to the Catholic Church or to Christian churches in general but to all religious communities with the status of a corporation of public law, like the Jewish synagogues, and it is of course possible for such corporations to opt out of it (as do some very small Christian denominations in Germany, such as the United Methodist Church or Church of Christ, Scientist). The term "tax" is also misleading, as it is not a national tax paid by all Germans but only by the members of the religious communities with this status. It is called "tax" because the assessment is bound to the income tax (church members have to pay 8 or 9 percent of their income tax as church tax) and because it is collected together with the income tax by the state, which receives a fee for this service. It is also, of course, possible for individuals to opt out of the tax. The German dioceses understand such a decision as a formal renunciation of the Church, but this is highly controversial—Pope Benedict XVI rebuked them for this position.

9. Professional lay ecclesial ministers are either *Pastoralreferenten* (PR) (with an academic degree comparable to that of the priests) or *Gemeindereferenten* (with shorter studies; usually these ministers work in a parish). In contrast to the United States they are hired and paid by the dioceses and not by the parishes. There are 3,171 PRs and 4,526 GRs.

10. The fates of the church buildings were very different. Some of them were torn down or converted into other buildings. A few are still used as churches with the help of private funding. For other church buildings, some of which remain under protection as historical monuments, no solution has yet been found.

11. Sinus is the name of a research institute in Heidelberg which is working on societal and cultural change in Germany. Their customers are both commercial enterprises and nonprofit organizations.

12. The term *Pfarrgemeinderat* (PGR) is difficult to translate, as there are some differences from the parish councils in the United States. It has to be noticed that the parish council as discussed in the 1983 Code of Canon Law (CIC 1983 §536) is *not* the reference point. After first attempts in different dioceses, the national German synod (named usually after the town where it met "*Würzburger Synode*") passed in May 1975 a resolution which was used by almost all German dioceses for the installment of the new council. In that way the PGR became mandatory for all parishes. In contrast to the parish council of the CIC 1983 it also has the formal right to pass resolutions. This formal right is in many ways restricted. The PGR, for instance, cannot decide on the budget of the parish. Another mandatory body has responsibility for these issues, a finance council, which is usually called "*Kirchenvorstand*."

13. Currently the parish of St. Urban in Gelsenkirchen-Buer, with its 38,000 members, *is* Germany's largest parish.

14. The Second Plenary Assembly of the Latin American Episcopal Conferences in Medellín, quoted following Böhnke, "Gemeindeleitung," in Böhnke and Schüller (eds.), *Gemeindeleitung*, 12, which presents the legal historical perspectives of this model of parish leadership.

15. Cf. Schüller, "Partikularrechtliche Umsetzung," in Böhnke and Schüller, *Gemeindeleitung*.

16. [Editors' note: The term "closeness" connotes both physical proximity and social intimacy.]

17. Böhnke, *Gemeindeleitung*, 29.

18. "Wenn das Leitungsteam zum Pastor wird,"*Aachener Zeitung*, March 6, 2015, http://www.aachener-zeitung.de/lokales/region/wenn-das-leitungsteam-zum-pastor-wird-1.1041724.

19. Second Plenary Assembly of the Episcopal Conferences of Latin America in Medellín, as cited by Böhnke, *Gemeindeleitung*, 12.

20. Parish priest Andreas Unfried reports effectively on his experiences with the merger process into a "community of a new type." He sees opportunities in the XXL-Parish that are being described here further. Cf. Andres Unfried et al., *XXL Pfarrei. Monster oder Werk des Heiligen Geistes?* (Würzburg, 2012).

21. Unfried, *XXL-Parish*, 145.

22. Jürgen Quante, "Fusion," in *Veränderung als Chance begreifen. Fusionsprozesse in Orden, Kirche und Gesellschaft*, Band 2: *Erfahrungsgeschichteaus Orden und Kirche*, ed. Markus Warode, Bernd Schmies, Thomas M. Schimmel (Münster, 2013), 60.

Chapter Eight

The Local Communities of Poitiers

Reflections on Their Reflection

Reinhard Feiter,
Translated by Robert Schreiter, CPPS

EDITORS' NOTE

The Archdiocese of Poitiers, France (about two hundred miles southwest of Paris) has become well known over the past twenty years, especially in Europe, for its innovative approach to the reorganization of its local church communities. Faced with dwindling numbers, rather than simply replacing parish priests with deacons, sisters, or trained lay ministers, the archdiocese—through a remarkably participative synodal process—made a momentous decision: they turned to canon 516.2, which allows a bishop to devise "another way" of providing pastoral care when parishes cannot be established or maintained. With priests assigned to "pastoral sectors" throughout the archdiocese rather than to parishes, and working with a pastoral council in each sector, local communities were given space to form within the sectors without direct reference to any particular physical plant or preestablished boundaries. Instead, the principle was that each community must be able to provide, and regularly renew, its own leaders for the three essential responsibilities of Church (to proclaim the Gospel, to pray, and to serve fellow human beings), as well as for material management (a treasurer) and overall coordination (a "pastoral delegate"). These local leaders are either called to their ministry by the pastoral council of the sector in which the community is located (in the case of the first three), or they are elected by the local community itself (in the case of the last two). Together, they form a team (*équipe*) that is formally installed as a delegation of the archbishop himself. Once installed, however, these leaders accept the serious responsibility not only of fulfilling their assigned tasks, but of identifying and calling others to their own roles of service and leadership in the local community.

The Poitiers experiment has been much admired in Germany, where it has influenced a number of dioceses' reorganization plans and sparked a great deal of pastoral discussion. Prof. Dr. Reinhard Feiter (see the biographical note below) has collected and translated a number of articles by pastoral leaders in Poitiers that had been previously published in two French volumes. The authors include the archbishop himself and several of those who have worked closely with him in establishing and developing this new pastoral approach. The chapter presented here is a translation from the German of Prof. Dr. Feiter's own commentary on these articles—what he means by "Reflections on Their Reflection." Prof. Dr. Feiter is particularly concerned with examining the meaning and implications of the Poitiers approach for the Church in Germany, but his insights and explanations help to make the overall approach accessible and in many ways are applicable to North America and other contexts as well.

The English translation of Prof. Dr. Feiter's German text has been provided by Prof. Robert Schreiter, CPPS (Chicago Theological Union), with some alterations for style and clarity by the editors. Translation of the French passages cited by Prof. Dr. Feiter has been made directly from the French originals by Prof. William A. Clark, SJ (with thanks for assistance from Prof. Thomas Worcester, SJ, College of the Holy Cross). In those few instances when the insertion of a few explanatory words within the text itself seemed advisable, these insertions are marked with square brackets. To assist the reader in understanding the context and meaning of certain passages, a number of "Editors' Notes" have also been added among the endnotes. Readers will be alerted to the presence of such explanatory notes with a parenthetical "see Editors' Endnote" before the relevant note number in the text.

Rev. Prof. Dr. Reinhard Feiter is professor of pastoral theology and religious education and director of the Institute of Pastoral Theology at the Faculty of Catholic Theology of the Westfälische Wilhelms-Universität, Münster, Germany. Prof. Dr. Feiter, a priest of the diocese of Aachen, studied Catholic theology in Bonn and Würzburg and earned a doctoral degree in Catholic theology (Dr. theol.) in 1993. His *habilitation* in pastoral theology followed in 2001. Since 2004 he has held the chair of pastoral theology. His ongoing research studies the development of parish life as well as pastoral work of the Church in France and its impact on pastoral theology and practice in Germany.

POITIERS: A MODEL?

The language of Archbishop Albert Rouet is always engaging and clear. But at some points he becomes very energetic, as when he comes to speak about imitations of the local communities of Poitiers:

A number of places claim to do "the same thing as in Poitiers"! Looking more closely, however, one notes important differences: the elections are done away with, and the priest alone appoints those to be responsible [for local ministries], the appointments do not have a fixed term, not all the important functions are guaranteed. . . . Such places act according to their own understanding and possibilities. Let them say, then, that they are inspired by [our] local communities, not that they are doing the same thing! [See editors' explanatory notes for author information and for further explanation about the arrangement of endnotes for this chapter.] [1]

This harsh reaction could stir up the feeling that the way the Diocese of Poitiers has dealt with its local communities is by no means uncontested. [For an important background point, see editors' explanatory note.] [2] Nothing endangers innovative pastoral methods in the Church so much as truncated imitations. Nothing burdens the "original" more than its being evoked and at the same time deviated from, by being put in place by others in an unreflective manner or set up prematurely.

Whoever goes into the reports and reflections from Poitiers in a deep and attentive manner will affirm, rather, that nowhere are these local communities recommended as a model *for* other local churches. Indeed they are never spoken of *as* models at all. . . . If the word "model" is used at all [by people from Poitiers], it is used in a critical manner. They speak of a "parish model" that has come up against its limits, [3] of a "clerical model" no longer functional in current contexts [author information in editors' explanatory note], [4] or a "model of an autonomous association" [5] inappropriate for an ecclesial community. It is denied expressly that the local communities comprise a "model" that would lead one astray into dreaming. [6]

What's behind this? Why the reluctance? Jean-Paul Russeil gives an indication by referring to the 1996 letter from the French Bishops' Conference "Presenting the Faith in Today's Society," where it says: "One world is being erased and another is emerging, without there being any pre-determined model for its construction." [For author information, see editors' explanatory note.] [7] But what does that mean? Are the Diocese of Poitiers and the local communities, the bishop, the councils, executives, priests, deacons, men and women in recognized ministries acting without a plan? No one would claim that if they had read the texts brought together here. [For context, see editor's explanatory note.] [8] In its *scope* the planning, organization, and development of pastoral structures evidently does not lag behind German dioceses, which, however, might be judged to be rather bureaucratic. But it could be that the *manner* in which the structures [in Poitiers] are put together and activities are organized is different.

If, therefore, Poitiers is presented in our German pastoral contexts as encouraging and stimulating, and if the local communities unavoidably take on the traits of a model for our own seeking and questioning, then of course concerns about that perception and its reasonableness require us to attend to Archbishop Rouet's reproach. The question is, Just how might the "model" character of the local communities of Poitiers provide new ways of community formation in Germany? In what follows, I try to give some answers to this question. This involves reflections on the reflection of the local communities that are documented here. (I make a selection of them.) That I am interpreting the presentations of the French authors goes without saying. I try to characterize the local communities in two separate rounds. The first round goes more thoroughly into the mode of action that the Archdiocese of Poitiers is trying to discern; the second round focuses more directly on individual elements in the process.

EXPERIENCE

Un nouveau visage d'Église ("A New Face of Church") was the title of the first book on the local communities of Poitiers, published in 2005 [see the works cited at the end of this chapter]. It is taken up again as the subtitle of a second volume, published in 2008, *Un goût d'espérance: Vers un nouveau visage d'Église* ("A Taste of Hope: Toward a New Face of Church"). In German one might speak without further reflection of a "new" face of Church and its way of doing things. That would not be incorrect, but it would be inexact. In doing so one loses the difference between *neuf* and the word used here, *nouveau*. It is the difference between "new" and "a new kind of"—not everything new is a new kind of something.

When the ways of doing things in Church life and pastoral activity change—something that is going on in German dioceses right now, where parishes are being merged or in various ways brought together into larger pastoral units—one needs to distinguish between "reproductive" and "productive" changes. When something new is brought forward, it may call forth a new way of doing things. The reports and reflections from Poitiers are showing us just what that means.

A New Way of Acting

By "reproductive changes," I mean that the "new" arising from these changes remains within preexisting procedures, oriented toward preestablished standards. What we call "the parish" is an example of such an established procedure, with its standards of measurement, as presented in the *Code of Canon Law*, canon 515.1:

> The parish is a certain community of the Christian faithful stably constituted in
> a particular church, whose pastoral care is entrusted to a pastor (*parochus*)
> under the authority of the diocesan bishop.

Reproductive action is on display when several previously independent parishes, each lacking its own pastor because of the shortage of priests, are put together into a new, larger parish, so that the canonically prescribed condition is reestablished: the "community of the faithful" so created once again has its own pastor.

The Church of Poitiers has taken a different path. The decision was made against "centralization"[9] and also against canon 517.2 (which so far has been the path that Germany has adopted—or at least what is always being discussed as the way to solve the problem):

> If, because of a lack of priests, the diocesan bishop has decided that participation in the exercise of pastoral care of a parish is to be entrusted to a deacon, to another person who is not a priest, or to a community of persons, he is to appoint some priest who, provided with the powers and faculties of a pastor, is to direct the pastoral care.

Archbishop Albert Rouet writes this about the possibility of nonpriests sharing in the pastoral responsibility for the parish:

> This permission locks us into a choice: either the exercise of pastoral responsibility flows necessarily into images of the lone parish priest, an idea which must evidently be rejected, given the multiple pastoral engagements that spill over territorial boundaries; or else we must recognize that this is only a temporary solution for a time of shortage, and ultimately unsatisfying.[10]

Instead of that, Poitiers suggests a way[11] already envisioned in canon 516.2:

> When certain communities cannot be erected as parishes or quasi-parishes, the diocesan bishop is to provide for their pastoral care in another way.

The path Poitiers has chosen has a double characteristic: the bishop remains personally responsible for the given community, since there is no priest who represents him in this charge or has responsibility as pastor. [See editors' explanatory note.][12] At the same time, the bishop gains the freedom to guarantee pastoral care—of course including a priest—in another way than in the traditional model of parish and parish priest.

Finding/Inventing Goals and Rules

From a pastoral-theological point of view, what is electrifying is that this is a *productive* rather than a *reproductive,* way of proceeding. That is to say, what happens here is not just pursuing goals and applying rules that already exist, but rather seeing the solution in finding and inventing new goals and rules. The local communities are the sites where this happens or, more precisely, each are the event in which it takes place.

Setting up local communities represents something other than subdividing a parish. The "sector" as pastoral unit in the Archdiocese of Poitiers is not the same as a megaparish, or an association or cooperative of parishes like those that are being or have been set up in Germany. [For background, see editors' explanatory note.][13] So if German dioceses try to subdivide their larger pastoral spaces, in which a priest functions as pastor, in order to somehow retain the old closeness and manageability of the parish community in the new large entities, and if in doing so they appeal to the local communities in Poitiers, then they are doing what Albert Rouet criticizes. In Poitiers it is about closeness—the local communities are even called "communities of closeness"[14]—not in the sense of closeness within the communities themselves, but closeness to others in the village or city neighborhood.

New kinds of goals and rules emerge in the local communities. The formation of the "basic team" (*l'équipe*) from members who are on the one hand *elected* in the local community, and on the other hand are *called* by the pastoral council is an example of how new rules are invented in Poitiers.[15] As an example of finding new goals, one can cite the saying, "The entrusted task is not a goal in itself."[16] It is not a matter of people managing predetermined tasks and positions, but rather of becoming active in ways corresponding to their abilities and moving along their personal journey of faith. [For author information, see editors' explanatory note.][17]

"It's Happening" and "That's How It's Going to Go"

Of course, productive action does not come as a flash of genius. Reports from Poitiers expressly state that the local communities did not fall from heaven, but rather have a prehistory.[18] They were not the invention of an individual, but owe their existence to a synodal process,[19] which is itself part of "the long development of a form for the Church of which, so far, we can perceive only the first features."[20] For whoever is looking for goals and rules in the process of productive change will, strictly speaking, not know *what* they are looking for.

Nevertheless, productive action is not without orientation and has some standards. What is *not* immediately available are preexisting standards, established patterns of action or *instructions* which can be applied from the outside as criteria for whatever practices are emerging. An example would be the prescription that in the ordering of a parish it must have "its own pastor." Rather, productive action latches onto—finds its guide in—*key experiences*. By these are meant experiences that one has for oneself, *in the midst of action*, that become decisive *for* action. In Poitiers these are the experiences of the basic teams. [See editors' explanatory note.][21] Indeed, the reports of the local communities make especially clear what key experiences actually are, precisely experiences that say, "It's happening," and, "That's how it's going to go!"

For example, such a key experience was the discovery of "It's happening!" when after three or six years—contrary to all prophecies of doom—

successors were found for the various positions in the basic teams.[22] That is not just any kind of success. Rather, the local communities discovered how they function and, through that, one of their very essential innovations: that successors were found happened *only* because people were asked, people who in the milieu of the old parish would simply not have been considered potential candidates for a ministry. So, "That's how it is going to go!"[23]

All this has an important consequence: renewal is not "made," but is experienced. Reproductive action is tendentiously activist and manipulative of life, whereas productive, creative changes that arise out of key experiences emphasize what is unexpected and can lead to a turnaround. This realization runs like a thread through the collected reports and reflections from Poitiers: those who together make up a local community must experience a turnaround. They must give up old certitudes and truisms, and experience at the same time what they did not hold to be possible either for themselves or for others.

For this reason it is also not accidental that the texts from Poitiers recount experiences over longer periods of time. To get on the trail of such procedures and changes one has to tell stories. Narrative is not merely a quirk of style with these authors. Rather, narrative is that style of pastoral reflection that corresponds to a productive action and promotes it. This happens in an exemplary way as Gisèle Bulteau carefully picks up and assembles the (prototypical) experiences of the basic teams. [For context, see editors' explanatory note.][24] In this way there comes into existence something of a "model" or rather a picture of a local community's self-realization. Productive action does not need instructions; rather, it produces an *example.*

Between Violation and Advance

In established ways of doing things, of course, one can relatively easily find what is "wrong" and "right" because standards have been formed that can be applied to action. But the *example* is a moment at the origin of a new way of acting.

A consequence of this is that the "old" and the "new sort of way" stand asymmetrically toward each other. One cannot compare the "new sort of way" as "old" is compared to "new." For a "new sort of way" that emerges is viewed as an "advance," but when viewed from the old way of doing things it is considered a "violation." To that extent the "new sort of way" has not yet been embedded in a new way of doing things and come to be considered "normal"; it will still have the character of a deviation from the older way. It is somewhat "unorderly." Concretely, according to the old way of thinking, that the vacant position of the parish pastor has not been filled with a parish priest has necessarily to be considered a violation in the logic of a parish. What is coming to be in and among the local community—that the vacant position of the parish priest is not filled and also the role is not taken up by laypersons or is slipped into various parts of their roles—brings about a new definition of the roles of *all* who participate in ministry.

That is why the struggle between the old and the new sort of way is both unavoidable as well as difficult to arbitrate. For on the basis of the old way, the new sort of way can neither be made intelligible nor can it be adequately justified. The new sort of way can only justify its own basis with hesitation, and can only be justified after the fact. As Éric Boone puts it, there remains a chasm:

> At this stage, a double desire moves us—these approaches testify to it: from the start, to hear the questions being addressed to us, taking them seriously, modifying our practices, and adjusting our attitudes; and then to ground our pastoral choices and think through our ecclesiology. In a context in which so many questions seem pressing and are presented as urgent, it seems to us fundamental to value a certain slowness which gives useful time for the reflection that should accompany our missionary zeal. In this way, we try to take seriously our historical condition, with its opportunities and limitations. [25]

The words of Boone make it clear how precarious this situation is. There is a lack of legitimation, at least within a certain time frame. The new must first emerge and find itself; this takes time, and it must be given time. Because the new sort of way breaks with what has been handed down, it carries with it the danger of being brought to a halt by greater or lesser acts of violence.

LEARN

Reading the texts from Poitiers brought to mind a story that Martin Buber passed along in his collection of narratives of the Hasidim: Levi Yitzchak of Berdichev seeks out a famous rabbi against the will of his father-in-law, and undertakes a long and potentially expensive journey. When he returns home, his father-in-law wants to know what the journey has accomplished and what Levi Yitzchak has learned. Levi Yitzchak answers: "That there is a creator of the world." The father-in-law stops the first passer-by and asks him if he was aware that there is a creator of the world. The passer-by answers affirmatively. But then Levi Yitzchak retorts: "Sure, everybody says this, but have they learned it?"

In the reports and reflections from Poitiers there is a lot of "what they all say": The Church is not there for itself. All believers by virtue of baptism and confirmation are called and charged with the proclamation of the Gospel. Office in the Church is always a ministry. A community is always and only a community together with other communities. Persons are more important than structures. But all this and much more of "what they all say" appears, in the journey of the Church of Poitiers, also to be "learnable." In what follows, I would like to point this out by way of a few seemingly "external" examples: organizational rules and concepts used [in Poitiers].

The Mix of Democratic and Hierarchical Ways of Proceeding

"The [formal] act of institution cannot 'come up from the base,'"[26] Archbishop Albert Rouet has said. It is a matter for the bishop to inaugurate the local communities and to erect each one of them. On the one hand, the Archbishop acutely recognizes and articulates here that such a decisive change as the local communities represent could not be brought about from a grassroots democratic action. The introduction of the local communities is carried out by the bishop with the vote of the councils in the diocese. On the other hand, by this decision the bishop makes clear his commitment that the teaching of the Second Vatican Council regarding the equal dignity of all the baptized is not only a "teaching" but is also translated into a concrete ecclesial reality.

> For many years, people tired themselves out helping the priests, giving service. Their long and faithful perseverance did not draw anyone to follow after them. Such service, as admirable as it is, does not bring about freedom in the Church.[27]

That there is volunteer engagement in the local communities does not distinguish them from the traditional parish in France or in Germany. It has been there and continues to be there in manifold ways in both places. There are also points of departure and connection for the formation of a local community.[28] What is different here is the "transition from helping to taking responsibility,"[29] which is initiated by the performative act of the bishop that then reproduces itself in a certain manner. Thus, the first or perhaps the foremost task of a person who, for example, has the responsibility for proclamation in the local community, is not to attend to this responsibility alone, but to recruit other persons in the community for the ministry of proclamation.[30] That is to say, their first task is the care of others in the community so that formation of community takes place.

Something similar happens in the formation of the basic team when those charged with pastoral ministry and those charged with the material needs are elected *in the community*; those charged with evangelization, with prayer, and with ministry in the neighborhood *are called by the pastoral council of the sector*. Here the real, theological meaning of the so often misunderstood concept of "hierarchy" is demonstrated. Put simply, the action of church governance does not mean deciding about all and everything, but rather means bearing the concern that the community fulfills those functions without which it is not a Christian community: proclamation, celebration of the liturgy, and care for those who are in desperate need or in difficult circumstances.

The Interplay of Local Community and the Sector

Above all, the interchange between local community and sector, between the basic team [in the local community] and the pastoral council of the sector, is of far-reaching significance.[31] This interchange ensures that the local communities do not mutate into mini- or quasi-parishes, understanding themselves juridically and factually as autarchic [self-governing] entities.

"No local community is an island," writes Bulteau,[32] and also at another place, "A community is not its own horizon. It is situated in a pastoral sector."[33] The bonds with the rest of the local communities of the sector as well as with the movements and associations and ministries in the sector, the collaboration of the sector in the formation of the basic [local] team, the representation of every basic team in the pastoral council of the sector, the coordination of the pastoral work in this council—all this ensures and supports that the local communities do not cut themselves off from one another.[34]

As Rouet puts it, "A parish naturally dreams of having everything."[35] But that is precisely not the meaning and purpose of the local communities. It is worth listening once again to the "dial tone" coming from Poitiers:

> The myth of juridical autonomy [of a parish] has engendered a pastoral independence. By contrast, a local community claims nothing but the good will of the people. It can meet at one home or another. It lives in visible poverty. And this is a good thing![36]

> This poses a real problem of faith. If we confuse the life of the Church with a contingent organization, the way the fall of Rome before the barbarians was taken to be the end of the world (and not of an era), then poverty appears as a dereliction in which God abandons his own. To preserve the same structures as the past, we are ready with all sorts of subterfuges: finding replacements, being less stringent on the criteria for priestly ordination (piety is enough). . . . In this case, poverty is a catastrophe: what becomes of the first Beatitude?[37]

I know that there is a great danger of spiritualizing the various forms of shortage and how they are shaping the situation in Germany, or of glamorizing the relevance of the shortages as the will of God. One should note, however, that in Poitiers (in contrast to Germany) there is no talk of a shortage of the *faithful.* "It is not that we are lacking in Christians, but that they lack confidence in themselves."[38] Nor does the shortage of priests constitute the reason for establishing local communities. These arise, rather, from the desire to build communities on the basis of the sacraments of initiation, of baptism and confirmation.[39] And under these two presuppositions, the short-age—or more precisely the lack of *one's own* possibilities—becomes in fact an important moment for building Church. What *are* lacking are the others without whom life cannot be shared. "It is important to avoid there being only one community in a sector for too long a time: with whom could they share?"[40] Thus a "spirit of mutual recognition"[41] grows and so do other ways of functioning in the community: a basic team is formed. "The responsibility to be exercised is shared, for practical reasons certainly (dividing tasks, not feeling alone with the responsibility, etc.), but equally from a theological and pastoral perspective: we are never the Church by ourselves."[42] What has to be done has to be achieved together. Faith happens in community, and the Church is a community of communities.

The priest is not someone alone either, although the office of pastor has promoted this conception or form of life and work. Setting up local communities is not about creating a Church without priests. Rather, it brings about a different form of priesthood. Here again the local communities have something to learn, something that no one contests theoretically, but which is not always well depicted in praxis: that the priest belongs to a presbyterate, that is, to the community of priests of a diocese that stand alongside the bishop "in the exercise of the mission they have received."[43] "Sent from elsewhere into the community, the priest prevents it from closing in on itself and continuously opens it to the apostolic dimension."[44]

At the same time, by doing this, the priest is of course also kept from lording it over the faith of other believers (cf. 2 Cor 1:23). His task is to serve the community of faith and the community among the communities.[45] In this way the celebration of the Eucharist in the communities becomes what it really is: it binds together the celebrating community with Jesus Christ *and* the other communities, together with whom it builds up the Church.

"Closeness"

There is something else very near to, indeed inseparably bound up with, this view and way of building the Church as *koinonia*, as a community of communities: "The local community keeps its horizons open for all women and men who expect ministry from the Church."[46] "It is indeed to this that the Council invites us when it says that the Church ought 'to be in the world and that she lives and acts with it.'"[47]

The question, "Bishop, what is to become of us?" was not the question of a parish without a pastor, but rather the question that the mayors in the villages of the Poitou would always ask the new bishop of Poitiers. [For context, see editors' explanatory note.][48]

Reinhard Feiter

The rural communities had seen the closure of streetcar lines, then of local
trains; bus services had been thinned out, except for school buses (themselves
a sign of the "pedagogical regrouping" which included the closure of many
schools). The postal service closed offices. Merchants in the smaller towns
lowered their curtains and the supermarkets, often modest, were attracting
customers to the main town of a region. . . . Overall, a climate of depression
struck the communities, who otherwise had done all they could to animate the
population and restore their churches. A network of human relationships was
unraveling.[49]

Setting up the local communities—first in the villages and later also in the
cities—was and is intimately bound up with the question of the lives and the
togetherness of the people, among and with whom the Catholics of the Diocese of Poitiers live. They share their life experiences, needs, and desires (cf.
Gaudium et spes, 11). The local communities constitute a "change of place"
for the Church insofar as they no longer are located at the center.[50] The
Church no longer lives as a corporate entity around which others are
grouped: people of no faith, people of other faith, or people who are church
members, but hardly take part in what is commonly called "community life."
Rather, the Church in the local communities discovers precisely the opposite:
that its life is to be close to the people in the village or city neighborhood.

Actually it is a quite simple thing that shows up again and again, and so is
learned in a very basic way: that community (*communio*) and mission (*mis-
sio*) belong together. The community of the faithful is not an end in itself, but
has a mission: to bear witness to the call of people to a life in and from
community with the triune God (*mysterium*): "the Church is in Christ like a
sacrament or as a sign and instrument both of a very close knit union with
God and of the unity of the whole human race (*Lumen Gentium,* 1)."[51] Here
the "goal" is also the "method," namely to create community and to share life
up to the very limits of birth and death.[52]

For this reason, the third dimension of the local community for which
every basic team carries responsibility alongside proclamation and prayer is
closeness. A "ministry of closeness" may sound odd. Why not just speak of
caritas or *diakonia*? Because here it is not about *caritas* or *diakonia* as a
function or as one of the community's ministries *alongside* others, but a
different self-understanding that changes how we act and, even beforehand,
how we access people's real needs. The French authors use the phrase, that
the life of the community is "inscribed" in the social and civic life.[53] Jean-
Paul Russeil explains:

What is close is not just the neighborhood. One can be a neighbor and a
stranger. . . . It is above all encounter and exchange that create closeness. This
mode of presence in a given place engages the depths of the faith in the

incarnation. The faith takes flesh in a given community in a [particular] place.[54]

The local community thus becomes a way of living in solidarity in the concrete life-spaces of people.[55] The reports and reflections from Poitiers are not silent about how demanding such closeness and solidarity is, but they nevertheless testify to how much vitality and real concrete help grows from these qualities in the local communities.

"Call"

I touch here upon a final point that needs to be addressed, because it is not only fundamental for the local communities, but also elementary: the "culture of the call."[56] It is elementary in that it is captured in entirely smooth gestures and in equally simple rules.

The five members of the basic team are given a commission for three years, a commission that may be renewed for at most three more years.[57] The meaning and purpose of this regulation is first of all that no one taking over responsibility for the local community end up becoming someone who is understood to be always there, or as a matter of course takes over the work of whatever comes along, and so builds up power in a special area of service and in the community as a whole. This prevents something that one can observe in German parish communities: someone becomes "indispensable" so that the rest of the people in the community are unburdened because they are relieved of responsibility, even though they are dissatisfied. For the respective person, many times a family, and many times even a "dynasty," assures that the desired ministry is performed, but in a way that blocks change and development, and above all, keeps other, newer people from "getting in the way."[58]

Of course, this is only the negative side. The positive side of fixed-term commissions is certainly also the manageability of the task for anyone taking it on. This also highlights the changes that are reshaping volunteer engagement today. Yet the consequences of having to find new people over and over again to take on these responsibilities have an even greater significance. Three—even six—years pass quickly. So local communities and the sector are forced to permanently look out for and ask people, and soon to have to ask even those who have not been previously "positioned." Trust must be built up: trust in people, trust in the abilities that are dormant within them, trust in the development that taking over responsibility will call forth from them.

This is not blind trust that fails to result in genuine recognition. A "discerning of spirits" is required here, both of those who are called to ministry and of those who are there as baptized and confirmed.[59] Again and again, the need for support and training is emphasized. Nonetheless, because of this elementary rule the local community becomes in a fundamental way a community that asks, that prays, that encourages. It becomes above all attentive to others and begins to question itself, to have experiences of being called and confirmed in an area of ministry, and to seek a language for this experience. Gisele Bulteau describes this in detail in her contributions. [60]

At this point a small parenthetical remark is necessary. Because of their financial situation, a French local church is not usually able to entrust pastoral ministry to someone on a full-time basis in a way similar to German dioceses that have their lay theologians and other laypersons with some professional training. [For background, see editors' explanatory note.][61] Nonetheless, such does happen; there is no fundamental rejection of professionalization in pastoral ministry. One thing, however, that the Diocese of Poitiers tries to avoid is giving assurance of "long-term permanence" to those who take over the tasks of recognized ministries because of the lack of a parish priest. Rather, all ministries, whether imparted by ordination (as priest or deacon) or through a commissioning letter of the bishop, are "in the service of developing the capacity for responsibility [in ministry] of all the baptized."[62] Professional ministers may not suppress ministries of the faithful in local communities—ministries that they have by virtue of their baptism and confirmation. Rather, the professional ministers' function is to support them. That could be called a "professional de-professionalization." Professionalism is placed here in service of the ministry so that the mission of all the baptized and confirmed is not allowed to wither due to the presence of professional oversight and responsibility. Rather, the professionals' task is the opposite: that more and more of the faithful come to perceive their own vocation.

It is precisely in this that the "call" described in the contributions and reflections from Poitiers truly comes to light. It is about more than "keeping communities running" by continually filling vacant ministry positions. Indeed, it is not about "seeking executives for predetermined positions."[63] Above all, "Even if the way of faith passes through tasks that need to be accomplished, it does not end there."[64] In the end, it is about the personal faith of people and the simple fact that faith is a gift that wishes to be received. Or to use the central biblical metaphor taken up in Poitiers: responding to faith is responding to a call. Jean-Paul Russeil explains:

> "Not that we are competent of ourselves to claim anything as coming from us; our competence is from God. . . ." (2 Cor 3:5) Who has never discovered unimagined possibilities, and yet at first felt themselves incapable of answering the call? Often we think that we are called because we are able to respond. For the Apostle, the reverse is true. It is because we are called that we become capable of responding. [65]

It is the call that makes the response possible. What is fundamental for faith, however—what makes it able to be experienced and able to be learned by the person who is so spoken to and called upon—is to participate in one way or another in the local community.

It is the call that makes the response possible. What is also the case is that the response comes to life in a person as the givenness of the call received. The Christian vocation has a "dialogical structure."[66] God's call seeks the human being's free response, and that is also realized in a very concrete manner:

> Of course, some people respond in the negative to the call they are given. Their choice is always carefully considered and the call taken seriously. Overall, we notice that, even if it is refused, a call has its effect.[67]

Naturally the call is intended to lead to service. "In the Scriptures there is no 'call-response event' without [the receiver] being sent. The stories of call speak clearly on this matter."[68] Thus in the local communities of Poitiers a request is always made for a particular service. The reports from Poitiers are very clear on this point, in order to clarify that such a request can be about a very "small" ministry. For this to succeed, it is vital that someone be approached about an as yet unnoticed need for help that they can tackle on their own: "It is precisely the fact of being called that elicits a responsible freedom and a quality of initiative."[69]

The call that has been heard, in which being addressed and having a claim made upon me coincide, and to which I am unable not to respond, is the "zero point" of human freedom:

> He who is not called is not able to arrive at his human responsibility. She is not able to discover her capacities, because there is no one to reveal them to her. His "yes" or "here I am" has not been called forth. No one calls herself to life, no one gives himself his name. . . . Every human life is thus made up of responses to calls. In this way, all of life is vocation.[70]

From all of this it is understandable why Gisele Bulteau would express her conviction, in the title of her contribution in the second book, that the local communities represent a way "of becoming ever more human." [For context, see editors' explanatory note.][71] That this does happen, and that community is the very way to it happening, is and remains bound up with "a de-centering of oneself"[72] for others.

SO IT GOES

The exemplary quality of the local communities of Poitiers or, more precisely, of the reflections of those who participated in their founding and their
journey, consists, from my point of view, in their showing *how* new sorts of
pastoral paths are discovered and *how* a community "model" *can* come about
that is not new wine in old wineskins.

These texts, which have appeared over the course of three years, also give
a look into that process by which the new kinds of ways are stabilized, or
how new types of experiences, in the course of time, create a new way of
doing things. Finally, they are also an astonishing witness to a local church
not only seeking solutions in difficult times—such as in realigning a budget
in the face of rapidly diminishing resources and then adapting pastoral structures to it—but rather taking the challenge as a theological task and developing an appropriate theological discourse from it.

To be sure there is the possibility of other local churches orienting themselves to Poitiers. It is not unthinkable that this might lead to the formation of
local communities or something like them in German dioceses. But if something comparable is to happen, these local churches, those who are involved
in them, must undergo a process comparable to that which the Diocese of
Poitiers has gone through and continues to go through. Poitiers is not offering
a set model that can be transferred without any further emendation into
another context and be implemented there. That is not a shortcoming, because without this model Poitiers gives the courage to place trust in making
our own experiences.

A final word: Gisele Bulteau writes, "Everyone active in the church
knows how difficult it is, even impertinent, to pretend to evaluate a completed pastoral journey. The local communities of Poitiers continue their
growth, modest, fragile and confident, at the heart of the Church of the
ages."[73] My reflections here are not intended to cover that over.

WORKS CITED

Boone, Éric. "Communautés locales et ministères: points d'appui, expérience et recherches." In
    Albert Rouet, Éric Boone, Gisele Bulteau, Jean-Pierre Russeil, and André Talbot. *Un gout
    d'espérance: Vers un nouveau visage d'Église II*, 99–126. Paris: Bayard, 2009.
Bulteau, Gisele. "Les communautés locales: un chemin d'humanisation." In Albert Rouet, Éric
    Boone, Gisele Bulteau, Jean-Pierre Russeil, and André Talbot. *Un gout d'espérance: Vers
    un nouveau visage d'Église II*, 49–73. Paris: Bayard, 2009.
———. "Mes responsabilités auprès des communautés locales." In Albert Rouet, Éric Boone,
    Gisele Buteau, Jean-Paul Russeil, and André Talbot. *Un nouveau visage d'Église.
    L'expérience des communautés locales à Poitiers*, 63–105. Paris: Bayard, 2005.
Feiter, Reinhard, and Hadwig Müller, eds. *Was wird jetzt aus uns, Herr Bischof? Ermutigende
    Erfahrungen der Gemeindebildung in Poitiers*. Ostfildern: Schwabenverlag, 2009.

Müller, Hadwig. "Ein Schimmer von Hoffnung—eine Einführung." In Reinhard Feiter and Hadwig Müller, eds. *Was wird jetzt aus uns, Herr Bischof? Ermutigende Erfahrungen der Gemeindebildung in Poitiers*, 9–15. Ostfildern: Schwabenverlag, 2009.

Rouet, Albert. "Les communautés locales comme institution." In Albert Rouet, Éric Boone, Gisele Bulteau, Jean-Pierre Russeil, and André Talbot. *Un gout d'espérance: Vers un nouveau visage d'Église II*, 75–98. Paris: Bayard, 2009.

———. "Vers un nouveau visage d'Église." In Albert Rouet, Éric Boone, Gisele Buteau, Jean-Paul Russeil, and André Talbot. *Un nouveau visage d'Église: L'expérience des communautés locales à Poitiers*, 19–61. Paris: Bayard, 2005.

Russeil, Jean-Paul. "L'itinéraire de foi des communautés locales." In Albert Rouet, Éric Boone, Gisele Buteau, Jean-Paul Russeil, and André Talbot. *Un nouveau visage d'Église. L'expérience des communautés locales à Poitiers*, 107–164. Paris: Bayard, 2005.

Vatican Council II. Dogmatic Constitution on the Church—*Lumen Gentium*, §1. Rome: Libreria Editrice Vaticana, November 21, 1964. http://www.vatican.va/archive/hist_councils/ii_vatican_council/documents/vat-ii_const_19641121_lumen-gentium_en.html.

NOTES

1. Archbishop Albert Rouet, "Les communautés locales comme institution," in Albert Rouet, Éric Boone, Gisele Bulteau, Jean-Pierre Russeil, and André Talbot, *Un gout d'espérance: Vers un nouveau visage d'Église II* (Paris: Bayard, 2009) (hereinafter cited as Rouet, "Les communautés"), 75–76: "Nombre de lieux affirment faire *«la même chose qu'à Poitiers»*! À y regarder de plus près, on note cependant des différences importantes: les élections sont supprimées et le prêtre seul désigne les responsables, les charges n'ont pas de durée prévue, les fonctions importantes ne sont pas toutes assurés. . . . Ces endroits agissent comme ils l'entendent et selon possibilités. Qu'ils disent alors s'inspirer des communautés locales, non qu'il s'agisse de la même chose!"

[Editors' note: Albert Rouet was the Bishop of Poitiers from 1994 to 2002, and Archbishop (after the diocese became an archdiocese) from 2002 to 2011. He succeeded Bishop Joseph Rozier, and was succeeded by Archbishop Pascal Wintzer.]

[Editors' note: The citations in Prof. Dr. Feiter's original chapter (which are given parenthetically in his text) refer only to the German translations of French documents, as found in Reinhard Feiter and Hallwig Müller, eds., *Was wird aus uns, Herr Bischof? Ermutigende Erfahrungen der Gemeindebildung in Poitiers* (Ostfildern: Schwabenverlag, 2009). These citations have been converted to endnotes for this translation. In cases in which substantial text has been quoted directly from the documents, the editors of this English version have translated from the original French and cited those original sources; the French text is given here in the endnotes. In cases in which Prof. Dr. Feiter has referred to a general idea without substantial quotation, references are to the German translations found in the Feiter-Müller volume. Prof. Dr. Feiter also refers readers to Reinhard Feiter, *Verantwortendes Handeln: Praktische Theologie als kontextuelle Theologie* (Münster 2002), for theoretical background and sources for it.]

2. [Editors' note: Because Poitiers was only designated an archdiocese in 2002, about ten years after the process of reimagining local church began, there remain many references to the "Diocese of Poitiers."]

3. Albert Rouet, "Vers un nouveau visage d'Église," in Albert Rouet, Éric Boone, Gisele Buteau, Jean-Paul Russeil, and André Talbot, *Un nouveau visage d'Église. L'expérience des communautés locales à Poitiers* (Paris: Bayard, 2005), 30 (hereinafter cited as Rouet, "Nouveau visage"): "modèle paroissial."

4. Éric Boone, "Communautés locales et ministères: points d'appui, expérience et recherche," in Rouet et al., *Un gout d'espérance* (hereinafter cited as Boone, "Communautés locales"), 107: "modèle clérical."

[Editors' note: Éric Boone is a lay teacher of theology and has been assistant director of the Centre Théologique of Poitiers.]

5. Boone, ibid., 99: "modèle associative autonome."

6. Cf. Boone, "Communautés locales," in Feiter and Müller, 145.

7. The Bishops of France, *Proposer la foi dans la société actuelle* (Paris: Éditions du Cerf, 1996), 22. Quoted in Jean-Paul Russeil, "L'itinéraire de foi des communautés locales," in Rouet et al., *Un nouveau visage d'Église* (hereinafter cited as Russeil, "L'itinéraire"), 127: "un monde s'efface et un autre est en train d'émerger, sans qu'existe aucun modèle préétabli pour sa construction."

[Editors' note: Jean Paul Russeil is a priest of the Archdiocese of Poitiers and has been the episcopal vicar of the archdiocese as well as a teacher of ecclesiology.]

8. [Editors' note: Prof. Dr. Feiter is referring here to his own work, which presents German translations of several essays by leaders of the Archdiocese of Poitiers, and in which the original version of this essay also appears. (See Note 1 above.)]

9. Rouet, "Nouveau visage," in Feiter and Müller, 22.

10. Rouet, "Nouveau visage," 31: "Cette permission enferme dans une alternative: ou bien l'exercice de la charge pastorale se coule obligatoirement dans les images du seul ministère presbytéral de type paroissial, idée qu'il faut à l'évidence rejeter, étant donné les multiples engagements pastoraux qui débordent ce quadrillage territorial; ou bien on reconnaît que ce n'est là qu'un cas transitoire par temps de pénurie et finalement insatisfaisant."

11. Cf. Rouet, "Nouveau visage," in Feiter and Müller, 24.

12. [Editors' note: As the next sentence makes clear, Prof. Dr. Feiter does not mean that there are no priests involved with these local communities. Priests in the Archdiocese of Poitiers are assigned to "pastoral sectors," with duties of oversight and animation of the various local communities in their sector, rather than as formally appointed "parish priests" of traditionally constituted parishes.]

13. [Editors' note: Many German dioceses have instituted pastoral plans similar to those seen in many US dioceses. Several formerly independent parish churches may be grouped as "communities" into a much larger parish, or into "clusters" of parishes that remain legally separate but share a pastor. However they are structured, these new entities function canonically (and, to a large extent, practically) in similar ways to their predecessors, with clerical leadership, some professional staff, and volunteers. The local communities in Poitiers have a more direct relationship both to the bishop and to the secular communities within which they are located.]

14. Cf. Hadwig Müller, "Ein Schimmer von Hoffnung—eine Einführung," in Feiter and Müller, 10.

15. Cf. Rouet, "Nouveau visage," in Feiter and Müller, 29–31.

16. Russeil, "L'itinéraire," 161: "la tâche confiée n'est pas un but en soi."

17. Cf. Gisele Bulteau, "Mes responsabilités auprès des communautés locales," in Rouet, Boone, et al., *Un nouveau visage d'Église* (hereinafter cited as Bulteau, "Responsabilités"), in Feiter and Müller, 52f.

[Editors' note: Gisèle Bulteau is a laywoman who has performed the ministry of "accompanying" local communities throughout the Archdiocese of Poitiers.]

18. Cf. esp. Bulteau, ibid., 44.

19. Cf. Rouet, "Nouveau visage," in Feiter and Müller, 18–21.

20. Boone, "Communautés," 124: "le long engendrement d'une figure d'Église dont on ne perçoit encore que les premiers traits."

21. [Editors' note: Prof. Dr. Feiter refers here to the "équipes," the leadership teams in each of the local communities.]

22. Cf. Bulteau, "Responsabilités," in Feiter and Müller, 57.

23. Ibid., 53; Russeil, "L'itinéraire," ibid., 98f; and Rouet, "Les communautés," ibid., 112f.

24. [Editors' note: See also Note 18. Prof. Dr. Feiter is here referring to Bulteau's article, already cited several times, the title of which translates: "My Responsibilities toward the Local Communities."]

25. Boone, "Communautés locales," 125–126: "Dans cette étape, nous sommes animés d'une double volonté—ces lignes en témoignent: d'abord être à l'écoute des questions que l'on nous adresse, en les prenant au sérieux, en modifiant nos pratiques, en ajustant nos attitudes; ensuite, fonder nos choix pastoraux et penser notre ecclésiologie. Dans un contexte où tant de questions semblent pressantes et sont présentées comme urgentes, il nous paraît fondamental de faire l'éloge d'une certaine forme de lenteur qui donne le temps utile à la réflexion qui doit

accompagner notre élan missionnaire. Par là, nous essayons de prendre au sérieux notre condition historique, avec ses chances et ses conditionnements."

26. Rouet, "Les communautés," 85: "L'acte d'instituer ne «montera pas de la base»."

27. Rouet, "Nouveau visage," 47: "Pendant de longues années, des personnes se sont usés à aider des prêtres, à rendre service. Leur ténacité longue et fidèle n'a entraîné personne à prendre leur suite. Un tel service, si admirable qu'il soit, n'engendre aucune liberté dans l'Église."

28. Cf. Rouet, "Nouveau visage," in Feiter and Müller, 36; cf. Bulteau, "Responsabilités," ibid., 48f.

29. Cf. Rouet, "Nouveau visage," 52: "Passer de l'aide à la responsabilité."

30. Cf. Rouet, in Feiter and Müller, 31; cf. Russeil, "L'itinéraire," ibid., 99.

31. Cf. Rouet, ibid., 35f.

32. Bulteau, "Responsabilités," 74: "Aucune communauté locale n'est une île."

33. Bulteau, "Les communautés locales: un chemin d'humanisation," in Rouet et al., *Un gout d'espérance* (hereinafter cited as Bulteau, "Les communautés"), 53: "Chaque communauté n'est pas son propre horizon. Elle est située au sein d'un secteur pastoral."

34. Rouet, "Les communautés," in Feiter and Müller, 115.

35. Rouet, "Les communautés," 95.

36. Rouet, ibid.: "Le mythe de l'autonomie juridique a engendré l'indépendance pastorale. Par contre, une communauté locale ne réclame rien d'autre que la bonne volonté des gens. Elle peut se réunir chez l'un ou chez l'autre. Elle vit une pauvreté manifeste. Et c'est une bonne chose!"

37. Cf. Rouet, "Nouveau visage," 33: "Car il se pose ici un véritable problème de foi. Si on confond la vie de l'Église avec une organisation contingente, comme la chute de Rome devant les barbares fut prise pour la fin du monde (et non d'un temps), alors la pauvreté apparaît comme une déréliction où Dieu abandonne les siens. Pour conserver les mêmes structures qu'hier, on est prêt à tous les subterfuges: trouver des supplétifs, être moins exigeant sur le critères pour l'ordination presbytérale (la piété suffit). . . . En ce cas, la pauvreté est une catastrophe: que devient la première Béatitude?"

38. Rouet, "Nouveau visage," 50: "Ce ne sont pas les chrétiens qui manquent, mais ils manquent de confiance en eux."

39. Cf. Rouet, "Nouveau visage," in Feiter and Müller, 34.

40. Rouet, "Nouveau visage," 46: "Il convient d'éviter que, trop longtemps, n'existe qu'une seule communauté dans un secteur: avec qui pourrait-elle échanger?"

41. Russeil, "L'itinéraire," 120: "qui se reconnaissent mutuellement."

42. Bulteau, "Responsabilités," 77: "La responsabilité exercée est partagée. Bien sûr, pour une raison pratique—démultiplier les tâches, ne pas se sentir seul face à la responsabilité . . . , mais également dans une perspective théologique et pastorale: on n'est jamais l'Église tout seul."

43. Rouet, "Nouveau visage," 54: "à l'exercice de la mission reçue."

44. Rouet, ibid., 56: "Envoyé d'ailleurs vers une communauté, le prêtre empêche celle-ci de se fermer sur elle-même et l'ouvre sans cesse à la dimension apostolique."

45. Cf. Rouet, "Nouveau visage," in Feiter and Müller, 39.

46. Russeil, "L'itinéraire," 138: "La communauté locale garde l'horizon ouvert vers ceux et celles qui attendent un service de l'Église."

47. Bulteau, "Les communautés," 55: "C'est bien à cela que nous invite le Concile quand il dit que l'Église doit «être dans le monde et qu'elle vit et agit avec lui.»"

48. [Editors' note: This question is the title of Prof. Dr. Feiter's book, in which this chapter originally appeared in German.]

49. Rouet, "Nouveau visage," 25–26: "Les communes rurales avaient vu se fermer les lignes du tramway, puis le voies ferrées secondaires, les services de cars se raréfiaient, sauf pour le ramassage scolaire, signe du «regroupement pédagogique» avec la fermeture de nombreuses écoles. La poste fermait des agences. Les commerçants des bourgs baissaient leurs rideaux et les «grandes surfaces», souvent modestes, attiraient les clients au chef-lieu de canton. . . . Surtout, un climat de neurasthénie frappait des communes qui, par ailleurs, faisaient tout leur

possible pour animer la population et restauraient leurs églises. Un tissue de relations humaines s'effilochait."

50. Cf. Russeil, "L'itinéraire," in Feiter and Müller, 99.

51. [Editors' note: Vatican Council II, Dogmatic Constitution on the Church—*Lumen Gentium*, §1 (Rome: Libreria Editrice Vaticana, November 21, 1964).]

52. Cf. Bulteau, "Les communautés," in Feiter and Müller, 125–130.

53. Cf. Bulteau, ibid., 58.

54. Russeil, "L'itinéraire," 121: "La proximité n'est pas seulement le voisinage. On peut être voisin et étranger. . . . C'est avant tout la rencontre et l'échange qui traduisent la proximité. Ce mode de présence en un lieu donné engage les profondeurs de la foi en l'incarnation. La foi prend corps dans une communauté donnée en un lieu."

55. Cf. Bulteau, "Les communautés," in Feiter and Müller, 130.

56. Esp. Russeil, "L'itinéraire," in Feiter and Müller, 98–100.

57. Cf. Rouet, "Nouveau visage," in Feiter and Müller, 29.

58. Rouet, "Les communautés," in Feiter and Müller, 107, 112.

59. Cf. Bulteau, "Les communautés," in Feiter and Müller, 121; cf. Boone, "Communautés locales," ibid., 139.

60. [Editors' note: See Bulteau, "Les communautés," and "Responsabilités," previously cited.]

61. [Editors' note: This arrangement is much less familiar to North American Catholics. The Church in Germany has for many years trained and employed many lay ministers who exercise various responsibilities in parishes but are hired and paid through the dioceses, rather than being either local employees or volunteers (as would be much more common in the United States).]

62. Boone, "Communautés locales," 116: "au service du déploiement des capacités de responsabilités de tous les baptisés."

63. Bulteau, "Responsabilités," in Feiter and Müller, 52f.

64. Boone, "Communautés locales," 72: "Même si le chemin de la foi passe par des tâches à accomplir, il ne s'arrête pas là."

65. Russeil, L'itinéraire," 118–119: "«Ce n'est pas à cause d'une capacité personnelle que nous pourrions mettre à notre compte, mais de Dieu que vient notre capacité» (2Co 3,5). Qui n'a jamais découvert des possibilités ignorées, alors qu'au départ il se percevait incapable de répondre à l'appel adressé? Souvent, nous en venons à penser que nous sommes appelés parce que *nous sommes* capables de réponse. Pour l'Apôtre, c'est l'inverse qui est vrai. C'est parce que nous sommes appelés que *nous devenons* capables de réponse."

66. Russeil, L'itinéraire," in Feiter and Müller, 76.

67. Bulteau, "Responsabilités," 80: "Bien entendu, certains répondent négativement à l'appel lancé. Leur choix est toujours réfléchi et l'appel entendu avec sérieux. Surtout on note que, même refusé, un appel produit son effet."

68. Russeil, L'itinéraire,"120: "Dans l'Écriture, il n'est pas d'appel/réponse sans envoi. Les récits de vocation sont à cet égard révélateurs."

69. Ibid., 159: "Or, c'est justement le fait d'être appelé qui suscite une liberté responsable et une qualité d'initiative."

70. Ibid., 162–163: "Celui qui n'est pas appelé ne peut pas advenir à sa responsabilité humaine. Il ne peut pas découvrir ses capacités, puisque personne n'est là pour les lui révéler. Son « oui » ou son « me voici » n'ont pas été appelés. Personne ne s'appelle lui-même à la vie, personne ne se donne lui-même son nom. . . . Toute vie humaine est ainsi faite de réponses à des appels. En ce sens, toute vie est vocation."

71. Cf. Bulteau, "Les communautés," 49.

[Editors' note: The subtitle of this article of Bulteau (which appears in the volume *Un gout d'espérance: Vers un noveau visage d'Eglise II*, translates as "a way of humanization."]

72. Russeil, "L'itinéraire," 159: "par un décentrement de soi-même."

73. Bulteau, "Les communautés," 49: "Tous le acteurs dans l'Église savent combien il est difficile, voire impertinent de prétendre évaluer un chemin pastoral accompli. Les communautés locales du diocèse de Poitiers poursuivent leur croissance, modestes, fragiles et confiantes au cœur de l'Église séculaire."

Chapter Nine

From Practice to Tradition and Back Again

Marti R. Jewell

EDITORS' NOTE

One of the most basic collaborations both represented by and promoted in this volume is that between theologians and other professionals with interest in pastoral ministry. In the United States in particular, it is a frequent complaint that theology has little applicability to "real-life" pastoral situations; theologians sometimes complain that, conversely, their expertise is not sought or appreciated by those responsible for pastoral life. The following chapter is a reminder that a basic theological orientation does ground pastoral practice, and that the practice also, in turn, shapes theology.

Dr. Marti R. Jewell is assistant professor of theology in the School of Ministry at the University of Dallas. She served as director of the Emerging Models of Pastoral Leadership Project, a national research project studying excellence in parish leadership, and coauthored *The Changing Face of Church* and *The Next Generation of Pastoral Leaders*.

Ministry is diverse and, at the same time, profoundly relational. This is so because ministry has its source in the triune God and because it takes shape within the Church understood as a communion. Ministerial relationships are grounded first in what all members of Christ's Body have in common. Through their sacramental initiation all are established in a personal relationship with Christ and in a network of relationships within the communion of disciples formed by and for the mission of Christ.

—*Co-Workers in the Vineyard of the Lord*[1]

When we talk about parish leadership and pastoral collaboration, what matters in the end? Walking with the faithful through the Paschal Mystery and sending them out as missionary disciples matter. Creating possibilities for parish communities to manifest God's mercy, forming structures that benefit society, and inviting the lay faithful to be sharers in the mission of Christ, all matter. How, then, do lay and ordained pastoral leaders work together to effectively fulfill this mission, allowing themselves "to be challenged in their efforts to advance the good of the church and her mission in the world,"[2] which is the very heart of collaboration?

When persons assume leadership positions in a parish they first and foremost accept the responsibility to facilitate an encounter with Christ. In order to carry out this commission, they must ensure the health and spiritual vitality of the parish community; work together to ensure sacramental, catechetical, pastoral, and social ministries; and animate the missionary discipleship of the baptized. In today's parishes these essential tasks are accomplished by pastors working with lay ecclesial ministers, permanent deacons, and other lay professionals. The ability of these leaders to work well together is critical to ensuring parish vitality,[3] so much so that the INSPIRE project, in working toward sustaining pastoral excellence, called collaboration the capstone of leadership practices.[4]

This was also one of the findings of Emerging Models of Pastoral Leadership (EMP),[5] a sister project to INSPIRE. In its research EMP asked over five hundred lay and ordained pastoral leaders, nationwide, to describe what they believe is needed for a spiritually alive and vital parish. Responses to this question suggest that what is needed is a "total ministering community," that is, the parish as an organic whole where the roles of pastor, staff, and parishioner are "critical, interdependent, and unique."[6] These pastors and pastoral leaders spoke of communities coming together as a whole in order to bring about the mission of the church.[7] This is collaboration that both projects came to understand and describe as the Spirit-led dynamic of achieving a shared vision and engaging the faithful in the mission of the Church, all according to their own gifts and abilities.[8]

The EMP research also discovered that while we speak easily of collaboration and empowerment, we don't always know how to integrate these powerful concepts into our ministry, or even what, exactly, these practices are. It was evident that when communities work collaboratively the parish seems to flourish, and on the other hand, where pastoral leaders don't see collaboration happening they describe themselves as less effective in their ministry as a whole. To discover the reasons, we asked pastoral leaders to talk about their own personal styles of leadership.[9] Some respondents focused on the pastor's responsibility for leading the parish, with staff and parish leaders supporting the pastor when he calls for consultation. Others spoke of pastor and parish staff as a "team" working closely together, ensuring the work of the community takes place through efforts such as sacramental programming, faith formation, and liturgy planning. A third, and the largest, group of parish leaders focused on their role as "animators" of the community: inviting parishioners to be involved in creating a vision for the parish and its mission, calling forth the gifts of the community, supported by pastor and staff. Each of these styles involves a form of collaboration, although differently understood in each case. And each has a basis in theology and the history of the Church.[10]

To understand the nature and history of pastoral collaboration we begin by acknowledging parish leadership as a public act, done by and for the sake of the community, under the authorization of the bishop. Good pastoral leadership must be rooted in Scripture and tradition, carried forward in lives faithful to the Gospel; rooted in prayer; focused on the call of the reign of God; and rooted in the conviction that we are a Trinitarian community called to participate in the "gracious invitation of the triune God to every human person, individually and communally, to enter into a mutual exchange of life and love with God."[11] Thus grounded, we model our pastoral relationships on the life of the Trinity, asking three questions: How are we stewarding God's creation? How are we sharing in Christ's mission to bring the kingdom of God into the world? And how are we calling the community to live out their baptismal call to missionary discipleship in the Spirit?

In seeking an answer to these questions, this chapter first focuses on a historical and ecclesiological look at collaborative leadership. As James and Evelyn Whitehead remind us, "In every age the community must discover the shape of its ministry."[12] As far back as the early church it was the assumption that "all believers would participate in the building up of the community and its mission in the world."[13] Lay and ordained have worked together to provide pastoral care and leadership throughout the millennia, sometimes more obviously, sometimes less. The reader who wants to trace the roots of collaboration in the life of the Church will want to begin with the history of collaboration. Those who prefer to start with today's realities might begin with the second part of this chapter, "Collaborative Practices Today," which looks at each of the three understandings of collaborative leadership that surfaced in the Emerging Models Project. These are described, rooted in a scriptural image, and followed by challenges named by today's pastoral leaders along with a suggestion for moving forward in each of these areas. The chapter concludes with the reminder that the ultimate model for collaborative ministry is indeed the Trinity and the baptismal call of all the faithful to participate fully in the mission of Christ.

HISTORICAL DEVELOPMENT OF COLLABORATION

Early Church

It would be disingenuous to say that collaboration, as we understand it today, existed as far back as the early church. It would be equally disingenuous to say the practice did not, as if collaboration were a thoroughly contemporary and newly discovered concept. The demands of leadership and ministry we face today are not so very different from those of the early Church where we see evidence of consultation, cooperation, and animation. All members of the new Christian communities shared in ministerial and missionary activity, each according to their ability and gifts. When the need for additional community stewards arose, the apostles, together with all the community, appointed seven deacons (Acts 6:2 ff.) whose task was the building up, or animation, of the community.[14] People came together in house churches to discern needs, sharing meals presided over by the host and hostess of the home in which they met. All were considered equals, no task exceptional, and no one ordained as we take that term to mean today.[15] As described by William Clark,

> It is precisely because the emphasis in apostolic-era communities did not fall
> on the structures of authority, but on the quality of Christian life in fidelity to
> the Christ proclaimed by the apostles, that these communities were able to
> inherit and display the authenticity of Jesus.[16]

As the early communities grew, leadership demands increased, and communities chose overseers (*episkopoi* in Greek) and elders or advisors (*presbyteroi*). All members of the community, men and women alike, performed the work needed. Over time, as post-apostolic Christians addressed institutional and leadership challenges, a distinction developed between the emerging *ordos* of the "clergy" and the "laity." Early bishops adapted the leadership models of the surrounding Roman and Greek worlds, these aligning well with cultic leadership found in the Hebrew scriptures. Eventually, bishops, such as Cyprian of Carthage who worked toward the sacerdotalization of ministry,[17] and Clement of Alexandria whose first letter made a clear distinction between the *klerikos* and *laikos*,[18] worked toward a leadership rooted in the rising clerical class. Lost was the sense of communal responsibility described so clearly in the early Pauline letters.[19]

Middle Ages

As the new Church moved through the first millennium organizational development continued, but did so in the face of the collapse of the Roman Empire in the West. In the absence of civic structures, the need for governance and pastoral care became the primary issues facing the young Church. Governance moved to the hierarchy but laity remained involved in pastoral care taken on by monastics, laymen and women, and priests who cooperated with one another in caring for the community.

By the start of the second millennium Europe came to be divided into great feudal estates ruled by feudal lords and ladies responsible for the people on their lands. Church leadership lay in the hands of bishops and powerful abbots and abbesses, who were closely aligned with—even chosen by—feudal lords. Parishes came to be housed on feudal estates often with uneducated curates. Monasteries rose and fell, yet withdrawal from the world and disdain of the secular continued. Clergy claimed the power of governance, often in conflict with secular authorities. In the shadow of the feudal system, bishops and lords, popes and kings, vied for control, curia or court advising them. The biblical sense of *diakonia* had long since been replaced by the Roman sense of office.[20] With the diaconate becoming a transitional order in preparation for priesthood, permanent deacons, both men and women, disappeared. By the time of Lateran IV (1215) ordination came to be described as giving the "power to" consecrate and perform sacraments, while the role of the laity devolved into one of passive reception.[21]

In this era, with the rise of cathedrals, cathedral schools, and then universities, an educated populace increased. As demands on bishops grew, they formed consultative bodies, developing models such as the Chapter of Canons, a structure designed as "a legal (corporate) body of priests whose purpose was to assist bishops as an advisory council."[22] Over the years notable men and women also advised the clergy. Francis of Assisi (1182–1226), a deacon, offered advice to pope and bishop alike. By the thirteenth century laity became active in tertiary orders such as the Third Order of St. Francis, which traces its approval to Nicholas IV in *Supra montem*.[23] This document approved the Franciscan third order or "seculars living in their own homes,"[24] instructing that tertiaries be faithful to the ministries and offices given them.[25] This is one of the earliest examples of laity outside of the monastery being formally involved in Church office, instructed in the duties required of them. A Dominican tertiary, Catherine of Sienna (1347–1380), later named a doctor of the church, advised political and military leaders as well as clergy, famously urging Pope Gregory XI to return to Rome from Avignon. Franciscan tertiary Angela Merici (1474–1540), founder of the Ursulines, also spent her life offering pastoral consultation. Living during the tumultuous time of the Reformation and the reign of the Medici popes, the sage counsel of Angela was courted by Church and secular leaders alike. Clement VII asked her to oversee charitable works in Rome, though she respectfully declined the invitation.

The sixteenth century saw Martin Luther and the Protestant reformers question priestly power and pose the common priesthood of the faithful. In reaction, the Catholic Reformation emphasized the ordained priesthood. While the concept of priest as "other" remained, the Council of Trent opened another avenue for the nonordained to serve the church. The council fathers had called for a catechism to be written in order to educate the laity in their faith, which surfaced the need for teachers. Religious women officially began cooperating in the teaching function of the church. One such instance came when Charles Borromeo, Archbishop of Milan, turned to the members of the Order of St. Ursula, twenty-five years after the death of their foundress Angela Merici, and asked them to teach the new catechism.

The Modern Era

By the seventeenth and eighteenth centuries the world and its needs again made new demands on the Church. Apostolic orders of religious women arose, serving the catechetical and pastoral needs of the faithful.[26] The church could no longer claim to be the sole authority as science and the arts came alive in the period of the Enlightenment, and access to education increased. As a result clergy increasingly became relegated to the margins while a newly educated laity held significant roles in society. John Cardinal Newman (1801–1890), speaking of the *sensus fidelium*, even suggested that the laity ought to be consulted in matters of doctrine, although he had to go to quite some lengths to defend this "radical" idea.[27] This era also saw the rise of the Industrial Revolution, which brought progress but also despair in the form of the urban welfare crisis, poverty, human misery, and an increase in alcoholism. Laity rallied around the social causes of the day. Recognizing this, Leo XIII, in his encyclical *Immortale Dei* (1885), called the lay faithful to take part in public affairs to the best of their ability in order "to infuse, as it were, into all the veins of the state, the holy sap and blood of Christian wisdom and virtue."[28] He animated the gifts of the laity, recognizing their expertise and ability to live out their faith in the world, the needs of the times once again requiring the collaboration of the laity in the mission of the Church as laity worked with their pastors and bishops in the development of social action.

By 1917 the newly written Code of Canon Law, based on an ecclesiology of church as a perfect society, "comparable to the state but independent of it,"[29] held as its primary image a society composed of those who governed and those who were governed but also active in pastoral, catechetical, and social concerns. Thus the church officially codified the ability of the laity to cooperate with the clergy in specific, though subordinate, capacities. The involvement of the laity was both welcome and troubling as questions surfaced about implications for the hierarchy, a tension acknowledged by Pope Pius XII in an address to the Second International Congress of the Laity, in 1957:

> Does not the layman who is entrusted with teaching religion—that is, with the *missio canonica*, the ecclesiastical mandate to teach—and whose teaching is perhaps his only professional activity, pass by this very fact from the lay apostolate to the "hierarchical apostolate?"[30]

While his answer to the question was a clear "no," Pius XII affirmed the role of the laity in consecrating the world, and suggested that the laity could receive the authority to teach, a power, he reasserted, held only by ecclesiastical authority which comes from Christ. He continued, "It is clear that the ordinary layman can resolve—and it is highly desirable that he should so resolve—to cooperate in a more organized way with ecclesiastical authorities and to help them more effectively in their apostolic labor."[31] His thoughts were shared by a number of theologians, such as Yves Congar who were studying the involvement of the laity in the mission of the Church.

The Second Vatican Council

The stage was set for the Second Vatican Council (1962–1965), its convener, John XXIII, realizing that the needs and realities of the twentieth century called for a clear look at the pastoral nature of the church. From the first promulgated document on, the Council recognized the essential role of all the faithful in the life of the Church. The path toward wider recognition of involving all the faithful in the life of the Church appears in the Constitution on the Sacred Liturgy, *Sacrosanctum Concilium,* which calls for the full, active, and conscious participation of all the baptized. Such participation as "a chosen race, a royal priesthood . . . is their right and duty by reason of their baptism."[32] The role of the laity is further developed in the Constitution on the Church, *Lumen Gentium* 10, which sheds light on the relationship between the priesthood of the ordained and the common priesthood, in which there is a renewed "emphasis on cooperation rather than obedience."[33]

> Though they differ from one another in essence and not only in degree, the common priesthood of the faithful and the ministerial or hierarchical priesthood are nonetheless interrelated: each of them in its own special way is a participation in the one priesthood of Christ.[34]

Significant to this development was an encyclical written by Pius XII in 1943: *Mystici Corporis Christi, The Mystical Body of Christ.* Rooting his thought in Pauline texts, Pius spoke of "laity who collaborate with the ecclesiastical hierarchy in spreading the kingdom of the Divine Redeemer."[35] Vatican II takes up the image of the "Body of Christ" in describing the mystery of the church, lay and ordained together forming "one complex reality which coalesces from a divine and human element."[36] The clergy are not expected to take on the entire salvific mission alone. On the contrary, according to *Lumen Gentium,* "they understand it is their noble duty to shepherd the faithful and to recognize their ministries and charisms, so that all according to their proper roles may cooperate in this common undertaking with one mind."[37] The Constitution goes on to affirm that some laity are called to serve within the Church in addition to their apostolate in the world.[38] In the records of the Council discussions, *Acta Synodalia Sacrosancti,* we see how the Council fathers understood this passage, a clear expression of collaboration:

> Pastors were instituted in the church not so that they take upon themselves the whole burden of building up the Mystical Body of Christ but that they might nourish and govern the faithful in a way that would result in everybody cooperating together (each in his own way and order) in accomplishing the common task.[39]

This theme is further illuminated in several of the Vatican II decrees. *Apostolicum Actuositatum,* the "Decree on the Apostolate of the Laity," calls the church to recognize a diversity of ministries but a unity of mission.[40] It states:

> The hierarchy entrusts to the laity certain functions which are more closely connected with pastoral duties, such as the teaching of Christian doctrine, certain liturgical actions, and the care of souls. By virtue of this mission, the laity are fully subject to higher ecclesiastical control in the performance of this work.[41]

This theme is also evident in *Christus Dominus, The Pastoral Office of the Bishop* (1965), which notes that laity are to be among the collaborators of the bishop, serving as consultors in the diocesan curia and on the diocesan pastoral council,[42] and that deacons are to work "in communion with" the pastors.[43] And all of this is to be understood in light of the evangelical mission of the Church: "[So] too the laity go forth as powerful proclaimers of a faith in things to be hoped for, when they courageously join to their profession of faith a life springing from faith."[44] After two millennia of understanding how to be the Church, we find ourselves once again, as we have so often in the past, returning to the apostolic nature of our tradition: the animation of the faithful, which is the ultimate goal of collaboration, and the primary function of the pastor in his task of presiding over the Church as a ministerial and missionary community.

Since the Council

The Vatican II shift from a monarchical church replicated in local and parish churches, to a missionary church of all the baptized faithful has not been without its challenges. By the 1980s parishes added consecrated religious and then laymen and women, as well as permanent deacons, working as pastoral teams, serving in official and stable ecclesial capacities. The 1983 Code of Canon Law, concretized this development. While the role of the pastor continued to be the canonical norm of parish leadership, addressing his ministry in collaborative terms was new. So, too, was the official recognition of the participation of laity and the new order of permanent deacons in the mission of the Church (e.g., canons 519, 528–529, 536–537, 545–548).[45]

Canon law presumes that the pastor will enlist the assistance of the faithful (ordained, consecrated, and lay) in the discharge of his responsibilities (e.g., CIC 519; 851.2; 776). With the exception of those rights and obligations which arise from ordination or the exercise of the power of governance, nearly all of the pastor's responsibilities can be broadly delegated to others within and outside the parish.[46]

Following the promulgation of the Code came a decade of Vatican attempts to understand and control this growing reality. Following the 1987 synod on the laity, John Paul II wrote *Christifidelis Laici,* which named the "new need for active collaboration among priests, religious, and the lay faithful."[47] Shortly afterward, in 1992, in the introduction of *Pastores Dabo Vobis,* "On the Formation of Priests," he wrote: "Brother priests, we want to express our appreciation to you, who are our most important collaborators in the apostolate. Your priesthood is absolutely vital. There is no substitute for it."[48] A year later, in 1992, the *Catechism of the Catholic Church* looked at how lay and ordained can work together without diminishing either priesthood, the ministerial priesthood in service of the common priesthood.[49] Finally, the 1997 curial instruction, "On Certain Questions Regarding the Collaboration of the Non-Ordained Faithful in the Sacred Ministry of the Priest," focused on the active ministry of the laity within the church, calling for appropriate collaboration between priests, deacons, and lay ministers in a continuing attempt to ensure the distinction between the ordained and common priesthoods.[50]

The dawn of the twenty-first century saw a shift in the tone of Vatican statements. With a Catholic population nearing one billion, the need for pastoral care had far exceeded the ability of pastors to be the sole providers of the life of the Church. John Paul II's important apostolic letter, *Novo Millennio Ineunte,* written for the close of the jubilee year in 2000, while calling for an increase in vocations to the priesthood and religious life, briefly, even cautiously, signifies a change of heart:

> Therefore the Church of the Third Millennium will need to encourage all the baptized and confirmed to be aware of their active responsibility in the Church's life. Together with the ordained ministry, other ministries, whether formally instituted or simply recognized, can flourish for the good of the whole community, sustaining it in all its many needs: from catechesis to liturgy, from the education of the young to the widest array of charitable works.[51]

Even though the revision of canon law had been written with the intent that a pastor would personally know, and hence be able to offer pastoral care to, each parishioner,[52] this was becoming less and less a possibility in many places. Acknowledging this in *Pastores Gregis* (2003), John Paul II called bishops to greater collaboration with the laity:

> A lived ecclesial communion will lead the Bishop to a pastoral style which is ever more open to collaboration with all. There is a type of reciprocal interplay between what a Bishop is called to decide with personal responsibility for the good of the Church entrusted to his care and the contribution that the faithful can offer him through consultative bodies.[53]

In 2005, US bishops published several calls for the collaboration of pastors, permanent deacons, and lay ecclesial ministers. Their document, *Co-Workers in the Vineyard of the Lord*, requires lay ministers to collaborate with pastors and deacons in providing for the life of the Church.[54] *The National Directory for the Formation, Ministry, and Life of the Permanent Deacons in the United States,* also published in 2005, repeatedly calls for collaboration of clergy and laity who "as members of the church, have an obligation and right to share in the communion and mission of the church."[55] And, in 2007, we hear this same solicitude offered pastors by Benedict XVI:

> I think it is very important to find the right way to delegate. . . . This should be done in such a way that on the one hand he (the pastor) retains responsibility for the totality of pastoral units entrusted to him. He should not be reduced to being mainly and above all a coordinating bureaucrat. On the contrary, he should be the one who holds the essential reins himself but can also rely on collaborators.[56]

While the Pope's call for collaboration both recognizes and attempts to alleviate the increasing burdens placed on pastors, the paradox of these admonitions lay in the continued attempt to retain the centuries-old understanding of the role of the pastor, even while recognizing today's understanding of a responsible leader as one who consults *and* delegates. In the end, Benedict, understanding the heart of *Lumen Gentium*, called for co-responsibility:

> I believe that this is one of the important and positive results of the Council: the co-responsibility of the entire parish, for the parish priest is no longer the only one to animate everything. Since we all form a parish together, we must all collaborate and help so that the parish priest is not left on his own, mainly as a coordinator, but truly discovers that he is a pastor who is backed up in these common tasks in which, together, the parish lives and is fulfilled.[57]

Today, we have come to understand that we are a community of "missionary disciples"[58] who answer the call to communion and mission found at the very heart of the mystery of the Church as expressed in *Ad Gentes*, the Second Vatican Council's "Decree on the Missionary Nature of the Church":

> The mission of the church is carried out by means of that activity through which, in obedience to Christ's command and moved by the grace and love of the holy Spirit, the church makes itself fully present to all individuals and peoples in order to lead them to the faith, freedom and peace of Christ by the example of its life and teaching, by the sacraments and other means of grace.[59]

Through the centuries, lay and ordained have had to learn to work together in one way or another to share in Jesus' mission to bring forth the kingdom of God. Whether by consultation, collaboration, or animation, the Spirit invites us all to serve the people of God.

COLLABORATIVE PRACTICES TODAY

Both by circumstance and preference some pastors today, because of their role as the designated leader, carry a strong sense of personal responsibility for ensuring the life of the parish,[60] a feeling often heightened by parishioners who believe the work of the parish belongs to "Father." Pastors with this strong sense of responsibility will speak of working with staff and/or parishioners by turning to them for consultation. Their staff will speak of "sharing in" the ministry of the pastor.

Collaboration as Consultation: The Responsible Leader

There are many leaders in Scripture, but the classic example of one who feels great responsibility for the task entrusted him is found especially so in the Exodus story of Moses, who led the Hebrew people out of Egypt. Moses meets the "God Who Is" in a burning bush, struggles with his own worthiness and ability to be a leader, and then, accepting the call given him, leads God's people to the Promised Land. In the process, he becomes responsible for a somewhat disparate band of nomads who share a common belief in one God, sets direction for the journey, leads worship, mediates rules, and provides nourishment. He cares deeply for the Hebrew tribes that follow him, becoming overwhelmed when he cannot find food and drink, crying out to God for help. He gets frustrated when the nomadic tribes return to their former ways, crafting a golden calf. And we see him speaking for God throughout the long journey. We also discover the consequences of shouldering such a burden, even though he consults Aaron, Joshua, and Miriam as he makes his decisions. Watching Moses as he listens to people's complaints day after day, adjudicating their issues, his father-in-law comes to him saying,

> "What is this that you are doing for the people? Why do you sit alone, while all the people stand around you from morning until evening?" Moses said to his father-in-law, "Because the people come to me to inquire of God. When they

have a dispute, they come to me and I decide between one person and another, and I make known to them the statutes and instructions of God." Moses' father-in-law said to him, "What you are doing is not good. You will surely wear yourself out, both you and these people with you. For the task is too heavy for you; you cannot do it alone." (Ex 18:14–18)

What would "collaboration" mean for Moses? Is he not the intermediary of God? Would he be disloyal to God's charge if others work with him? Underneath these questions we see a subtle, real, and very human concern about identity. We see it today. Clergy express concern that there may be confusion between ordained and lay ministry, even to the point of wondering if laity can do ministry at all. Lay ecclesial ministers worry that their sense of vocation is disregarded, relegated to administrative rather than pastoral work. Permanent deacons get caught in between. Although they are clergy, some call them "lay deacons," an ecclesial impossibility; while others think of them as a sort of a mini-priest, also theologically incorrect. Add to this the presence of other professional parish staff, serving the many needs of a parish, often well trained in their own disciplines, and one begins to understand why collaboration is challenging. How can we come to recognize the ministry of pastor and staff, not as adversarial, but as mutually enriching the community and one another?

Rather than struggle to rank or separate ministries, we can distinguish between a person's role in the parish and their state-in-life, each person fulfilling the designated tasks they are called to do. Hence a person can function as the one pastoring, the catechetical leader, youth minister, and so on, whether the person filling the position is ordained, religious, or lay. In other words, we can respect the uniqueness and gift of each state in life while working together in designated positions to care for the community. There are certainly times when strong, responsible leadership is necessary. We need those who can set a course, part seas, feed the hungry, and prophetically lead a community into the unknown. Yet, for a pastor keenly aware that he is ultimately the one responsible, the stage is set for the very real toll this can take. With the increasing demands of pastoring: multiple parishes, growing pastor-to-parishioner ratios, multicultural communities, and increased demand for ministries and services in addition to the requisite sacramental ministry, one can see how the priest who chooses to bear all the responsibility himself can pay a heavy price. Too many men find themselves becoming overwhelmed, burned out, or sick.

Pastoral leaders would do well to heed the sage advice of Moses' father-in-law when he suggests Moses share the burden of leadership: "Enlighten them in regard to statutes and instructions, showing them how they are able to conduct themselves and what they are to do" (Ex 18:20). Pastors who turn to a team approach in their pastoral leadership focus less on the heavy responsibility of leading a parish and more on training staff, ensuring they assume their rightful responsibilities in order to serve the life of the parish. It is to this way of collaborating that we now turn.

Collaboration as Team Leadership: Serving the Community

Pastors and staff who work closely together to coordinate pastoral, liturgical, catechetical, and administrative ministries, and to ensure the community's sacramental life, describe themselves as "collaborative teams," believing the ability to work together is critical to the life and health of the parish.[61] Core teams include lay ecclesial ministers, known by a variety of titles worldwide, such as "pastoral agents" and "catechists." By their vocation, position, and gifts they provide leadership and ministry in "close mutual collaboration with the pastoral ministry of bishops, priests, and deacons."[62] Also included on teams are permanent deacons, a growing constituency in the US Church, who represent the bishop in word, worship, and service to persons in need within the parish and in the community. Other lay professionals on staff include a wide range of personnel who bring the expertise needed for successful parish management. Pastors collaborate with staff through training, planning, and empowerment: staff persons work closely with one another and the pastor to move forward the work of the parish.

Looking to Scripture, this idea of both preparing and working with those who serve the community can be seen in the Gospel accounts of Jesus calling men and women to be his disciples. In ways radical for his time, Jesus, the rabbi, gathers followers: fishermen, housekeepers, and tax collectors, rather than religious leaders,[63] teaching in word and deed that the kingdom of God is already among us. He lives with, walks, and works with his disciples, instructing them to do as he did, and sends them out. Jesus shows his disciples how to heal, as he did the daughter of the Syro-Phoenician woman (Mk 7:25–30); how to nourish, as he did the five thousand (Mt 14: 13–21); and how to go out and evangelize, as he sent the seventy (Lk 10:1–23). He charges the disciples with the duty to proclaim the reign of God and empowers them to heal, teach, and nourish just as he did. Jesus clearly expects his disciples to be able to do as he had taught them. So great is this expectation that when they fail he expresses disappointment, even anger. For example, returning from the transformation on the mount, when Jesus discovers his followers are unable to heal a father's son (Mt 17:17), he wonders aloud whether they had learned anything . . . the time-honored plaint of a teacher!

Even though today's pastors and staff may be well trained theologically, one of the challenges to working collaboratively comes from what they often are *not* trained for . . . the day-to-day challenges of working together. One of the most frequent questions on collaboration heard by the Emerging Models Project was how to collaborate as supervisor/supervisee, male/female, or lay/

ordained. Pastors find themselves needing unfamiliar skills. Staffs discover they must learn what is required to work within Church structures, not only ministering to others but representing the Church as well.

Yet, sometimes in the process of learning to work together, a sense of ownership develops. It is not unusual to hear pastors and staff using organizational or corporate language to describe their ministry. The community is seen as "those who come to be served," a relationship parishioners can all too readily accept. "This is Father's parish," parishioners will say. "The parish must decide how best to provide for *us*," others claim. Parish staffs talk about "our programs" as in, "Why don't people come to *our* programs?" Parishioners are seen as "members" and are called on to "help" the staff and the pastor in "their" work. In fact, we call them "volunteers" when they come to participate in the parish—that place on the corner of 4th and Vine, or in the country, or buried in a suburban neighborhood. But the parish is not, at least not often, spoken of as the Body of Christ, as "we, the faithful."

Whether lay ecclesial ministers whose "functions of collaboration with the ordained require of [them] a special level of competence and presence to the community"[64] or permanent deacons who are formed "to contribute a collaboration based on mutual respect and dialogue, in a spirit of faith and fraternal dialogue,"[65] pastoral staff, along with other professional and administrative staff, are mandated to collaborate with the pastor in serving the community. Collaboration, done well, is about learning to respect one another and work together, each using their own gifts and training, but with the single-minded purpose of co-responsibly serving the Body of Christ and seeking to bring the kingdom of God into the world. The healthier the relationships of the pastor and staff are, the healthier the parish is,[66] and their care for the community is a blessing. Like the disciples after Pentecost, we are called to do more than care for the needs of the community. We are to engage the community in mission.

Collaboration as Engaging the Community: Animating for Mission

Collaboration at its best is about calling forth each person's gifts in order to animate the baptized for mission because we believe the "Church which 'goes forth' is a community of missionary disciples."[67] Pope Francis, picking up on the evangelization themes of his predecessors, calls us to realize the Church is "missionary by her very nature, since it is from the mission of the Son and of the Holy Spirit that she draws her origin, in accordance with the decree of the Father."[68] This is one of the most significant teachings of Vatican II: the missiological nature of the church, in which ordained and lay alike are called by Jesus himself into the salvific mission of the church "as living members, to expend all their energy for the growth of the church and its continuous sanctification, since this very energy is a gift from the Creator and a blessing of the Redeemer."[69]

This style, too, reflects an ancient form of leadership. The Gospel writers tell us Jesus acknowledged Peter as their leader, but sent the Spirit, who came at Pentecost bringing grace and power and animated the disciples, including the twelve, to go forth and share the good news (Acts 2, ff.). The twelve were soon joined by Paul who, along with his co-workers, moved from place to place, working alongside members of each community in their daily duties. They witnessed their faith in the risen Jesus, the primary act of discipleship, and set up house churches. Paul taught the new communities to discern the gifts of each member and devote those gifts to the good of the whole (1 Cor 12). He then moved on, leaving the community in place, animated and led by the Spirit, to live out the mission he gave them. His letters and messages served to encourage the young Christians to work together in proclaiming the Gospel and caring for one another, while also providing us with a vision of pastoral leadership.[70]

In the Pauline letters we discover an understanding of the Spirit as the power of God at work in the community.[71] Paul teaches the early Christians to discern and respect the gifts given, no gift more important than another, each essential and necessary to the life of the community. We follow this teaching to this day, believing that the gifts are given for the sake of the community. Many of the pastoral leaders encountered by both INSPIRE and the Emerging Models Project named "animating the community" as the primary focus of their collaboration: engaging "the faith of all the baptized, working together towards a shared mission. They respect the Spirit that is present and active in the community and in its members."[72] These collaborative leaders engage parishioners in the mission of the Church, seeing as essential parishioner-led ministries, strong pastoral councils, committees, and commissions, with pastor and staff taking supportive and guiding roles. Parishes working under this style of collaboration develop many opportunities for service within the parish, and work to serve the neighborhoods in which they find themselves.[73]

This sense of collaboration as mission-based pastoral leadership is distinctive in two significant ways. First, these leaders focus primarily on the mission of the baptized rather than on their own personal responsibility or service to the community, even though these are not ignored. The second difference lies in the relationship between the parish leaders and the community. Rather than discussing differences, rank, or sources of authority they see the parish as a systemic whole, a missionary community in which each person plays a distinct role and contributes to the whole.[74]

When seen as engaging the life of the community, this style of collaboration calls us to think of the parish, not as an institution, but as a community of missionary disciples committed to Jesus and to one another, and sent out on mission. In doing this, we recognize a people animated and led by the Spirit for the purpose of bringing the reign of God into the world. In other words, the life of the parish is not primarily an individual endeavor, rather a mutual interdependence by which all work together.[75] Called to do as Paul and his co-workers did, we serve the mission of Jesus, facilitating the many ministries inside and outside of the Church needed to build up the Body of Christ, working together to realize the coming reign of God, the ultimate emerging future!

The challenge for both pastor and staff is to move from thinking they are the ones who do all the ministry to realizing that their primary task is to animate the ministry of others. It is their responsibility to call forth and facilitate the gifts of the faithful, thus animating disciples for mission. Pastors who share this vision of collaboration have an overview of their parish. They understand how the various groups and ministries work together, what the needs of the parish are, and how the parish can serve the larger community. In a sense they see the proverbial "forest" as a whole. It is the parish staff who know the "trees": the parishioners and their gifts, their needs, and whom to call on to meet those needs. Parishioners are invited to be present to one another, sharing faith, and caring for the community. They function as a total ministering community.[76] Being animators of the gifts and ministry of the baptized and forming missionary disciples is, therefore, not a particular form of leadership that can be chosen or not. It is intrinsic to the life of the Church. It is the demand of the Gospel.

CONCLUSION

Collaborative ministry and leadership are, in fact must be, modeled on the triune God. As Trinitarian people we model our ministry on God the Father who leads us to create healthy and vital parishes. We follow God the Son who draws us deeply into community and there teaches and heals us, sending us out on mission. And we receive God the Holy Spirit who impels us toward the present and coming kingdom. The message is clear. We are called to work together. We always have been. We need pastors who not only understand what is needed in their parishes but also how to work with staff and parishioners to make those things happen. We need parish staff—lay ecclesial ministers, permanent deacons, and other lay professionals—who care for the daily needs of the parish while calling forth and animating the gifts of parishioners. This work is not easy. In the end, in the many ways we work together with all of our gifts and challenges, we must respond to the invitation of the triune God to collaborate, personally and communally, in bringing forth the kingdom in our time.

BIBLIOGRAPHY

Acta Synodalia Sacrosancto, II/1, 256–257. Quoted in John W. O'Malley, *What Happened at Vatican II?* Cambridge, MA: Belknap Press of Harvard University Press, 2008.

Benedict XVI, "Meeting of the Holy Father Benedict XVI with the Clergy of the Dioceses of Belluno-Feltre and Treviso, Church of St. Justin Martyr," *Auronzo di Cadore*. Rome: Libreria Editrice Vaticana, July 24, 2007. http://w2.vatican.va/content/benedict-xvi/en/speeches/2007/july/documents/hf_ben-xvi_spe_20070724_clero-cadore.html.

Catechism of the Catholic Church (CCC), 2nd ed. Washington, DC: United States Catholic Conference, 2000.

Clark, William A. *A Voice of Their Own: The Authority of the Local Parish*. Collegeville: Liturgical Press, 2005.

Code of Canon Law (CIC). Latin-English Edition. Washington, DC: Canon Law Society of America, 1999.

Collins, Raymond F., *The Many Faces of the Church: A Study in New Testament Ecclesiology*. Spring Valley, NY: Crossroads Publishing Co., 2004.

Congregation for the Clergy et al. Instruction: "On Certain Questions Regarding the Collaboration of the Non-Ordained Faithful in the Sacred Ministry of Priest." Rome: Libreria Editrice Vaticana, August 15, 1997.

Coriden, James A. *The Parish in Catholic Tradition: History, Theology, and Canon Law*. Mahwah NJ: Paulist Press, 1997.

Drilling, Peter. *Trinity and Ministry*. Minneapolis: Fortress Press, 1992.

Euart, Sharon. "Structures for Participation in the Church." *Origins* 35, no. 2 (May 26, 2005): 17–25.

Gaillardetz, Richard R. "The Ecclesiological Foundations of Ministry Within An Ordered Priesthood." In *Ordering the Baptismal Priesthood*. Edited by Susan Wood. Collegeville: Liturgical Press: 2003.

Hahnenberg, Edward P. "A Theology of Lay Ecclesial Ministry." *Origins* 37, no. 12 (August 30, 2007).

Jewell, Marti R., and David A. Ramey. *The Changing Face of Church: Emerging Models of Parish Leadership*. Chicago: Loyola Press, 2010.

Kaslyn, Robert J. "Introduction to Book II: The People of God (cc. 204–329)." *New Commentary on the Code of Canon Law*. Edited by John P. Beal, James A. Coriden, and Thomas J. Green. Mahwah, NY: Paulist Press, 2000.

Newman, John Henry. "On Consulting the Faithful in Matters of Doctrine." *The Rambler*, July 1859, para 2.5. http://www.newmanreader.org/works/rambler/consulting.html.

Pope Francis. "Address to the Leadership of the Episcopal Conferences of Latin America during the General Coordination Meeting." July 28, 2013. https://w2.vatican.va/content/francesco/en/speeches/2013/july/documents/papa-francesco_20130728_gmg-celam-rio.html.

———. Apostolic Exhortation *Evangelium Gaudium*, The Joy of the Gospel. Rome: Libreria Editrice Vaticana, November 24, 2013.

Pope John Paul II. Post-Synodal Apostolic Exhortation *Christifidelis Laici*, The Christian Faithful. Rome: Libreria Editrice Vaticana, December 23, 1988.

———. Post-Synodal Apostolic Exhortation *Pastores Dabo Vobis*, I Will Give You Shepherds. Rome: Libreria Editrice Vaticana, March 25, 1993.

Pope Leo XIII, Encyclical Letter *Immortale Dei*, Immortal God. Rome: Libreria Editrice Vaticana, November 1, 1885.

Pope Pius XII, "Address to the Second World Congress on the Laity," 1957. http://www.papalencyclicals.net/Pius12/P12layap.htm.

———. Encyclical *Mystici Corporis Christi*, The Mystical Body of Christ. Rome: Libreria Editrice Vaticana, June 29, 1949.

Pope Urban II, Council of Clermont, 1095. http://legacy.fordham.edu/halsall/source/urban2-5vers.html.

Rademacher, William J. *Ministry: A Theological, Pastoral, and Spiritual Handbook*. New York: Crossroads, 1991.

Secondo, L., and G. Schinelli. "Franciscans, Third Order Regular." In *New Catholic Encyclopedia*, 2nd ed., vol. 5, 906–908. Detroit: Gale, 2003.

US Conference of Catholic Bishops. *Co-Workers in the Vineyard of the Lord: A Resource for Guiding the Development of Lay Ecclesial Ministry*. Washington, DC: USCCB, 2006.

———. *National Directory for the Formation, Ministry, and Life of Permanent Deacons in the United States*. Washington, DC: USCCB, 2005.

Verbeek, Siobhan. "A Shepherd's Care: The Parish and the Pastor In Canon Law." In *Multiple Parish Pastoring in the Catholic Church in the United States* (Project Report, 2006), 10. http://www.emergingmodels.org/doc/reports/Symp%20Report%20Final%20w%20Gautier%20article%20chg%2010%2012%2006.pdf (accessed June 15, 2008).

Whitehead, James, and Evelyn. *Method in Ministry: Theological Reflection and Christian Ministry*. San Francisco: Harper & Row Publishers, 1980.

VATICAN COUNCIL II DOCUMENTS

Ad Gentes, On the Mission Activity of the Church. Rome: Libreria Editrice Vaticana, December 7, 1965.

Apostolicum Actuositatum, Decree on the Apostolate of the Laity. Rome: Libreria Editrice Vaticana, November 18, 1965.

Christus Domini, Decree on the Pastoral Office of Bishops. Rome: Libreria Editrice Vaticana, October 28, 1965.

Lumen Gentium, Dogmatic Constitution on the Church. Rome: Libreria Editrice Vaticana, November 21, 1964.

Sacrosanctum Concilium, Constitution on the Sacred Liturgy. Rome: Libreria Editrice Vaticana, December 4, 1963.

NOTES

1. US Conference of Catholic Bishops, *Co-Workers in the Vineyard of the Lord: A Resource Guide for Lay Ecclesial Ministry* (Washington, DC: USCCB, 2006), 21.

2. Pope Francis, "Address to the Leadership of the Episcopal Conferences of Latin America during the General Coordination Meeting," July 28, 2013, https://w2.vatican.va/content/francesco/en/speeches/2013/july/documents/papa-francesco_20130728_gmg-celam-rio.html (accessed August 9, 2015).

3. Marti R. Jewell and David A. Ramey, *The Changing Face of Church: Emerging Models of Parish Leadership* (Chicago: Loyola Press, 2010), 78.

4. Daniel Gast and Peter Gilmour. See chapter 2 in this book.

5. The Emerging Models of Pastoral Leadership Project was a joint effort of the National Association for Lay Ministry, Conference for Pastoral Planning and Council Development, National Catholic Young Adult Ministry Association, National Association of Church Personnel Administrators, National Association of Diaconate Directors, and Nation Federation of Priests' Councils, funded by the Lilly Endowment Inc. in its *Sustaining Pastoral Excellence* program.

6. Jewell and Ramey, *Changing Face*, 78.

7. Ibid., 80.

8. Gast and Gilmour.

9. For a description of these findings see Jewell and Ramey, *Changing Face*, 94–100.

10. Thanks to David DeLambo for conversation on the possibility of varied understandings of collaboration.

11. Peter Drilling, *Trinity and Ministry* (Minneapolis: Fortress Press, 1992), 24.

12. James and Evelyn Whitehead, *Method in Ministry: Theological Reflection and Christian Ministry* (San Francisco: Harper & Row Publishers, 1980), 11.

13. Richard R. Gaillardetz, "The Ecclesiological Foundations of Ministry within an Ordered Priesthood," in *Ordering the Baptismal Priesthood*, ed. Susan Wood (Collegeville: Liturgical Press: 2003), 29.

14. Paul Bernier, *Ministry in the Church: A Historical and Pastoral Approach* (Mystic CT: Twenty-third Publications, 1992), 26.

15. William J. Rademacher, *Ministry: A Theological, Pastoral, and Spiritual Handbook* (New York: Crossroads, 1991), 54.

16. William A. Clark, *A Voice of Their Own: The Authority of the Local Parish* (Collegeville: Liturgical Press, 2005), 121.

17. Bernier, *Ministry*, 57, 59.

18. Edward Schillebeeckx, *Ministry: Leadership in the Community of Jesus Christ* (New York: Crossroads, 1981), 70.

19. Raymond F. Collins, *The Many Faces of the Church: A Study in New Testament Ecclesiology* (Spring Valley, NY: Crossroads Publishing Co., 2004), 10.

20. Thomas J. O'Meara, *Theology of Ministry: Revised Edition* (Mahwah, NJ: Paulist Press, 1999), 108.

21. Bernier, *Ministry*, 138

22. Sharon Euart, "Structures for Participation in the Church," *Origins* 35, no. 2 (May 26, 2005): 17–25.

23. L. Secondo and G. Schinelli, "Franciscans, Third Order Regular," in *New Catholic Encyclopedia*, 2nd ed., vol. 5 (Detroit: Gale Virtual Reference Library, 2003), 906–908.

24. Nicholas IV, Apostolic Exhortation, *Supra Montem* (1289), http://www.franciscan-archive.org/bullarium/smonteme.html (accessed April 6, 2016).

25. Ibid., chap. XV.

26. Edward P. Hahnenberg, "A Theology of Lay Ecclesial Ministry," *Origins* 37, no. 12 (August 30, 2007): 178.

27. John Henry Newman, "On Consulting the Faithful in Matters of Doctrine," in *The Rambler* (July 1859), para 2.5, http://www.newmanreader.org/works/rambler/consulting.html (accessed August 24, 2015).

28. Leo XIII, Encyclical Letter *Immortale Dei*, Immortal God, no. 45 (November 1, 1885).

29. Robert J. Kaslyn, SJ, "Book II: The People of God (cc. 204–329)," in *New Commentary on the Code of Canon Law* (Mahwah, New York: Paulist Press, 2000), 1530.

30. Pius XII, Address to the Second World Congress on the Laity (1957), para. I, http://www.papalencyclicals.net/Pius12/P12LAYAP.HTM (accessed July 6, 2015).

31. Ibid.

32. Vatican II, *Sacrosanctum Concilium*, 14.

33. Bernier, *Ministry*, 206.

34. Vatican II, *Lumen Gentium*, 10.

35. Pius XII, *Mystici Corporis Christi*, 17.

36. Vatican II, *Lumen Gentium*, 8.

37. Ibid., 30.

38. Ibid., 31.

39. *Acta Synodalia Sacrosancti* II/1, 256–257, quoted in John W. O'Malley, *What Happened at Vatican II?* (Cambridge, MA: Belknap Press of Harvard University Press, 2008), 186.

40. Vatican II, *Apostolicum Actuositatum*, 2.

41. Ibid., 24.

42. Vatican II, *Christus Dominus*, 27.

43. Ibid., 15.

44. Vatican II, *Lumen Gentium*, 35.

45. James A. Coriden, *The Parish in Catholic Tradition: History, Theology, and Canon Law* (Mahwah, NJ: Paulist Press, 1997), 97.

46. Siobhan Verbeek, "A Shepherd's Care: The Parish and the Pastor in Canon Law," in *Multiple Parish Pastoring in the Catholic Church in the United States* (Project Report, 2006), 10, http://www.emergingmodels.org/doc/reports/Symp%20Report%20Final%20w%20Gautier%20article%20chg%2010%2012%2006.pdf (accessed June 15, 2008).

47. John Paul II, *Christifidelis Laici*, 2 ff.

48. John Paul II, *Pastores Dabo Vobis*, 4.

49. *CIC*, no. 1547.

50. Congregation for the Clergy et al., Instruction: "On Certain Questions Regarding the Collaboration of the Non-Ordained Faithful in the Sacred Ministry of Priest" (Vatican City: Libreria Editrice Vaticana, August 15, 1997), Preface.

51. John Paul II, *Novo Millennio Ineunte*, 46.

52. Verbeek, "A Shepherd's Care," #10.

53. John Paul II, *Pastores Gregis,* 44.

54. US Conference of Catholic Bishops, *Co-Workers in the Vineyard of the Lord: A Resource for Guiding Lay Ecclesial Ministry* (Washington, DC: USCCB, 2005), 14.

55. US Conference of Catholic Bishops. *National Directory for the Formation, Ministry, and Life of Permanent Deacons in the United States* (Washington, DC: USCCB, 2005), 30.

56. Benedict XVI, Meeting with the Clergy of the Dioceses of Belluno-Feltre and Treviso (July 24, 2007), http://w2.vatican.va/content/benedict-xvi/en/speeches/2007/july/documents/hf_ben-xvi_spe_20070724_clero-cadore.html (accessed July 6, 2015).

57. Ibid.

58. Francis, *Evangelium Gaudium*, 120.

59. Vatican II, *Ad Gentes*, 25.

60. Jewell and Ramey, *Changing Face*, 98.

61. Ibid., 97.

62. USCCB, *Co-Workers*, 10.

63. Gerhard Lohfink, *Jesus of Nazareth: What He Wanted, Who He Was*, Linda M. Maloney, trans. (Collegeville: Liturgical Press, 2012), 74.

64. USCCB, *Co-Workers*, 12.

65. USCCB, *National Directory*, 60.

66. Jewell and Ramey, 71.

67. Francis, *Evangelium Gaudium,* 24.

68. Vatican II, *Ad Gentes,* 2.

69. Vatican II, *Lumen Gentium,* 33.

70. Collins, *Many Faces*, 59.

71. Ibid., 10.

72. Jewell and Ramey, *Changing Face*, 104.

73. Ibid.

74. Ibid., 75.

75. Kaslyn, "Book II," 263.

76. Jewell and Ramey, *Changing Faces,* 77.

Chapter Ten

Collaboration in a Pastoral Key

Daniel Gast and William A. Clark, SJ

EDITORS' NOTE

At the conclusion of the main body of our volume, the editors offer reflections on how the collaboration called for and, one hopes, demonstrated in each chapter might be pursued in ordinary pastoral situations. The perspective here is decidedly North American, but may hold insights relevant to pastoral work in other areas as well. (See Editors' Notes prior to chapters 1, 2, and 4 for biographical notes on the authors.)

While they differ essentially, the ordained priesthood and the common priesthood of the faithful are ordered to one another and thus are intimately related. (LG 10) Lay ecclesial ministers, especially those serving in parishes, look to their priests for leadership in developing collaboration that is mutually life-giving and respectful. [1]

"WE NEED TO TALK"

This stark declaration conveys strong emotional and intellectual admissions. It is one of those "need to talk" moments for those who lead in today's Catholic parishes, whether they do so as pastors and ordained clergy, lay ecclesial ministers, or as parishioners who take on leadership and ministerial roles. It really matters that their conversations follow high standards of conduct that assure personal safety, invite thoughtful assertions and honest questioning, seek informed observations and projections, and every so often are punctuated by shared silences instead of reactive outbursts. Such interchanges among two, three, or even a roomful of people ought always to allow and encourage emotional intelligence that welcomes expressions of sorrow and longing, impossible dreaming, discoveries, wonder, laughter, and rejoinders. On Luke's Emmaus Road (24:13–35) two distraught companions suffered no reluctance to leverage Greek expressions that would give a sailor pause. Still, hearts were burning, and near nightfall, the two formerly disconsolate companions offered safety and sustenance to the Stranger. He then sat at their table and made a stunning final assertion with just a familiar blessing and ritual gesture.

As were the two dazed companions abruptly lost on a familiar road, we who serve and lead in Catholic local communities of "resident aliens" (*paroikia*) find ourselves at a threshold few of us ever sought. We along with our parishes stand together in liminal space. We look back to the communities we knew with longing. We wonder just how "stably established"[2] we can be on this changing ground of communal and institutional transition. We can be tempted to wonder whether "the parish" will constitute a core experience for Catholics only a generation from today.

Somehow it must, contend the authors in this volume, so as we near its closure we offer the following reflection with talking points for deliberations among parish staff and laypersons. We believe that parishes will find new ways to form themselves for worship, witness, and service, especially if there can be leadership-level conversations on the ground of parish life and ministries, among pastors, ordained priests and deacons, religious and laity. We need to practice the art of restorative conversation, not entering into discourses about problems to be solved, but possibilities we shall live our way into, says community learning designer Peter Block:

> We begin the process of restoration when we understand that our well being is defined simply by the nature and structure and power of our conversation.[3]

As faith-oriented collaborators, we contend that expressions of collaboration in the work everyone does in the Name of Father, Son, and Holy Spirit have enormous potential for communal regeneration. Ministry shared among co-workers seems to create natural spaces for shared reflection. There is work to do, a certain kind of generative work that cannot go unexamined if we are to perform and lead well. That is, pastoral work shared in collaborative expressions of leadership.

LIVING THE PASTORAL LIFE

Pastoral work is the essence of *good* work. Pastoral work creates safe, nurturing space for life and human relationships. It models and invites recognition of divine presence. It enlightens and calls, makes demands and respects human freedom; and it leads celebrations, reconciliations, mourning, and thanksgiving. Pastoral ministers express compassion and understanding. Their efforts enable people to leverage talents in commitments that express faith, hope, and the greatest charism, love. Pastoral work, say the over-whelming majority of those who have committed themselves as church min-isters, is worthwhile, rewarding, and highly satisfying work.[4]

That is, on a good day. At the end of a good day, one can look at the work one is doing and call it *good*. During the ten-year run of Project INSPIRE, parish ministers—ordained pastors, associate pastors, deacons, and men and women lay ministers—sorted out their good days and explored what made them so. With the help of coaches and facilitators, parish-based pastoral ministers grew collaborative leadership practices that generated both pastoral excellence and life-giving, respectful relationships. The aim was to increase everyone's anticipation of good days. To this end, parish staffs formed them-selves as Pastoral Leadership Teams.

COLLABORATION IN A PASTORAL KEY

Collaboration is a skilled performance. A working definition of collaboration expressed in pastoral leadership includes disciplined, aligned performances guided by a common mission that alternates its focus between Church tradi-tion, Sacred Story, and the story, situation, and dedications of the local parish community. The mission is probed and provoked by sharing a vision that includes personal and communal desires. Nevertheless, it challenges every-one to surpass the boundaries of comfort and the status quo. Named and exercised values help determine priorities, allocation of resources, action, and evaluation. Collaboration of any kind requires personal and shared re-flection, communication, and accountability. All this requires practice, sub-stantive conversations, more practice, and evaluation. Eventually collabora-tion becomes praxis: everyone learns as everyone practices and shares reflec-tion on both the learning and the doing.[5] The learning generates new com-mitments and new practice, and often grows new collaborations.

These days, the work that goes on in Catholic parishes is of many hands. A pastor, his pastoral associates, and staff may each provide distinct but complementary skilled services such as counseling, teaching, religious for-mation, liturgical and music ministry, social service and outreach, home and hospital visitation, and so on. Inevitably, each will also be called upon to supervise parish activities that are sometimes well ordered and sometimes only loosely networked. Staff members enlist parishioners and help them develop skills for exercising various forms of lay leadership including partic-ipation in councils, commissions, committees, ministries, and volunteer pro-grams.

Many of these parishioner engagements are relatively new to American parish life. Over the past fifty years parishes have evolved into complex communities. A typical parish website in Chicago now lists several staff persons and dozens of ministries in which persons of all ages may join. US Catholics have seized upon Church teaching about baptismal priesthood. They are eager to perform good works—unabashedly identified as ministries—that often require support and oversight from the pastor or delegated members of the pastoral team. Providing such attention demands new allocations of time in the already busy schedules of pastoral ministers. It also calls for new skill sets to sustain ministerial delegations and collaborations, and provide administrative support—all this, and one big thing more.

Collaborative pastoral leadership is profoundly about *spiritual* leadership. It demands presence in the community that exudes the joy of the Gospel. It attracts, nurtures, and orients everyone to the core values and the community's religious mission. As an act of leadership, one's collaborative posture demands a personal spirituality that goes public and accepts the vulnerability of transparency. Pastoral spirituality shines through skilled performances of counseling, preaching and teaching, community presiding, interventions, and stabilizing presence at the edges and crisis moments of people's lives.

As an expression of community leadership, pastoral spirituality may be manifested in precious few lofty moments of exhortation during prayer and worship. Much more often, spiritual leadership engages gritty realities in response to a community's social, physical, and spiritual poverty. It matters greatly when communities experience coherent proclamations of the Gospel from each of their parish ministers. Moreover, when those ministers are transparent in fervently expressing a common mission informed by shared spiritual values, they attract others to join with them. Working together is always a matter of personal growth and shared forbearance.

PATHWAYS TO COLLABORATIVE PRACTICE

If collaboration were quick and easy, few would ever collaborate. If true collaboration were accomplished in short order, the sudden shock to one's ego would be more than most could bear. To collaborate, one must cross borders that protect one's safe space, dispel illusions of being invulnerable and in total control, and surrender the inviolability of one's good idea. One must learn another's professional or ministerial language, and appreciate another's gifts, value, and contribution to the work, and allow others to stand in spotlights. One must suspend assumptions and talk, take time to listen, ask questions that could possibly betray ignorance, and seek criticism of one's own work. One must negotiate budgets, reshape programs and services to complement other ministries and calendars, and adjust goals, objectives, and values to accommodate others. One must be willing to learn new facts and new practices, make commitments, and follow through on them. Those who work together while adopting such routines also understand that conflict is inevitable, but possibly a portal to discovery, and therefore is to be met with constructive disciplines of inquiry and testing.[6]

Meanwhile, there is also good news about the pathway to collaborative pastoral leadership. While collaboration isn't achievable with one-minute-management efficiency, positive feedback and deepened personal integrity are nearly immediate outcomes for those who commit to its practice. While learning how to listen and understand, for instance, one learns that she is being listened to and is becoming better understood. Further, an early discipline for pastoral collaboration comes naturally to most in pastoral ministry, as they adopt habits and practices of personal and shared spirituality. It shouldn't be amazing, but most say it is: a few minutes spent together in safe, unguarded offering of prayer, intentions, and reflection tends to bring balance and affirmation that *I and we* are doing good, important work. Spirituality blossoms and grows through intentional practice. Learning to collaborate builds resiliency in persons and teams, grows spiritual and relational capacity, and brings to the work profoundly more adept, coherent, and disciplined performances, ordered by shared proclamations of common mission, vision, and values.[7] It attracts persons to shared workspaces and even to meetings, where each person's contribution is invited and appreciated. As good works align and complement each other, ministerial synergies enable team members to experience the whole as greater than the sum of its parts.

CONFRONTING THE BURDENS

Nevertheless, does anyone really have time to learn collaborative pastoral leadership? INSPIRE's field consultants and researchers witnessed the modern-day pains that plague ministers. Pastoral people are busy, burdened with tasks and deadlines that preoccupy the sense of urgency that ought to belong to mission. They report episodes of being drained spiritually. As a landmark ecumenical study of clergy including Roman Catholic priests discovered, the experience of loneliness is common and a key stressor.[8] Consultants learned that lay ministers have similar experiences of abandonment, even as they build for themselves protective "silos" to keep their work undisturbed and to distance themselves from others. Transitions and periods of change frustrate pastoral ministers. They manage to find little time for continuing education. They may acknowledge awareness of not being on the same page with their co-workers with respect to priorities and mission, but tend to avoid dealing with such elephants in the room. It came as little surprise then, that two pastors took it upon themselves to turn down invitations to participate in INSPIRE. Without internal conferral, they were sure their staffs were too busy. A few other staffs considered participating but

demurred, expressing anxieties about the loss of time and potential distur-
bance of the status quo.

So a fair question begs an apologia: Are collaborative ministries worth
the effort? Can collaboration spread out from staff into the community? Can
it happen among persons, even among parishioners in ethnically blended
parish communities, or among adjacent, clustered or recently merged parishes? Ten years of data and reflection suggest resounding affirmatives! Collaboration brings back to the individual pastor, pastoral minister, and parishioner much more than it asks of them. In the spirit of Paul's admonition that
charisms—extraordinary spiritual gifts expressed as virtues—are never given
just for the sake of an individual, we have learned that collaborative pastoral
leadership is primarily about bringing animation to parish life and engaging
everyone in common mission. Paul's understanding that a community's gifts
need ordering, coherence, and purpose applies as much to us with our larger
parishes today as it did in Corinth, Rome, and his early small communities.
Collaborative pastoral leadership is for and about the community, and the
community's fidelity to mission.

ROLES AND REALITIES

The INSPIRE project identified leadership broadly, recognizing that leadership qualities—and opportunities to apply them—reside throughout a pastoral staff and the parish community. Project leaders therefore allowed pastors
and staff persons to define those who would participate in forming themselves as "collaborative pastoral leaders." One staff, to their ultimate reward,
enlisted the parish maintenance supervisor (self-identified as "just the jani-
tor") as a valued member of the pastoral leadership team. At a critical moment of decision, he would read the social justice commitment in the parish
mission and then call the staff and community to accountability with respect
to ecological stewardship. In some parishes where the delegated and salaried
pastoral ministers were in smaller numbers, administrative support persons
and key parishioners were included in some of the team development work.

Asserting more inclusive parameters for participative pastoral leadership,
however, makes necessary some agreements about ground rules. There are
"rights and duties" that a pastor may not relinquish. Besides the institutional
authorization given in canon law (canons 515 ff.), the pastor of a Catholic
parish receives additional social and cultural deference. He exercises authority by leveraging both institutional and sociocultural empowerment. Meanwhile, pastors hire and delegate persons to perform particular pastoral and
leadership services. "Pastors cast the longest shadows," observed one of the
project's consultants. So it is unsurprising that pastors must be proactive
about forming collaborative working relationships.

Expressing ecclesial and pastoral authority through collaborative forms of leadership allows a pastor no tolerance for abdication of requisite duties, canonically or legally. In fact, one who wishes to lead coaccountable associates must model for them the ownership of specific duties, due diligence, and the taking of initiatives consistent with one's role and office. That is because collaboration is as much about overtly taking initiative as it is about stewarding shared decision making, executing performances cooperatively, and cultivating alignments of shared mission, vision, and values.

ORDERING FOR ABUNDANCE

Collaborative expressions of leadership generate ownership and coaccountability. In parishes it can be a contagious discipline. INSPIRE leaders were transparent in expressing the working assumptions that not only can *everyone* lead, but everyone can learn to collaborate in pastoral leadership. There are situations that occasion independent action by one or another person: the pastor, the youth minister, the rectory office receptionist. One's initiative gains leverage and consequence when it is known, understood, and valued— and particularly when it is expected. Such initiative may well generate complementary subsequent actions by other team members. As collaboration routines become rooted in the daily life of a pastoral leadership team, it is a short and natural step to identify and develop collaborative lay leaders from among parishioners, an outcome likely to enrich parish life, outreach, and mission in many forms.[9]

NAMING THE ELEPHANTS IN THE ROOM

Parish consultants reported common obstacles to collaborative leadership. Some impediments, unsurprising to the consultants, remained hidden or taken for granted by most participants. The project's first research specialist identified the most common impediment as a strong "culture of task." Imprinted deep in most parish staffs, we found a relentless, nearly addictive drive to be at work, on task with or without deadlines.[10] "We work and work without taking a step back to see and hear."[11] Task orientation in ministry surfaced as an unholy sacred busyness. In some parishes, staff meetings were perceived as keeping persons away from "doing my work," and were begrudgingly tolerated only if the proceedings organized work and deflected potential conflicts.

Addiction to task prompted other unhealthy habits: inattention to mission, vision, and values; loss of perspective abetted by lack of reflection; perfunctory prayer or no prayer shared with colleagues; workplace silos; curtailed or abandoned continuing education, reading, and spiritual direction; alternately compliant or fractious engagements among staff; suppression of conflict; "fixing" behaviors in lieu of systemic examination to get at underlying dynamics; resistance to change, and ungraceful transitions. The losses were both personal and corporate.

CALLING FORTH CONSEQUENTIAL GIFTS

However, healthy patterns and best practices also emerged with increasing clarity, suggesting pathways to aligned, complementary ministries, to intellectually and emotionally coherent persons and teams, and to appealing expressions of parish mission and vision. As persons and teams grew collaborative competencies, they were able to deconstruct the disabling patterns of task orientation, faulty communication, incoherent or conflicting values, and ministerial isolation. More important, they learned to name each other's gifts and call one another to pastoral leadership based on shared ecclesial mission, and to propagate discipleship, enlisting parishioners in the good work of forming vibrant local parish communities of faith, stewardship, and evangelization.

We close with a summation of the critical leadership performances we observed and recorded as we watched pastoral teams express "pastoral excellence" as leadership teams. First though, an admonishment that excellence as a human achievement usually occurs only after passages of trial, struggle, and even failure. One should read, therefore, with certain cautions in mind: that there is no linear progression, that different staffs bring to the work unique assets and deficits, that blockages and stalling episodes are common (usually a sign of critical work to be addressed), and that skilled performances are matters of both personal and team learning. There is, however, a common starting point, and it usually occurs in private moments of unguarded assessment among one or more staff persons.

Express Longing

The first steps, we learned, are taken as one or more parish staff members—one of them often the pastor—admit and share a sense of longing. "We could sure communicate better." "We really need to get organized." "We have the same meeting over and over." "Sometimes it seems like we're working very hard, but not working together." Note in these most commonly heard introductory assertions that the malaise involves task. Sometimes there is a sense of great busyness that occludes or obscures core values and mission. What then is the longing for? Could it be for assurance that the work we do here really witnesses to a true community of faith in service to the Reign of God? One enrolling pastor referred to discussions on staff about their work seeming to uphold a contented "beige faith" among themselves and in their upper-middle-class community. Whatever the focus, the discomfort prompted by longing is a necessary driver. Astute pastoral leaders fan that flame rather than suppress it.

Build Safe Space for Discussion and Learning

Pastors and staffs find ways to talk about how to move from longing to discoveries of new ways to serve together in faith. While initial conversations are usually problem-focused, successful sessions keep the subject matter open and move toward sharing preferred scenarios. Early insights often occur at routine business or organizational meetings, often picked up and recorded for consideration by an outside observer, as described below. However, a healthy practice is to eventually move discussions into more informal settings where everyone agrees to maintain respect and confidentiality. As staffs move forward, their understanding and ability to create safe space for sharing and learning deepen and become skilled practices.

Bring in the Safe Outsider

An accomplished facilitator, someone who understands group dynamics and is trusted to hold confidentiality, becomes a vital asset. While it is human nature to begin explorations by focusing on problems, skilled helpers move persons toward appreciative inquiries about assets and human potential. They learn what and when to challenge, and while they may often form long-range prescriptions, they help group members to focus just on the work at hand and next steps. Adept facilitators hold and maintain safe space until group members are ready to become its co-owners and regulators. Especially at stages where confidentiality and trust building are essential to assure the integrity of the process, facilitators and consultants should not be a pastoral team's own parishioners or persons who supervise anyone on the team.

For on-site facilitation, our project developed and designated a "parish consultant" role. The name implied recognition that pastoral teams would own and determine their own destinies in the process of becoming collaborative pastoral leaders. Parish consultants came from the ranks of professional consultants in leadership, organizational, and managerial development. They were particularly skilled in facilitation and executive coaching performances. However, as we learned early on, it was essential that these persons also have personal experience in church ministry—preferably in parishes—so that they could readily discern and interpret church language and culture, and understand the values and assumptions that support persons in ministry. We found that several religious orders had cultivated such expertise, and that credentialed laypersons with personal histories in church settings were also available.

Grow Spiritual Integrity

Corporate leadership literature often acknowledges the importance of spiritual maturity—usually in later chapters and sections. Unlike the standard team development pathways in corporate settings, pastoral team development inverts the agenda. Spirituality as a requisite personal practice and as a corporate discipline is most often the gateway and sustaining resource for pastoral teams. Early on in their team development work, individuals chose from four learning areas: personal development, spirituality, Catholic theology and tradition, and ministerial skills.[12] The vast majority of laypersons prioritized options like spiritual direction, retreats, or learning reflective and meditational practices. Ordained and religious ministers had many of these practices built into daily and annual rhythms; most had priestly, community, or diaconal prayer groups in place. Nevertheless many ordained and religious also reflected on the need to get themselves to firmer spiritual ground.

When consultants asked staffs to assess how they prayed together, though, there were many accounts of perfunctory efforts. To questions like, "How would you describe yourselves as a spiritual community?" there were moments of silence and then epiphany. A consultant to a suburban parish team reported:

> It just blew them away. They hadn't thought of that. It's amazing that this parish that has almost everything, that has the staff members with the credentials they had, that they had just forgotten this element of what brings us together.

A very few staffs scheduled annual retreats for themselves. A survey of area retreat centers revealed that none offered programs for parish staffs. Remedies were not that difficult, however. These were persons who spent their days tending to parishioners' prayer and spiritual lives. Reported one pastor of an Anglo/African American parish about his decision to push his pastoral team to routinely make connections between spirituality and the works they do:

> If we lost track of that, if we lose track of why we're doing what we're doing, if we're only connected to the institution, we'll get way lost.

The perception of "finding the way" through repeated rhythms of shared reflection and prayer orients a pastoral team and positions them for fidelity to mission. Pastoral persons know full well the counterintuitive value of shared silence, of abiding together in acknowledgment of Presence. Nevertheless, given their more activist inclinations, they find it challenging to make spiritual sharing a routine priority. When teams ground themselves in prayer, silence, and reflection, however, everyone is prepared for conversations at deeper levels, for listening and sharing as skilled performances among co-ministers.

Talk

Easily the number one presenting problem of pastoral staffs was difficulty with communication. "We could sure learn to communicate better," was often an understated cry for help with conflict. When communication episodes are restricted to work-focused meetings or to texts and e-mails, staffs will avoid learning and practicing skilled conversations. Work-focused meetings are both necessary and performance-related. Thus they pose abundant temptations to expend energies on conflict avoidance and face-saving, to allow "expedient" (minimal or superficial) evaluation, and to keep problem solving only at the surface and away from systemic issues. Some staffs had taken to reducing meetings or eliminating them altogether.

While INSPIRE consultants brokered learning plans for staff members to develop skills in personal and corporate conflict management, they were also present for observation at routine staff meetings. They helped their clients negotiate rules of engagement such as building and circulating an agenda, showing up, being on time, practicing listening and feedback, sending reports out beforehand, and documenting decisions and commitments. Over time, setting and shaping routine practices and structures made room for assessing the quality of discussions: Do we stay on topic? Do we repeat ourselves for fear of not having been heard the first time? Do we come to closure? Members could also consider the content of those discussions: When decisions and commitments are made, are they documented and assigned evaluative markers, indicators that will signal that an objective has been met, and persons who will lead implementation?

Building and practicing efficient, productive work-focused meetings was, however, only the groundwork for learning advanced forms of team communication. Some teams learned how to evaluate and prioritize through cycles of study, evaluation, and planning. Some assigned themselves books or articles to read and discuss at gatherings scheduled with no other activity aside from prayer. Many teams arranged brief weekly morning gatherings to share reflections on the upcoming Sunday readings. Similar check-in activities featured requests for prayer from staff members or for parishioners and families. Some teams also set aside time for team learning events, such as an afternoon presentation from a seminary or university professor followed by discussion. Unsurprisingly, many teams discovered that finding ways to enjoy socializing and playing together led to new conversations and learning.

Such activities set the stage for learning and practicing particular skilled forms of interchange like discourse and debate, discussion, conversation, and finally, dialogue. Note the progression. Each form calls for particular listening, messaging, and reflection skills. As collaborating team members move forward with these disciplines, persons actually learn to "think slower," suspend assumptions, and delay asserting solutions in order to uncover deeper levels of possibility, imagination, learning, and meaning. Inquiries become appreciative in tone, and persons become secure in expressing transparency, puzzlement, or personal convictions. As thoughts get tested, stretched and challenged within climates of safety, persons understand that they and their contributions really matter. The stage is set for increasing conversations of consequence, as named in the next performance.

Talk Mission

When pastoral teams grew collaborative competencies, they didn't simply talk, they talked mission. Higher forms of communication, conversation and dialogue got them away from the focus on themselves and their tasks, and to consideration of what all this programming and ministering was really about. With that reference there could be qualitatively improved decision making and evaluation, reshaping programs for complementarity, and selection of collaborative projects.

> [Facilitated team meetings and planning sessions] . . . helped us to more concretely understand our guiding statement, what it means to Unite, Enlighten, Form, and Accompany the People of God. [13]

A well-articulated mission inspires, orders, and attracts participation. Starting with pastoral team members themselves, individuals see themselves not only as joined in something greater, but as making valued contributions as well.

Imitate Paul

Both persons and missions attract people to join communities and take on roles of witness and service. Pastoral leaders can bring charisma to parishes and model the way. That is, they are the public leaders whom members watch and from whom they learn. Their roles are crucial. When their charisms are strong and ordered to mission, persons engage with them. When personal charisms go unchecked either by communities or leaders themselves, celebrity can replace the focus on a community's sense of mission and values. Paul the Apostle became keenly aware of this. There was mischief afoot in Corinth.

In his *First Letter to the Corinthians* Paul writes from Ephesus a stern but loving reprimand. It seems that people are siding up with Paul himself, the community planter, or with Apollos, the one who waters. Paul admonishes the fractious community for their foolish attempts to elevate him or Apollos at all, emphasizing their lowliness as apostles (4:9 ff.). The contests have led to further bad behavior, starting with argumentation over whose gifts (charisms) count more. Things have deteriorated so much that celebrations of the Lord's Supper leave some filled to the point of drunkenness and others hungry, likely the late-arriving slaves and servants. They are eating and drinking to their own damnation!

This eclectic band of Corinthian Christians could have been a beacon of the new Faith, had they realized that charisms are given freely and to all, but never for the aggrandizement of one over another. They are given only for the sake of building up the Church, and at that a Church that abides in love, the greatest gift. After all the correction and admonishments Paul recites the Gospel proclamation, closing the recitation with exhortation to hold firm and "do the work of the Lord" (15:58). The very last words of his letter, "written in my own hand," leave the little community with Paul's assurance of "my love to all of you in Christ Jesus" (16:24).

Things today haven't changed much; personalities still make poor lodestones for community orientation. A pastoral leader might well model himself or herself after Paul, who regularly exhorts his hearers to become his imitators. Note, however, the de-estimation of his ministerial status in the ecclesial order (1 Cor 4:9–16, 15:9; 2 Cor 5:4). With modest self-worth intact, Paul calls attention to what really matters: Gospel as Good News; love of Christ; the Lord's work. However, out of the same posture he makes no hesitation to call a community's attention to its disconnection from what matters, to its failures of deed and acts of negligence and avoidance.

Proclaim and Call Everyone to Take Up the Mission

Pastoral leaders own the difficult work of calling attention to themselves, but only as reflectors of the mission, and sometimes as accountants of failures to live the mission. Their work joins ministries of proclamation and call, inviting everyone to see themselves as important working members of the same Body (1 Cor 12). When they are successful in expressing pastoral voice it is nevertheless tempting to collude with occasional expressions of adulation and to hunger for more. With roles susceptible to patterns of isolation exacerbated by siloed work, and minimal time for reflection and examination of the wider view, staffs and their communities can emulate the early Christians at Corinth.

Effective (pastorally excellent) ministers nurture, challenge, and grow the Body, paying special attention to the Body's mind and will, hungers and sorrows, goodness and potential. This requires extraordinary everyday spirituality that fosters a healthy sense of self and life work, both placed squarely in communal efforts at living the life in Christ, offering thanks and praise, and exercising stewardship. Pastoral excellence in local parish communities requires co-laboring with peers and parishioners to grow healthy values and attractive visions of how it could be in neighborhoods, regions, and a world animated by and reconciled to the Gospel.

> To highlight the last lines of the Liturgy that "sends us out" we began to explore Social Teachings with parishioners through both educational and prayerful events. Each month we explored a different Social teaching in ways that called for a collaborative effort between several departments within the parish and brought many parishioners to a new involvement in their parish. [14]

So, we all need to talk! [15] Mission matters most of all when "talking mission" aligns a community's efforts and inspires living the mission into our world. Pastoral leadership teams are challenged when they yield to task orientation, isolation, and its inevitable results: guarded perceptions of worth and status, unaligned performances and incoherent proclamations, unexamined conflict, inattention to continuing formation and education, and forestalled growth in personal, spiritual, and ministerial competencies. When pastoral teams resolve to talk mission, vision, and values, they leverage common personal assets characteristic of ministers: awareness of call, inherent generosity and inclinations to care for others, spiritual depth, and dedication to Gospel, Church, and apostolate. They can then draw from the ministerial commons that animate their lives and expressions of Church mission: tradition, scripture, sacrament, liturgy and Christianity's historically rich and abundant forms of prayer and reflection.

"At the end of the day" for persons dedicated to baptismal and ordained ministry, there may rarely be contentment, but there ought always to be quiet, graced utterance of thanksgiving and praise. There ought to be gathered around our pastoral ministers whole communities who also remain "firm, steadfast, always fully devoted to the work of the Lord, knowing that in the Lord your labor is not in vain" (1 Cor 15:58). [16]

BIBLIOGRAPHY

Carroll, Jackson W., with Becky R. McMillan. *God's Potters: Pastoral Leadership and the Shaping of Congregations*. Grand Rapids, MI: Wm. B. Eerdmans, 2006.

Hoover, Brett. "When Culture and Ministry Collide." INSPIRE Archives at Loyola University Chicago, 2011.

Hughes, Jonathan, and Jeff Weiss. "Want Collaboration? Accept—and Actively Manage—Conflict." *Harvard Business Review* 83, no. 3 (March 2005).

Karlgaard, Rich, and Michael S. Malone. *Team Genius: The New Science of High-Performing Organizations*. New York: Harper Business, 2015.

CHURCH DOCUMENTS

Catechism of the Catholic Church (CCC). English text on-line at http://www.vatican.va/archive/ccc/index.htm.

Codex Iuri Canonici, Code of Canon Law (CIC). English text on-line at http://www.vatican.va/archive/ENG1104/_INDEX.HTM.

Francis. *Evangelii Gaudium*, Joy of the Gospel (EG). Apostolic Exhortation. 2013. English text on-line at http://w2.vatican.va/content/francesco/en/apost_exhortations/documents/papa-francesco_esortazione-ap_20131124_evangelii-gaudium.html.

Paul VI. *Evangelii Nutiandi*, Evangelization in the Modern World (EN). Apostolic Exhortation. 1975. English text on-line at http://w2.vatican.va/content/paul-vi/en/apost_exhortations/documents/hf_p-vi_exh_19751208_evangelii-nuntiandi.html.

US Conference of Catholic Bishops. *Co-Workers in the Vineyard of the Lord: A Resource for Guiding the Development of Lay Ecclesial Ministry*. Washington, DC: USCCB, 2005.

Vatican Council II. *Lumen Gentium*, Dogmatic Constitution on the Church (LG). 1964. English text on-line at http://www.vatican.va/archive/hist_councils/ii_vatican_council/documents/vat-ii_const_19641121_lumen-gentium_en.html.

NOTES

1. US Conference of Catholic Bishops, *Co-Workers in the Vineyard: A Resource for Guiding the Development of Lay Ecclesial Ministry* (Washington, DC: USCCB, 2005), 24.

2. Code of Canon Law, 515 §1. "A parish is a certain community of Christ's faithful stably established in a particular Church, whose pastoral care, under authority of the diocesan Bishop, is entrusted to a parish priest as its proper pastor." The Code in English is accessible at http://www.vatican.va/archive/ENG1104/_INDEX.HTM.

3. Peter Block, *Community: The Structure of Belonging* (San Francisco: Berrett-Koehler, 2008), 53.

4. Jackson W. Carroll and Becky R. McMillan, *God's Potters: Pastoral Leadership and the Shaping of Congregations* (Grand Rapids, MI: Wm. B. Eerdmans, 2006), 169–172. Carroll and McMillan surveyed pastors of several Christian denominations, including Roman Catholics. The authors reference Howard Gardner's (et al.) understanding of "good work" as "work that combines both excellence and ethics, work done expertly that is also socially responsible" (32). Pastoral "good work" is skilled and redemptive.

5. Praxis is used here as learning informed by action, practice-focused, intentional reflection that grows actionable knowledge, discipline, better-understood principles and theories, and application.

6. INSPIRE parish consultant Dominic Perri saw among parish staffs typical tacit agreements to suppress, avoid, and deny conflict as behaviors invoked by a powerful "culture of *nice*" in church and religious organizations. Consultant Phyllis DiFuccia identified a consequence of avoidance as working with "elephants in the room." But corporate literature has long identified the hidden value of conflict: "The disagreements sparked by differences in perspective, competencies, access to information, and strategic focus within a company actually generate much of the value that can come from collaboration across organizational boundaries. Clashes between parties are the crucibles in which creative solutions are developed and wise trade-offs among competing objectives are made." Jonathan Hughes and Jeff Weiss, "Want Collaboration? Accept—and Actively Manage—Conflict," Harvard Business Review (March 2005). Recent work on productive teams acknowledges the essential dynamics of cognitive diversity, divergence, dissent, and even "creative abrasion." Rich Karlgaard and Michael S. Malone in *Team Genius: The New Science of High-Performing Organizations* (New York: Harper Business, 2015).

7. See Peter Senge's schema describing the collaborations involved in team learning. Performances in teams include thinking together insightfully about complex issues; engaging in innovative, coordinated action; fostering other teams through inculcating the practices and

skills of team learning more broadly. *The Fifth Discipline: The Art and Practice of the Learning Organization* (New York: Doubleday Currency, 1990), 236–238 ff.

8. Carroll and McMillan, 178–180.

9. See Pope Paul VI, *Evangelii Nutiandi,* Evangelization in the Modern World; Catechism of the Catholic Church, §910; *Lumen Gentium,* Dogmatic Constitution on the Church, §10, §32; Code of Canon Law, canon 228ff; Pope Francis, *Evangelii Gaudium,* Joy of the Gospel, §28, §120, §130.

10. Cf. Brett Hoover, "When Culture and Ministry Collide," Visiting Professor Report (2011), INSPIRE Archive at Loyola University Chicago, McNamara Center for the Study of Religion.

11. Ibid. (Observation of a woman pastoral staff member.)

12. Detailed descriptions of the learning agendas are found in chapter 2 of this book.

13. Report from a pastoral team of three merged parishes. The succinct reference to their mission was imprinted on staff and parish council business cards.

14. Letter from pastoral team of a large suburban parish to the Lilly Endowment Inc., the project's sponsor.

15. [Editors' Note: We built this and the previous chapter (Jewell) to be accessible to the widest possible array of participants in this critical conversation about how parishes shall be. We envision border-crossing discussions, for instance, parish staff persons and parish councils, theologians and pastors, bishops and academics, and so on. We expect outcomes that may include appreciative awareness, learning, and collaborative action.]

16. New Revised Standard Version (NRSV) translation.

Afterword

Further Notes on a Theology of
"Collaborative Leadership"

William A. Clark, SJ

EDITORS' NOTE

> This brief theological reflection is a final consideration, from the point of view of an ecclesiologist particularly focused on local church communities, of the underpinnings of the attitudes toward community, collaboration, and mission that pervade the essays presented in this volume. (See Editors' Notes at the introduction of chapters 1 and 4 for biographical details.)

PASTORAL COLLABORATION
AND THEOLOGICAL REFLECTION

Christian pastoral practice both relies upon basic theological orientations and raises important questions about them. Among the most foundational: Who is Jesus? What does it mean for Christians to follow or be in communion with Him? How does Christian doctrine evolve and how do we determine its authenticity?

The practical experience of collaborative pastoral leadership raises still other theological issues, including, What is the relationship between communion and communities? What is the relationship between the Truth of Christ and the constantly shifting contexts of local church communities? How do these communities, in all their aspects, contribute to the ongoing renewal of Christian understanding and Christian life?

The preceding chapters having scrutinized various manifestations of collaborative pastoral practice. I propose here to examine these general theological issues with a look at relevant scriptural perspectives on three pairs of concepts that bear directly on the work of parishes: communion and revelation; incarnation and sacramentality; mission and collaboration. I will then conclude with a discussion of how the pastoral work of local church communities can be understood within the framework of these concepts.

COMMUNION AND REVELATION

> [Jesus said to his disciples:] "And you know the way to the place where I am going." Thomas said to him, "Lord, we do not know where you are going. How can we know the way?" Jesus said to him, "I am the way, and the truth, and the life. No one comes to the Father except through me." (John 14:4–6)[1]

The fundamental question, "Who is Jesus?" is answered succinctly by the Lord himself, when Thomas asks literally about "how to follow" him. Jesus solemnly declares himself to be, in effect, both the path to salvation, and salvation itself. If he is "the Way," to be with him is to be "on the way"— specifically on the way to the Father who has sent him, who is the eternal source of both Truth and Life. Arrival at this destination is as good an expression of the meaning of salvation as we could hope for.

Yet, Jesus does not limit his self-defining statement to pointing out a *means* to the salvific end. He identifies himself with that end by calling himself both "Truth" and "Life." Salvation is not merely following Christ, but "abiding in him" (John 15:5), sharing essentially the same relationship with him as he shares with the Father (John 15:10). This invitation into the life of the Trinity is completed when Jesus promises the disciples, "When the Spirit of truth comes, he will guide you into all the truth; . . . He will glorify me, because he will take what is mine and declare it to you" (John 16:13–14).

What begins as an answer to Thomas is received by the whole Church through John's gospel, and leaves us with a foundational understanding about the work of salvation that belongs to all communities of Christians. Salvation comes to us through an ongoing relationship with Christ that is thorough and intimate, so that disciples may share his own intimacy with the Father. This intimate communion is the Way that leads us, by "the Spirit of truth," to "the Truth and the Life," and we come to realize that communion with Christ is not just some sort of passive reward, but reveals to us the very inner life of the triune God. How to keep this revelatory communion living and authentic is the underlying question when we discuss the meaning of the Church, how to understand its mission, and what practical decisions to make in its regard.

INCARNATION AND SACRAMENTALITY

> The words that I say to you I do not speak on my own; but the Father who
> dwells in me does his works. Believe me that I am in the Father and the Father
> is in me; but if you do not, then believe me because of the works themselves.
> Very truly, I tell you, the one who believes in me will also do the works that I
> do and, in fact, will do greater works than these, because I am going to the
> Father. (John 14:10–12)

The concept of communion at the heart of Jesus' discourse to the Twelve in
the Gospel of John could be preserved in an abstract, academic form. But the
same source (in concert with the entire New Testament) makes it clear that
Jesus offers communion to his disciples in what could be called, rather, a
sacramental form, the same form in which we continue to receive it today.
Communion is offered to the first disciples not as a theological exercise, but
in the concrete life of Jesus himself—in the words he speaks, the actions he
takes, the signs he performs. To treat this intimate communion, to which
Christians are invited to be witnesses, as a mere concept somehow distant
from the community's daily life is, therefore, self-contradictory. What Jesus
offers to disciples of every age he offers through his own Incarnation, the
enfleshing of the divine life that transformed the lives of its first witnesses
and continues to transform lives in the sacramental practice of the Church to
this day.

The Baltimore Catechism defined a sacrament as "an outward sign instituted by Christ to give grace."[2] Today's Catechism of the Catholic Church
expands somewhat: "The sacraments are perceptible signs (words and actions) accessible to our human nature. By the action of Christ and the power
of the Holy Spirit they make present efficaciously the grace that they signify."[3] The emphasis here on the *perceptibility* and *accessibility* of sacramental signs reflects the language of Vatican II's Constitution on the Sacred
Liturgy, *Sacrosanctum Concilium*, in which customary legal-style language
is shaped by a more personalist sacramental theology:

> Rightly, then, the liturgy is considered as an exercise of the priestly office of
> Jesus Christ. In the liturgy the sanctification of the man is signified by signs
> perceptible to the senses, and is effected in a way which corresponds with each
> of these signs; in the liturgy the whole public worship is performed by the
> Mystical Body of Jesus Christ, that is, by the Head and His members.[4]

All of this points out once again that the sacramental perspective is rooted in
the Incarnation—Christ's coming in the flesh to a particular place at a particular time. This particularity, unavoidable for any flesh-and-blood creature,
suggests an essential link between authentic sacraments and the particular
forms of meaning in any given community. Because the sacramental signs

are also performed in a particular place and time, access to them is given through the community's own way of understanding itself, the world, and God; because the sacrament is given by Christ to the whole Church, its saving character enlightens and enriches a community's particular understanding. In this way, the ordinary life and outlook of the community becomes the context within which it receives grace, the very life of God, by the action of the Holy Spirit. Sacrament brings communion.

It is from this point of view that we can come to understand Vatican II's frequent insistence that the Church itself be understood as a sacrament. As the Dogmatic Constitution on the Church, *Lumen Gentium*, teaches in its opening paragraph, the Church shows Christ to the world as "a light brightly visible on the countenance of the Church." Therefore, "the Church is in Christ like a sacrament or as a sign and instrument both of a very closely knit union with God and of the unity of the whole human race."[5] The claim that Christ is visible in the Church is made even more explicitly at the beginning of the second chapter as the Council Fathers begin to unfold the concept of the "People of God." God brings about the Church by gathering believers in Jesus, in whom they find their "source of unity and peace," so that "for each and all" the Church "may be the *visible* sacrament of this saving unity."[6] The document then turns implicitly to the "perceptible" and "accessible" qualities of a sacrament by reminding us that despite its transcendent qualities, "the Church is destined to extend to all regions of the earth and so *enters into the history of mankind*."[7] The Church's claim to sacramentality is not, then, based on a mere "pointing toward" the savior, but upon its genuine union with him. This union, moreover, is not simply a future hope, but a living reality: "He sent His life-giving Spirit upon His disciples and through Him has established His Body which is the Church as the universal sacrament of salvation."[8]

MISSION AND COLLABORATION

He said to them, "What are you looking for?" They said to him, "Rabbi, . . . where are you staying?" He said to them, "Come and see." They came and saw where he was staying, and they remained with him that day. (John 1:38–39)

Preparation for the transformation of a specific body of believers into the "universal sacrament of salvation" begins with the "perceptible and accessible" elements of the life that Jesus shared with his disciples. In particular, it begins within the human community that he formed around himself, especially (but not exclusively) among his closest disciples. From the beginning, this is a community marked by sharing of spiritual and material goods and, soon enough, by participation in Jesus' ministry.

In the Synoptic accounts of the call of the first disciples, Jesus tells the fishermen, "I will make you fish for people" (Matthew 4:19 and Mark 1:17; cf. Luke 5:10). This declaration begins to be fulfilled even before the Resurrection, in his sending first the Twelve (Matthew 10:5–15; Mark 6:7–13; Luke 9:1–6) and later "seventy others" (Luke 10:1). While their instructions are clear and the goals explicit, Jesus does not merely give these first missionaries a task along the lines of a training exercise. Their being sent is above all a manifestation of the communion that has already been established between the Master and the disciples. ("I do not call you servants," he will tell them later, "but I have called you friends." See John 15:15.) These apostles ("those who are sent") take on the very mission of Christ, that for which *he* was sent. Their work is deeply shaped by Jesus's own ministry, marked by healing of physical and spiritual maladies and by their announcement of the Gospel's fundamental hope in the reign of God. Although the seventy are sent ahead of him, preparing the way, they are more than simple messengers. It is they, as well as Jesus, who bear responsibility for building up the work by "asking the Lord of the harvest to send out laborers" (Luke 10:2). The authority he gives them is not a matter of legal warrant (which even Jesus does not have, particularly in the pre-Resurrection setting of this story), but the charismatic authority of the Spirit. They heal and cast out demons because they are in communion with Jesus. Mission thus becomes a primary way of revealing the authentic relationship of love that Jesus has established with his disciples.

Just as the communion among Jesus and the disciples implies also the wider communion of the Church's members with one another, so the mission of the disciples implies not only sharing in the work that is the Lord's, but mutual collaboration in that work. They will not travel alone (and this teamwork remains a feature of almost all the evangelistic endeavors described in the New Testament, with only a few notable exceptions). They are to approach their mission with simplicity, as indicated by the restricted list of items that they should carry with them. They go expecting to be dependent on the communities they visit for their basic physical necessities. Importantly, this renders their hosts accountable for the mission as well: the receiving communities must recognize that "the laborer deserves to be paid" (Luke 10:7), and that the Gospel they hear proclaimed demands their response. Embedded in the mission that Christ gives his disciples, then, is not only the disciples' cooperation with the Lord, but their collaboration with one another, and the collaboration of the communities that receive them.

This understanding of mission requires us to recognize that the communion that Jesus offers us as his disciples, by its incarnational, sacramental, and collaborative character, is embedded in ordinary human life. Given the realities of human lives, this would seem to guarantee that our communion with Christ and one another will be "messy" in actual practice. Virtually every experience of collaborative pastoral practice can verify the hunch. Whatever approach is taken to building a pastoral team and a culture of shared responsibility, questions of custom and even of canonical legality are inevitably raised. Innovations may jeopardize people's sense of security and put them on the defensive. This is particularly true when deeply embedded religious symbols are at stake, from the reverence due a priest to communal affinity with the parish's history and traditions. Further, destabilizing demographic, economic, and other conditions can amplify parishioner resistance to new forms of pastoral leadership and organizational structures. Nor are local church communities immune to ethnic, linguistic, and socioeconomic tensions that exist in the wider society.

As a local parish community attempts to face such challenges, it can also happen that professionally trained and responsible lay ministers with experience and "good ideas" find themselves pitted against longtime members who express a keen sense for the realities of their communities. The professionals resent being resisted by members who are less formally educated and authorized, and the longtime parishioners resent being told what is best for them by people they see as outsiders. Connected to many of these other problems is a basic issue of identity, unresolved since Vatican II despite many positive developments: ordained clergy struggle to define an essential role worthy of their training and sacramental distinction, in the face of laypeople (whether "progressive" or "traditionalist") who, in the light of the Council's teaching, feel empowered to demand at least a hearing and, often, to demand serious participation in decision making.

Though it disturbs the outward peacefulness of our communities, evokes soul searching and questioning, and demands seemingly undue time and attention, this messiness in the struggle to build new structures and forms of ministry is not ultimately a weakness but genuine witness to Christ's love. The ultimate expression of that love is the Incarnation itself: Christ took on human flesh, lived through an earthly life in that flesh, and was crucified in it by others with whom he shared that bodily existence. Throughout his life, Jesus ministered with full reliance on that incarnate life, seeking out those suffering in the flesh, laying his hands on them, speaking words of comfort and challenge, using material signs—mud, spittle, water, wine, fish, bread— and announcing the coming of the Reign of God through his acts of healing. In this way, Jesus bequeathed to us the material elements, gestures, and words of the sacraments, which cut through all the mess and bind us together despite our struggles. The sacraments are not mere religious rites, distractions from the difficulties of daily life, but paths to larger meaning, exposing the smallness of so many of our personal concerns. In them, the Lord continues to reveal himself and to deepen our communion with him and, as a result, with one another. In this way, we are continually prepared and renewed for the mission he shares with us.

CONCLUSION: PARISH LIFE AND THE
"SACRAMENTAL—COLLABORATIVE MISSION"

Recent literature on the Church illustrates a pronounced division between pastorally oriented treatments of parish life and administration on the one hand and on the other, ecclesiologies focused more readily on the universal Church that often bypass treatment of local church communities. The tension suggests that some leaders and thinkers in the Church may consider the parish or other local church community incidental to the process of communion and revelation that I have been discussing here. A parish's very identity as a local institution may suggest a too narrow and, frankly, "parochial" perspective to allow for serious expression of the profound mystery that the Church presents to the world. From this point of view, it is the universal Church with its institutions, from scripture to sacraments to hierarchy, that are taken to be the truest demonstrations of the nature of the Church.

Pope Francis is by no means the first to take a different approach to this question, but his writing and speaking have been extraordinarily evocative of the centrality of concrete, local manifestations of Church, both pastorally and theologically. As we pointed out in an earlier chapter, his 2013 Apostolic Exhortation *Evangelii Gaudium* calls everyone to more grounded lives of faith:

> [T]he Gospel tells us constantly to run the risk of a face-to-face encounter with others, with their physical presence which challenges us, with their pain and their pleasure, with their joy which infects us in our close and continuous interaction. True faith in the incarnate Son of God is inseparable from self-giving, from membership in the community, from service, from reconciliation with others. The Son of God, by becoming flesh, summoned us to the revolution of tenderness.[9]

Through the day-to-day, "enfleshed" life of believers and those to whom they reach out, parishes and other local church communities participate in the essential mission of the Church, through which the incarnate Christ continues to reveal himself. Since ancient times this has been the parish's purpose. The very name "parish" evolves from a Greek expression for a neighborhood of foreign sojourners. As the numbers of Christians grew in the early centuries of the Church, bishops found these gathered communities of believers useful for maintaining, through authorized elders (presbyters), the local pastoral ministry that was their original charge. Vatican II's mention of parish ministry in the Dogmatic Constitution on the Church[10] carries forward this dual perspective on a community that is at once an expression of the episcopal ministry and an assembly of believers that itself deserves the name "church." The Council further finds in the parish both an arena for and a support to the exercise of lay responsibility for the whole Church.[11]

In reminding the whole Church that "Jesus Christ is the face of the Father's mercy,"[12] that "Mercy is the very foundation of the Church's life,"[13] and that the parish is "the Church living in the midst of the homes of her sons and daughters,"[14] Pope Francis has brought forward this understanding of the local church community as a place of central importance for the universal Church. In doing so, the pope reminds us that, if we now tend to think of our arrangements for local leadership in institutional terms, and study them sociologically and statistically, these are still tools and measures for essentially human, pastoral ministry. Tools cannot be allowed to obscure—rather than illuminate—the enfleshed human reality where the mercy of God is both received and reflected.

A good description of the work of pastoral ministry, then, is developing and using appropriate tools and measures in such a way that they remain clearly at the service of the lived faith, the communion with Christ, that comprises the core of the community's existence. The first step toward this service orientation is, in fact, the effort to work together. As outlined in our introduction, this volume itself has been a collaborative work among ordained and laypeople; North and Latin Americans, and Europeans; theologians, pastoral leaders, sociologists, organizational development professionals—all presenting the products of their experience and reflection with an eye toward deeper understanding of the Church and its members. Yet, once again, this is not simply an academic exercise. It is a "conversation of consequence" (see chapter 1) like that between Jesus and his disciples, moving toward transformation. Moreover, this similarity is not merely coincidental or generic but is deeply conditioned by the communion with Christ in which local church communities are immersed by faith.

This communion provides the context within which we appropriate the usefulness of "secular" models such as Organizational Development (OD) for grasping the human qualities of a local church community. Dan Gast and Peter Gilmour (chapter 2) point to the subtle but essential differences between OD approaches applied in business situations and the same tools used by a community anchored in its faith in Christ. They recall Dr. Craig Dykstra's definition of "pastoral imagination" as a "peculiar intelligence." Within the experience of communion—among Christians and between them and Christ—we can find a properly theological explanation of this intelligence. Marti R. Jewell (chapter 9) adds the essential Trinitarian dimension of that communion: in the end, the living presence of Christ through which the community develops and exercises its pastoral imagination leads to a sharing of the divine life that Christ himself enjoys with the Father and the Spirit.

The invitation to join the divine communion in all its aspects undergirds the day-to-day relationships upon which the life and work of the local church community rely. Bryan and Mary Froehle (chapter 3) describe "horizontal relationships" (complementing hierarchical accountability structures) among members of parish teams, and the "learning networks" grown inside and outside the parish through collaborative pastoral arrangements. Dan Gast and Peter Gilmour (chapter 2) stress the essential role of such working relationships in counteracting the temptation to isolate and construct ministerial "silos." The practical challenges of the call to become co-workers must of course be met, but it remains indispensable to the peculiar intelligence of pastoral imagination to understand that concrete responses flow from the very real spiritual communion which is the community's taproot.

The pastoral relationships communities must form are therefore more than simple responses to a local situation. They are an essential aspect of the enfleshed communion to which all Christians are called. Development and growth of this communion is the very purpose of the Church. Although our discussion here has been particularly focused on qualities of pastoral *leadership*, the bonds developed through collaboration within a pastoral team have a visible effect in the general life of the community, as the Froehles point out (chapter 3). In this vein, both Brett Hoover (chapter 5) and I (chapter 4) discuss the influence of leadership's respect for—and willingness to cross—cultural and linguistic lines, and the connection between such community practice and the universality of the Church's mission. Andreas Henkelmann and Graciela Sonntag (chapter 7), Elfriede Wedam (chapter 6), and Marti R. Jewell (chapter 9) all point to the need for shared skills, innovative approaches, and transformed attitudes in their discussions of encounters among ordained clergy, lay ministers, and local communities themselves. In such engagements, we can see the potential of the day-to-day communion, upon which parishes are built, continually and more practically revealing the meaning and the implications of faith in Christ.

Ultimately, the mosaic of these local communities opens the concrete reality of some of the broadest and most essential characteristics of Christian pastoral practice. Dan Gast and Peter Gilmour (chapter 2) write of "areas essential to pastoral leadership teams" that include both personal development and spiritual formation, rootedness in tradition, and skills for ministry. The Froehles (chapter 3) underscore that without "vision" and "leadership" parishes do not flourish despite the attention of programs such as INSPIRE. In comparing the results of two parish mergers, I (chapter 4) highlight four "salient factors," including the style of the process, the quality of pastoral leadership, attention to community identity, and the presence of strong social ministry. Reinhard Feiter (chapter 8) focuses on experience, learning, closeness, and a sense of call. In each of these overlapping areas, we can see the mutual reflections of the universal Church and the local church community. We begin to realize that they are aspects of one another within which Christians express their lives of communion in Christ.

Collaborative leadership in parishes can be seen in this way as a kind of sacramental incarnate response to the mission which the Spirit of Christ reveals continually to his Church.

NOTES

1. All biblical quotations are from the New Revised Standard Version (NRSV).

2. *Baltimore Catechism, No. 2.* Revised Edition (1941), §304, http://laudate-dominum.net/files/cat.pdf.

3. *Catechism of the Catholic Church* (1993) §1084, http://www.vatican.va/archive/ENG0015/P2W.HTM.

4. Vatican Council II, *Sacrosanctum Concilium*, Constitution on the Sacred Liturgy (December 4, 1963), §7, http://www.vatican.va/archive/hist_councils/ii_vatican_council/documents/vat-ii_const_19631204_sacrosanctum-concilium_en.html.

5. Vatican Council II, *Lumen Gentium*, Dogmatic Constitution on the Church (November 21, 1964), §1, http://www.vatican.va archive/hist_councils/ii_vatican_council/documents/vat-ii_const_19641121_lumen-gentium_en.html.

6. Ibid., §9. Emphasis added.

7. Ibid. Emphasis added.

8. Ibid., §48.

9. Francis, *Evangelii Gaudium*, Apostolic Exhortation (November 24, 2013), §88, http://w2.vatican.va/content/francesco/en/apost_exhortations/documents/papa-francesco_esortazione-ap_20131124_evangelii-gaudium.html.

10. Vatican Council II, *Lumen Gentium,* §26.

11. Vatican Council II, *Apostolicam Actuositatem*, Decree on the Apostolate of the Laity (November 18, 1965), §10, http://www.vatican.va/archive/hist_councils/ii_vatican_council/documents/vat-ii_decree_19651118_apostolicam-actuositatem_en.html.

12. Francis, *Misericordiae Vultus*, Bull of Indiction of the Extraordinary Jubilee of Mercy (April 11, 2015), §1, http://w2.vatican.va/content/francesco/en/bulls/documents/papa-francesco_bolla_20150411_misericordiae-vultus.html.

13. Ibid., §10.

14. Francis, *Evangelii Gaudium*, Post-Synodal Apostolic Exhortation, §28 (quoting Pope John Paul II, *Christifideles Laici*, December 30, 1988), §26, http://w2.vatican.va/content/Francesco/en/apost_exhortations/documents/papa-esortazione-ap_0131124_evangelii-gaudium.html.

Index

Aachen (Germany), Diocese of, 148, 149
accountability and coaccountability, 36, 37, 42, 48n32, 58, 61, 197, 200, 201, 218
Ad Gentes, Decree On the Missionary Nature of the Church (Vatican II), 184, 188
Apostolicum Actuositatum, Decree on the Apostolate of the Laity (Vatican II), 182
Argyris, Chris, 29

Baltimore Catechism, 213
Baltzell, E. Digby, 136
Bator, Joseph, 26
Bauman, Zygmunt, 137
Benedict XVI (Pope), 153n8, 184
Bergoglio, Jorge Cardinal, 128. *See also* Francis (Pope)
bishops: and conversation about parish ministry, 14, 20, 210n15; in early and medieval church, 2, 178, 179–180, 217; in France, 155, 156, 157, 165; in Germany, 142, 144, 149–150, 172n13; and lay ecclesial ministry, 11–12, 26, 184, 187; in Mexico and Latin America, 127–128, 147, 149–150; and parishes, 109, 112, 139n10, 177, 209n2; and parish restructuring, 75, 77, 79, 82–83, 145, 147, 150, 155, 156, 158, 159, 163, 168, 171n1; and priests, 165; and social

ministry, 90; and US parishes, history of, 135; and Vatican Council II, 182
Boone, Éric, 162
Bordas, Juana, 29
Borromeo, Charles (Saint), 180
Briggs Myers, Isabel, 30
Brown, Juanita, 30
Buber, Martin, 162
Bulteau, Gisèle, 161, 164, 168, 169, 170

Calhoun, Craig, 136
call, 43, 168, 177, 184, 185, 215; and church mission, 166; and social ministry, 90; as a work of pastoral leadership, 207–208; in the Church of Poitiers, 167–169. *See also* vocation
Canon Law. *See* Code of Canon Law
Capraro, James, 133, 135
Carroll, Jackson W., 104, 209n4
Catechism of the Catholic Church (CCC), 183, 213
Catherine of Sienna (Saint), 179
Catholic social teaching, 35, 90, 208
Catholic Theological Union, Chicago (CTU), 34
Center for Applied Research in the Apostolate (CARA), 15, 16, 47n21, 106
Center of Applied Research in Pastoral Theology (*Zentrum für Angewandte Pastoralforschung*) (ZAP), xiv, 7, 141
Chapter of Canons, 179

221

emotional intelligence, 30
Engaged Scholars project, x, 4
Evangelii Gaudium, The Joy of the Gospel
(Pope Francis), 10, 217, 218
Essen (Germany), Diocese of, ix, 145, 150

France, Church in. *See* Poitiers, Archdio-
cese of
Francis (Pope), 9, 11, 97, 188, 217, 218;
and parish renewal, 10. *See also*
Bergoglio, Jorge; *Evangelii Gaudium*
Francis of Assisi, 179
Froehle, Bryan, 5, 51, 218
Froehle, Mary, 5, 51, 218

Garanzini, Michael, 26–27
Gast, Daniel, 4, 9, 23, 218, 219
Gaudium et Spes, Pastoral Constitution on
the Church in the Modern World
(Vatican II), 143, 166
Gemeindereferent. See lay ecclesial
minister, in Germany
Genn, Felix (Bishop of Essen, Germany),
145
Germany, Church in, 141–152, 158, 159,
164, 167, 168, 172n13, 174n61; crisis
in, 142–146; leadership in, 147–150;
and Poitiers experiment, 156, 157, 159,
167, 170. *See also* bishops; deacons; lay
ecclesial minister; pastoral council;
pastoral leadership team; pastoral
ministry; priests
Gilmour, Peter, 4, 23, 25, 218
Gleick, James, 47n14
God the Father, 188, 190, 212–213, 218
Goleman, Daniel, 30
Gregory XI (Pope), 179

Hammond, Philip, 131
Henkelmann, Andreas, 7, 141, 219
hierarchy, 163, 178, 180, 182
Hispanic Catholics in the US. *See* Latino
Catholics in the US
Holy Spirit, 72, 176, 189, 196, 212, 213,
214, 215, 218, 220
homophily (social phenomenon), 112, 113,
115, 132. *See also* social
Hoover, Brett, 6, 40, 73n2, 103, 219

Immortale Dei, On the Christian
Constitution of States (Leo XIII), 180
immigrants in the US, 6, 15, 87, 89, 91, 93,
107, 109, 130; Mexican, 6, 88, 89, 114,
116, 126, 134. *See also* Latino
Catholics in the US
immigration, 6, 103, 105, 110, 125, 135,
136
incarnation, 166, 213–214, 216
INSPIRE, Project, 4–6, 23–43, 51–72; data
collection and management, 15, 24, 36;
financial support of personal and team
development, 61–62; funds, 71–72;
future opportunities, 68–72; and higher
education, 69–70; as institutional
partnership, 26, 69; learning areas and
plans, 31–36; learning reports, 39;
Milestone Conference, 53, 99; origin
and vision, 52–53; parish communities,
impact on, 67–68; parish staffs, impact
on, 66–67; promise, 26–27; and
qualitative social research, 3, 15, 24,
39, 41, 42, 53. *See also* parish
consultation; personal learning; team
learning
Institute of Pastoral Studies (IPS). *See*
Loyola University Chicago
Isaacs, William, 30
isolation in ministry, 12, 13, 14, 25, 34, 40,
48n28, 56, 73n2, 202, 207, 208, 218.
See also pastoral ministry; pastors

John Paul II (Pope Saint), 32, 97, 183
John XXIII (Pope Blessed), 181
Johnson, Homer, 28, 29
Jovenes para Cristo, 107. *See also* young
adults; youth ministries
Jung, Carl, 30
Juran, Joseph, 47n15

Kirchensteuer. See church tax
King, Martin Luther, 112
Kuhn, Thomas, 47n14

laity, 180, 181–182; Congress of the,
Second International, 180; in pastoral
leadership, 16, 26, 120, 128, 146, 147,
149, 182–183. *See also* lay ecclesial

About the Contributors

Rev. Dr. William A. Clark, SJ (coeditor, author of chapter 4 and Afterword, coauthor of chapters 1 and 10), INSPIRE's visiting research professor at Loyola University Chicago from 2011 to 2013, is associate professor of religious studies at the College of the Holy Cross, Worcester, Massachusetts, offering courses in Catholic life and doctrine, Christian prayer, and local church community. His doctoral degree in systematic theology is from the Weston Jesuit School of Theology, Cambridge, Massachusetts (now Boston College School of Theology and Ministry). His book, *A Voice of Their Own: The Authority of the Local Parish*, was published by Liturgical Press in 2005. Fr. Clark has served in pastoral ministry roles in New England and in Jamaica (West Indies), including pastor, priest-in-residence, pastoral associate, and music minister.

Prof. Dr. Reinhard Feiter (author of chapter 8) is chairperson and professor of pastoral theology and religious education, and director of the Institute of Pastoral Theology at the Faculty of Catholic Theology of the Westfälische Wilhelms-University Münster, Germany. Prof. Dr. Feiter, a priest of the diocese of Aachen, studied Catholic theology in Bonn and Würzburg, and earned a doctoral degree in Catholic theology (Dr. theol.) in 1993. His *habilitation* in pastoral theology followed in 2001. His research is particularly focused on parish life development as well as on pastoral work of the Church in France and implications for pastoral theology and practice in Germany.

Dr. Bryan Froehle (coauthor of chapter 3) is professor of practical theology at the School of Theology and Ministry, St. Thomas University (Miami, Florida), where he directs the PhD program in practical theology. He previously served on the faculty of Dominican University, River Forest, Illinois, and at the Center for Applied Research in the Apostolate (CARA). With a doctorate in sociology (University of Michigan, 1993), Dr. Froehle conducts much of his research at the intersection between theology and the social sciences, focusing on Catholic pastoral life and public theology. He has been active in a number of professional organizations, boards, and projects including the International Academy for Practical Theology, the Association for Practical Theology, the Society for the Social Scientific Study of Religion, the Center for the Study of Church Management at Villanova University, and the Center for the Study of World Christian Revitalization Movements at the Asbury Theological Seminary, Wilmore, Kentucky.

Dr. Mary Froehle (coauthor of chapter 3) is assistant professor of practical theology, St. Vincent de Paul Regional Seminary, Boynton Beach, Florida, where she is director of the Office of Institutional Research and Evaluation (OIRE) and Instructional Technology. She is also a licensed clinical professional counselor and a pastoral counselor in private practice. She has been an adjunct faculty member of the Institute of Pastoral Studies at Loyola University Chicago.

Daniel Gast, (coeditor, coauthor of chapters 1, 2, and 10) directed Project INSPIRE from its launch in 2004 until 2012 when he retired. (The Lilly Endowment Inc. *Sustaining Pastoral Excellence* (SPE) program supported INSPIRE, providing two generous grants to Loyola University Chicago and the Archdiocese of Chicago.) Gast has served in several church settings, including parish ministry, Catholic schools, higher education, diocesan ministry, and Catholic publishing. He remains active with a variety of projects and initiatives in the Archdiocese of Chicago, and consults locally and nationally in Catholic leadership ministry. He was an adjunct faculty member of the Loyola University Chicago Institute of Pastoral Studies. Dan is coauthor with Dr. Barbara Fleischer of the course book on Pastoral Leadership and Organization for the Loyola Institute of Ministry (LIM) at Loyola University of New Orleans. He holds a master of science degree in theology from St. Xavier University, Chicago.

Dr. Peter Gilmour (coauthor of chapter 2) collaborated with colleagues from Loyola University Chicago and the Archdiocese of Chicago to design Project INSPIRE, and thereafter convened the project's Lead Team, serving as the project's principal investigator. He is professor emeritus at Loyola University Chicago's Institute for Pastoral Studies. Prior to his retirement Dr. Gilmour served as graduate program director of the master of arts degree in religious education. He is the author of *The Emerging Pastor* (1986), *The Wisdom of Memoir* (1997), *Growing in Courage* (1998), and other publications.

Dr. Andreas Henkelmann (coauthor of chapter 7) was research associate for CrossingOver (www.crossingover.de) from 2004 to 2016. He served on the leadership team of the Centre of Applied Pastoral Theology (ZAP) in Bochum, Germany (www.zap-bochum.de). He studied Catholic theology and history in Vienna, Münster, Tübingen, and Bochum, and wrote his dissertation in Catholic theology on the history of Catholic youth care in Germany in the nineteenth and twentieth centuries. He is currently working on his *habilitation* on the history of lay ecclesial ministers in Germany and the United States, and serves as pastoral associate in the diocese of Aachen.

Dr. Brett Hoover (author of chapter 5) is assistant professor of pastoral theology at Loyola Marymount University in Los Angeles. He has spent the past decade involved in qualitative research in Catholic parishes. He is the author of *The Shared Parish: Latinos and the Future of U.S. Catholicism* (2014). He has written and spoken on parish life and various other topics. Dr. Hoover cofounded *BustedHalo*, an Internet ministry for young seekers. He served as INSPIRE's first visiting professor at Loyola University Chicago's Institute of Pastoral Studies, where he organized and laid out the foundations for the project's research and reporting mission.

Dr. Marti R. Jewell (author of chapter 9) is associate professor of theology in the School of Ministry at the University of Dallas. She directed the Emerging Models of Pastoral Leadership Project, a national research project studying excellence in parish leadership, funded by the Lilly Endowment Inc. *Sustaining Pastoral Excellence* (SPE) program, and coauthored *The Changing Face of Church* and *The Next Generation of Pastoral Leaders* and authored *Navigating Pastor Transitions: A Parish Leader's Guide.* She served as an agency director in the Archdiocese of Louisville, Kentucky, from 1990 to 2003. She is the recipient of the 2011 "Spirit of the Conference" award from the National Association for Lay Ministry (NALM) and the 2013 "Called and Gifted Award" from the Association of Graduate Programs in Ministry (AGPIM). Dr. Jewell holds a bachelor's degree in mathematics from the University of Dayton, Ohio, a master's in theological studies from St. Francis Seminary School of Pastoral Ministry, Milwaukee, Wisconsin, and a doctor of ministry degree from the Catholic University of America, Washington, DC.

Rev. Dr. Robert Schreiter, CPPS, translated chapters 7 and 8 from texts submitted in German. He is Vatican II Council professor of theology at Chicago Theological Union. Rev. Dr. Schreiter served as a distinguished participant and speaker at CrossingOver conferences in Germany and the INSPIRE Milestone Conference.

Graciela Sonntag (coauthor of chapter 7) has been a research associate for the CrossingOver project at Ruhr University of Bochum since 2011 while also serving as a pastoral associate for the Diocese of Münster. She studied Catholic theology and mathematics in Münster, Germany. She is currently developing her dissertation in pastoral theology, a comparative study on the future of lay ecclesial ministry and its contribution to the pastoral work of the Church in the United States and in Germany.

Dr. Elfriede Wedam (author of chapter 6) is advanced lecturer in the Department of Sociology at Loyola University Chicago, and research associate at Loyola's McNamara Center for the Social Study of Religion. She is also the current principal investigator of Project INSPIRE, with oversight of the database of Chicago parishes compiled during the active years of the Project. Prior to arrival at Loyola in 2006, she taught courses at the University of Illinois at Chicago (UIC), Indiana University–South Bend, and Indiana University–Purdue University, Indianapolis (IUPUI). Her areas of research and publication also include urban sociology and race and ethnic studies and, as an Austrian national, German sociology and cultural history. Dr. Wedam was a member of the Religion in Urban America Program at UIC from 1993 to 1997 and from 2001 to 2004, and field director for the Religion and Urban Culture Project of The Polis Center at IUPUI from 1997 to 2001.